The Mong
Oral Tradition

The Mong Oral Tradition

Cultural Memory in the Absence of Written Language

YER J. THAO

Foreword by Lourdes Arguelles
Afterword by Marianne Pennekamp

McFarland & Company, Inc., Publishers
Jefferson, North Carolina, and London

All photographs are by the author.

LIBRARY OF CONGRESS ONLINE CATALOG

Thao, Yer J., 1970–
    The Mong oral tradition : cultural memory in the absence of
written language / Yer J. Thao [; foreword by Lourdes Arguelles ;
afterword by Marianne Pennekamp].
        p.   cm.
    Includes bibliographical references and index.

    ISBN-13: 978-0-7864-2749-9
    ISBN-10: 0-7864-2749-3
    (softcover : 50# alkaline paper) ∞

    1. Hmong [sic] (Asian people)—Laos.   2. Oral tradition—Laos.
3. Oral tradition—California.   4. Hmong [sic] Americans—
Cultural assimilation—California.   5. Hmong [sic] Americans—
Ethnic identity—California.   I. Title.
DS555.45.M5 T53   2006
305.895'972—dc22
                                                    2006026723

British Library cataloguing data are available

Cover image ©2006 PhotoSpin

Manufactured in the United States of America

McFarland & Company, Inc., Publishers
    Box 611, Jefferson, North Carolina 28640
    www.mcfarlandpub.com

Acknowledgments

My elders, you taught me so much. This book would not have been possible without your stories, experiences, knowledge, and the information that you shared with me. I thank you for opening your hearts, lives, homes, and world to let me in to understand your wisdom, integrity, and faith. I will never forget you, your love, and your remarkable voices.

I would like to acknowledge and thank my mentors Dr. Lourdes Arguelles, Dr. John O. Regan, Dr. Doty Hale, Dr. David Drew, Dr. Christine Sleeter and Dr. Antonia Darder for your encouragement and teaching me the values of honoring my elders.

I want to thank The Paul & Daisy Soros Fellowships for New Americans, School of Educational Studies and Minority Mentorship Program at Claremont Graduate University for your wonderful gift of a fellowship to support me while I was doing this research.

I could never have finished this book without the support of my mother Ying Yang, my lovely wife Vilay S. Thao, and my wonderful children Jenny Thao, Andy Thao, Lisa Thao, Mike Thao and Kyle Thao. From the bottom of my heart, I want to say thank you for everything. I love you all very much.

Finally, I would like to thank all the Nhia Yen Thao families for your encouragement, blessing, and faith in my work. I dedicate this book to all the Mong who suffered for thousands of years to preserve the Mong oral cultural tradition and sacred knowledge.

Contents

Foreword
by Lourdes Arguelles

I was raised in a storied world, a world in which it was not extraordinary or rare for a teenager to willingly spend hours listening to elders verbally handing down the individual and collective wisdom they had received and developed in their lifetimes. Looking back, I feel that these stories and the storytellers themselves stimulated my imagination in a special way. I believe that they enabled me to see things that I might have ordinarily overlooked. Indeed, the stories and the memories of my elders have sustained me throughout my life and have helped me in defining myself as a scholar and as an activist.

Over the years I have repeatedly called to mind these old stories, particularly when faced with seemingly unsolvable difficulties. When I have done so, the faces of my elders have vividly appeared in my imagination and have helped to make me feel that I am not alone. As a result, the temptation to immediately fight or flee tends to subside and I am able to stay in the present moment long enough to work things through. When this happens I feel that these elders have created for me a relatively stable ground on which I can stand amidst the forces of incessant change and social injustice. Their narratives have proven to be some of the best tools that I have at my disposal in dealing with issues and situations that would have been unimaginable to me when long ago I sat mesmerized listening to stories in the warmth of many Caribbean nights.

Growing into elderhood both chronologically and academically in a society where the gifts of story and storytellers are desperately needed but difficult to encounter, I often find myself looking among my students for young scholars who have roots in storied worlds. I have hoped and trusted that I would find some who had not forgotten or rejected these roots and who would be willing to critically document and integrate these stories and the memory of their own storytellers into the modernized culture of their academic and everyday lives. More specifically, I am always seeking to facilitate the work of scholars who are willing to identify and mobilize through their teaching and research two powerful assets, storytelling elders and their stories, assets which remain unavailable for most people in the modern world. Several years ago I was very fortunate to find such a person in my former doctoral student and Mong scholar Yer Thao.

Professor Thao has labored intensively for many years to insure the preservation and the further development of his culture. In doing so he has faced many obstacles and has often found himself torn between the forces of modern critical ideologies and the static traditionalism of some members of his own and other refugee and immigrant communities. Undeterred by these obstacles, Professor Thao chose to chart a middle path that challenged the Enlightenment claims that still dominate the modern academy and that posit that understanding depends upon detachment from tradition.

In this book Professor Thao deftly articulates his scholarly middle path, anchoring it in a multiplicity of horizons of meaning from his past, his present, and his future. In his mode of inquiry he has blended the assets of his own oral culture, of his critical print scholarship, and of his image of a more just and sustainable future world. Rather than in method, he has grounded his approach in conversation by engaging with the horizons of meaning of elders of his own community of origin. He proceeds to document the stories that they chose to tell him. These are stories of wisdom and also of despair at the loss of culture and the devaluing of their traditional roles. Seemingly oblivious to the time pressures of academic life, Professor Thao respectfully listened to his elders for many consecutive days and nights. With the elders themselves he dialogically negotiated and re-negotiated his own horizons as a modern scholar and as a young Mong. His approach is one that can be likened in part to the "fusion of horizons" perspective pioneered by the German philosopher Hans-Georg Gadamer. The thought here is that a horizon of meaning can be brought into contact with various other horizons. Instead of one horizon obliterating the others, a process of temporary and productive fusion can take place.

Throughout the book Professor Thao elegantly continues to fuse his own and his elders' past and present horizons and begins to project this fusion into the future. He understands that it is his embeddedness in the Mong tradition that facilitates his encounter with the elders and that allows for the retrieval of their wisdom in the context of a despairing perception of cultural decline and generational conflict. His re-enactment and retrieval of these stories insures as much as possible that the stories remain devoid of the constraints of alphabetic culture. They are precious accounts of kinship systems, material tools, and spiritual values that in the past sustained Mong culture and that may, improbable as it seems to our modern sensibilities, do so in our peril-ridden future here in the West. Professor Thao then relays his understanding that his modern scholarship can complement this work of re-enacting and retrieving cultural memory. His modern conceptual tools assist in the elucidation of the problems created by the gap between past and present in Mong everyday life. Carefully, with the print tools of his scholarship, Professor Thao insures a deeper understanding of a culture that has been as much neglected as it has been misunderstood in the academy. It is Professor Thao's implicit image of a very different world based on stories and dialogue that gives this work a ring of the future.

I have little doubt that this first book by Professor Yer Thao will be broadly appealing to a multiplicity of audiences, but in particular to a younger generation of scholars of color. These new scholar-activists are often re-enacting and retrieving the wisdom of the elders from many post-colonial cultures. They see these elder men and women holding understandings that are very much alive and never seem to ossify. They are finding in these critical understandings practical elements that help them in resisting and going beyond the problematic worlds that they have inherited. In an era of increasing academic fundamentalisms, the continued devaluing of oral traditions and of those who embody those traditions, along with the possibility of unimagined terrors, Professor Thao's work should give them hope and point to a balanced way to do what needs to be done.

Lourdes Arguelles, Ph.D., is Professor of Education and Cultural Studies, Claremont Graduate University, Claremont, California.

Preface

This book explores the lives of thirteen Mong Elders through stories about their unique oral tradition and cultural practices. Also, this work attempts to explain the dilemma Mong Elders encounter living in a literate society, imbued as they continue to be with a non-literate tradition. It is important to understand the Mong Elders' worldview, oral reality and the predicaments they face within the written culture. I use the term "Mong" rather than "Hmong" because I speak Mong Leng dialect. Since there is no standard term officially approved by both the Mong Leng (Moob Leeg) and White Hmong (Hmoob Dawb) in the nation or the world I do not want to confuse my readers with Hmong. Hmong is the pronunciation and preferred term used by White Hmong, whereas Mong is for Mong Leng or Blue Mong.

The Mong Elders featured in this book came from Laos, where they were an ethnic minority. They came to the United States as political refugees after the Lao Communist government took control of Laos in 1975. In the 1960s to 1970s the Mong were recruited by the United States Central Intelligence Agency (CIA) to join the U.S. secret armed forces in Laos. The Mong involvement with the United States going to war with the Communist regime forced them to become refugees. They left Laos to escape Communist government prosecution.

In this work, I want to share the life-stories of the Mong Elders living in an oral tradition while they still lived on the mountains in Laos. Over a period of six months, I met with thirteen Mong Elders who live in California. I visited each Elder several times before my formal interviews began. I started with one open-ended question to engage the Elders in conversation. Additional, essential questions arose during conversations with the Elders in which I asked them to elaborate on emerging themes. Also, the questions were used as guidance to move from a non-literate to a literate society. As a Mong scholar and a professor in higher education teaching multicultural education theoretical foundation, I am interested in the ways that oral culture can contribute to the field of multicultural education in today's diverse American society.

When I met with the Elders we explored many topics through our conversations. We talked about their lifestyles on the mountains of Laos, Mong rituals, customs, beliefs, etc. The Elders told me stories and shared their memories of living in a primarily oral culture. They shared with me much important and valuable information about the Mong oral tradition. The Elders described their experiences of being educated, and how they obtained information and knowledge. Some themes that emerged during the conversations and stories were their childhood experiences, lifestyles, practice of customs religious beliefs, their experience with industrialization and school, and cultural conflict with their grandchildren. These became the central and focused topics in the conversations and stories for this work.

With respect to the unique customary system of my people, I used it to help me find my participants. The connection I established with the Elders was through the marriage custom and/or clan ties. For example, I respect the Yang clan as much as my mother. Her name is Ying Yang. Ying is my mother's name and Yang is her clan. When I talked to an Elder who is in the Yang clan I mentioned my mother. Then, the Elders quickly accepted me as a family member through my mother's kin. Since I am already in the Thao clan, when I talked to an Elder who was a Thao clan member, all we needed to do was to find a way to address each other. When I talked to an Elder from a different clan, such as the Hang, Her, Lee, Moua, or Vang, we could find our connections through his or her side of the family that married into my clan, or my side of the family that married into that specific clan. Kinship and clan structures are ways to define the Mong relationships. All Mong are related in the Mong society. We have great loyalties to our patrilineage clan and kinship system.

In the conversations with my Elders they talked about the beauty, harmony, and happiness in their mountains of Laos. They said the oral traditional lifestyles allowed them to stay closely connected to the souls of their ancestors, the natural world and to their own bodies. They missed their lives on the Mong Mountains, which included hunting, gathering, farming, New Year celebrations, raising stock, and rituals. The Mong grandfather, grandmother, father, mother, uncles and aunts played a very important role making sure that their grandsons, granddaughters, sons, daughters, nephews and nieces maintained their tradition and history, so I present these Elders as examples of practitioners of the traditional Mong lifestyle.

Formal education was first introduced to the majority of Mong people in the United States and those Mong who live in other western countries after 1976. Since then written literacy has invaded the sacred knowledge of the Mong people. The values of their oral tradition are slowly being replaced by a written tradition. The revelation of Mong sacred knowledge in a secular setting or in writing creates serious conflicts with tradition. Currently, the majority of the Mong Elders do not read and write in Mong or any other language. Even though many Mong live in a literate society and in technologically advanced countries such as the United States, they still maintain a strong oral tradition. The skills that Mong passed from generation to generation are inherently a part of this oral tradition. Therefore, the Mong Elders believe that oral tradition is only the positive way to maintain their sacred knowledge. The Elders make it clear throughout this book that they do not favor the idea of transforming their sacred knowledge into text, especially their chants and ritual songs, because this process could harm the spirits. To them, writing down the sacred knowledge is a form of forgetting the tradition because people no longer carry the knowledge with them in their heads.

The continuation of oral tradition practices by the Mong Elders in the United States is a hope that the Mong children will have a sense of oral culture, kinship and family values. In addition, it could provide understanding for Mong children to have respect for their elders, to be able to live a healthy life and to balance themselves with people and nature. The Mong believe that the tradition of oral culture and sacred spirits needs to be maintained so their souls can be protected from the evil spirits. The Elders believe that the process of knowing how to honor souls is very important to the Mong younger generation. They need to preserve their oral tradition in order to pass down these values to the next generation. According to the Elders, if a Mong person no longer values spirits as protectors, he or she no longer believes the Mong tradition. These spirits are the souls of dead ancestors, grandparents and parents. The Mong who rejected their ancestors' traditions are ashamed of the old beliefs, and shame themselves by dishonoring their ancestors. The souls and spirits from outside the family culture are considered evil. They are not the souls that will protect you. These are the evil souls that will haunt you. Mong need to worship their own ancestors' spirits, not ancestors of other people, because the others' ancestors are not friendly. It is important not to separate yourself and your body from the protecting souls of your family. Souls maintain the health, happiness, harmony, fortune and prosperity of the people, and keep the Mong connected to their cosmology.

The goal of this book is to enable readers to appreciate the Mong cultural tradition and the values of their oral culture. This work demonstrates that the minds of Mong elders function differently than those of people from other cultures. The knowledge and information they provide is relative to their having lived in an oral society; they experienced tremendous difficulties adjusting to a written society and maintaining their sacred knowledge and culture. They believe that knowing traditional values gives a sense of cultural balance and identity to Mong in this diverse American society. Mong should not lose their language, culture and customary belief system. Therefore, teaching oral culture values through multicultural education brings a richer curriculum to help members of this diverse society understand American cultural pluralism. Chapter One will help readers understand the important contribution of oral culture to multicultural education. The chapters that follow are about the Mong people and the importance of their oral culture. In Chapter Six, the thirteen Mong Elders share their own stories, and the concluding chapter explores the tenuous future of their age-old oral tradition and the importance of preserving this way of life — a difficult challenge for an oral culture in the midst of a literate society that too often forgets the old ways as it embraces the new.

1

Oral Culture and Multicultural Education

Over the course of our history some people have worked hard to preserve their traditional cultural values while others have attempted to adopt new values. Therefore, many different cultural values existing in this society render people unable to keep up with their culture. The main concern people have about culture in the United States is maintaining its privilege. Freire (1993) would call this concern "critical consciousness." It is an action approach that people make against each other's important culture norms and beliefs. Multicultural education has been the focus across the American education curriculum for almost four decades to try to level the playing field of culture representations. Some educators are wondering what kinds of contents and subjects should be included in the multicultural education field. Most of the cases of multicultural education in the United States are dealing with culture, gender, classes, disabilities and racial differences. People are being marginalized because they are labeled as fitting into one of the above categories. According to Banks and Banks (1993) multicultural education grew from the civil rights movement in the 1960s with a notion to eliminate discrimination in education. In the early 1970s the development of multicultural education became an important field. Banks and Banks (1993) stated, "A major goal of multicultural education is to help students to develop the knowledge, attitudes and skills needed to function within their own microcultures, the U.S. macroculture, other microcultures, and within the global community" (p. 24). If oral culture becomes part of the goal for multicultural education it will

5

have great benefit to the American diverse community. Oral culture values have important significance to this multicultural society. Therefore, throughout this book readers will find oral culture to be interesting and value Mong oral culture as a contribution to American multicultural society. This chapter provides an overview of how oral culture is so important to multicultural education in modern diverse American society.

Living the Vision of Oral Culture in Modern Society

Culturally determined norms guide our language, behavior, emotions, and thinking in different situations; they are the do's and don'ts of appropriate behavior within our culture [Gollnick and Chinn, 2002, p. 6].

The culture of America came from all around the world. Some Americans still have strong ties to their oral culture but others are completely disconnected from the oral culture values. The Native American and indigenous groups and most people who came from underdeveloped countries still celebrate their oral tradition in America. Cajete (1994) points out that Native American ceremony is a form of indigenous education. In addition, Mong Americans are another group that values oral tradition. The Mong people have a strong oral culture. Even though their children are going to school to study the printed word, at home oral culture practices still remain strong. Thao (2002) notes that oral tradition has been a part of Mong culture for thousands of years. This is an important tradition to the Mong people. They have taken their cultural values with them wherever they have resettled. The Mong use oral culture to educate and pass knowledge on to the younger generation (Thao, 2002). Cajete (1994) notes that similar values are passed down by the Native American Indians. The Native American Indians are struggling in the American educational system because it alienates Indians from their natural world and culture. It is important to study cultures in schools. This will help multicultural education meet the criterion from Banks and Banks' definition of multicultural education, which it is a "reform movement that is trying to change the schools and other educational institutions so that students from all social-class, gender, racial, and cultural groups will have an equal opportunity to learn" (p. 4). The daily language people use through stories, folktales, legends, plays, songs, chants, oratory and other forms of nonverbal communication are aspects of oral culture. Nowadays, Americans are so adapted to the print culture values and how the print culture operates that they have forgotten the important values of oral culture. There are many values that carried over from the oral culture. Communication through multi-media is one example from both the oral culture and print culture. We communicate through technological equipment like the telephone and computer microphone without producing text messages as a form of oral culture. To make my point short, we use oral communication on a regular basis without knowing that it is passed down from the oral culture. Ong (1980) called it "Secondary Orality." Media allows people to speak and to address one another with no text required. This technological revolution brings the capacity for people to communicate orally in not only one way but several ways.

In current society, print culture values make people unaware and become used to the low-context culture rather than a high-context culture. People who are most associated with oral culture operate in a high context of culture. Hall (1976) defines context of culture as the many ways in which people look into things. People who rise in the high-context culture are in positions of personal authority whereas the people who rise in the low-context culture are not. The context of cultures creates a system for that culture. According to this information the high-context culture system allows people to build a stronger relationship between one another, involves more collective thinking, maintains a harmonious relationship with the environment and has communal supports, whereas the low-context culture encourages individualism and puts more emphasis on profit-making.

The author came from an oral culture. He did not attend school until he was at the age of twelve. During his childhood period he learned things through oral teaching and accessed information face to face with another human being. He had a big family and extended family, and retains strong ties with his kinship system. From his oral culture experience, things do not come in packages, have no copyright permission label and no form of currency. Oral culture is not a linear operation. It is completely non-linear. Oral culture does not buy or sell things. It is a culture of trading. The author is from the Mong culture. The Mong are open, humble and courageous people. The Mong culture will have a great benefit to the American modern diverse society if Americans are to accept oral values.

There are so many elements to the oral culture religion. Religion has an important role to all cultures. Some people are willing to die for their religion rather than lose it. The oral culture religion that the Mong, Native American and indigenous groups believe must be understood by the print culture society. It may be difficult for some people to explain oral culture religion because nothing comes in text. Often print culture people did not take time to do research to understand how oral culture works. This topic was ignored. Therefore, oral culture people's religions are not clearly identified in this modern diverse society. Oral culture religion associates with spiritual entities. It emphasizes harmonizing with places, plants, animals, people and other physical features. It is not like other types of religions. It requires oral culture sacred knowledge in order to understand the religion. For example, the Mong believe that everything existing on earth has a soul. To become a spiritual healer one must be chosen by the spirits. See Chapter Four for detailed explanation. The Native Americans and other indigenous groups have similar beliefs. In order to have a comprehensive religion discussion for multicultural education one must include the religion of oral culture people. Gollnick and Chinn (2002) remind us that we live in a society that has become increasingly diverse and no one should ever underestimate another's religion beliefs.

When the author first arrived in the United States he quickly discovered that Americans do not place much emphasis on oral culture values. His oral culture background was not being recognized at school. School was very foreign and difficult for him. It took the author many years to adapt to the school culture. His mother faced a similar dilemma. She cannot obtain a job in this print culture society with her oral credential. She receives support from the author. It is sad to see how this society has forgotten the values of oral credential. To make sure this does not happen to future oral culture background students and parents, Americans really need to understand oral culture values. Including oral culture values in multicultural education curriculum in schools and providing oral culture training to peer professionals is the foundation to introduce all culture values. This will help the American diverse society develop greater understanding for American cultural pluralism.

Oral Culture and Written Culture Together in One Society

It is important to recognize both oral and written cultures. People may have different views of interpreting, learning and processing information based on the cultural society that they belong to. There are many culture representations in American society and each culture has its own unique system to maintain the importance of culture creativity. Hall (1976) reminds us that culture is an identification of people and it draws a line separating one thing from another. Printed words convey meaningful information to oral culture people as to print culture people. Oral culture people see print words as a mark and this mark means nothing to them. For example, "elephant" in print may not deliver the same message to oral culture people that a picture of an elephant does. If the print culture people see the word "elephant" they would immediately know the meaning that it is an animal. However, if one would ask a member of the print culture to recite any story about an elephant he or she might need to research from books in order to tell the complete story. The member from an oral culture would not need such books to help him or her. Ong (1982) points out that a person who has never seen a car in his or her life may think of a car as a horse. A horse provides similar services as to the car.

People cannot assume that in this modern diverse American society all people function the same way because everyone attends school to study print culture values. Even though some cultures may believe in going to school they have high expectations to keep their oral values. For example, Native American Indian education incorporated many cultural values from indigenous tradition (Cajete, 1994). In addition, some minority American communities have afterschool and weekend classes that teach heritage values to their children. Importantly, school is a place where many cultures including oral and written meet. School should promote heritage, language and culture. School needs to be a place that helps people reinforce different culture orientation. Since the American society is moving in the direction of transdisciplinary pedagogy, the American people need to understand oral and written cultural diversity. Both oral and written cultures are equally valuable to the American pluralistic society as knowledge becomes more transnational and globalized. People no longer live in isolated communities. There are all types of cultures living together in one community throughout the United States. Therefore, it is extremely important to address the issues raised by the differences in oral culture and written culture in modern society. With this information it will help the American people to be conscious about the different dimensions of culture. There are many culture modalities and forms that evolved in the various cultures now found in the United States. Many Americans do not know about the Mong culture, and the Mong are often lumped in with a larger Asian group such as Chinese, Japanese or Korean and other groups from Southeast Asia. It is time to have an open discussion about the American cultures. Representations of all cultures must be recognized by the American people in order for the United States to continue to be a strong nation.

Summary

Oral and print cultures have differences and similarities, and they both have important values that benefit this society. Oral culture has different norms and values than print culture. Multicultural education in this current society must include all cultural perspectives from oral and print cultures. No culture should be neglected or marginalized. The way to understand our past is through the contribution of oral culture values. One must not forget this oral culture. It is one of the oldest existing cultures and some people have great respect for it. In some communities throughout the United States, oral culture is still kept strong as a way to attain knowledge and wisdom. It is important for one to understand both the oral and print cultures in order to deliver effective multicultural education. Society needs to stay connected to past historical values, and oral culture can help people make this connection.

2

The Mong Oral Tradition and Cultural Practices

Members of the Mong culture are raised without knowing that they have been taught, because they learn from what they live in everyday life. The Mong maintain a strong oral cultural tradition. The culture is passed down orally from generation to generation by the nuclear family. This chapter provides an introduction to the early history of the Mong, information about the importance of their oral tradition, and the significant values of oral cultural practices. These are some of the values that inform oral tradition and cultivate knowledge associated with conserving the Mong family kinship systems, social responsibilities, religious doctrines, ceremonial rituals, and community customs and traditions.

Theories of Mong Origin

According to researchers, China used to be the homeland of the Mong people for thousands of years before they migrated to Southeast Asia (Geddes, 1976; Mottin, 1980; Lewis, 1984; Quincy, 1988; Thao, 1999a). Geddes (1976) describes Father Savina's early account in *Histoire des Miao* which was published in the 1930s about the origins of the *Miao* (Mong) people stating that "The Miao are first mentioned in Chinese history, he says, about the twenty-seventh century B.C. when they were living in the basin of the Yellow River. At first they had some success, but then the Chinese grouped together under Huan-yuan and defeated the Maio who

11

were led by Tcheou-yu" (p. 3). However, there is very little research about the Mong's early history, and the studies that exist are all very different. No one knows for sure about the real history of the Mong. Rev. Sam Pollard first documented the *Miao* (Mong) in China in the late 1800s. Pollard (1919) describes the *Miao* people, "For generations these Miao have lived without a history, mixing only with each other, quite ignorant of the outside world" (p. 45). Pollard's 1919 account stated that these *Miao* lived in the hill country of Yunnan and Kweichow Provinces, China. Geddes (1976), Mottin (1980), Smally (1994), Quincy (1988), and Thao (1999a) support the belief that the *Miao* lived mainly in the southern region of China in Yunnan, Kweichow and Kwangsi. The Mong lived near the Yellow River that runs in China. Thao (1999a) describes four different theories of the Mong origin. Each theory about early Mong history differs.

• The Theory of Mesopotamian Origin was developed by a French Catholic missionary called Savina. Savina claimed that Mong's ancestors are the Turanians. The Mong migrated to China because they were forced out by the Aryans (Quincy, 1988; Thao, 1999a). According to Savina's account, the Mong migrated from Iran and the Mong are a Caucasoid race (Quincy, 1988).

• The Theory of Ultimate Southern Origin was developed by a man called Eickstedt. He claimed that the Mong migrated to China from the south (now India and Myanmar). Eickstedt's theory is also supported by Father LaRocca who believes that he was a Mong in a previous life.

• The Theory of China Origin was a collective agreement by Mottin, Bernatzik, Graham, Linh Yeuh-Wah, and Geddes. They argued that Mong originally lived in the southern region of China on the basin of the Yellow River. This location is present-day Yunnan, Kweichow and Kwangsi, China.

• The Theory of the Russian Origin was developed by a man called Largéguy. He claimed the Mong migrated to China from Russia.

Thao (1999a) believes that Mong always lived on the basins of the Yellow River and the Yang-tse Kiang River. This region is the Mong ancestors' land. The Mong migrated in every direction in China when the Han Chinese invaded the Mong homeland. Thao's research supports the China Origin Theory.

Quincy (1988) states that the Mong faced government persecution in China because they did not want to assimilate into the Chinese culture and to be controlled by the Chinese. Therefore, they retreated to live on the mountains where the Chinese could not find them. The Mong who rebelled against Chinese authority continued fighting the Chinese until they were pushed out of China. These are the people who crossed over the border to Vietnam, Laos, Thailand, and Myanmar (Mottin, 1980; Quincy, 1988; Thao, 1999a). A 2000 article in *The Los Angeles Times* reports that a Southern China Great Wall was discovered in Fenghuang, China, that was about 400 years old. It was built to keep the *Miao* (Mong) out and to protect the Chinese emperor's capitals (Ni, 2000). Mottin (1980) states, "The Hmong first arrived in Laos shortly after their entry into Vietnam, that is to say around 1810–1820, which shows that some of them at least did not stay long in Vietnam and just passed through" (p. 47).

The Mong Elders whom I interviewed said they were from either the third or fourth generation born in Laos. They told me that their parents gave them this information. Elder Tong Yao Her remembered seeing one of his great granduncles who came from China. Elder Chai Xiong said she too remembered seeing one of her great granduncles who came from China. The Elders explained that according to the information passed down from their parents, grandparents, and legends, when the Mong fled China, many family members were left behind. The Chinese were very restrictive and only a few people in each group that lived in the same region could escape. As Elder Tong Yao Her described:

> My grandfather told me that only two of my great granduncles could make it to Laos. They came with a lot of Mong. He said the mountains between the border of China, Vietnam and Laos were very high. The Mong that escaped to Laos got stuck on these mountains and the Chinese caught up with them. They either killed the Mong or captured the Mong and the Chinese took the Mong back to China. The Mong who managed to escape from the Chinese — some made it to Laos, Vietnam, Myanmar and Thailand. There were some that never make it to Laos because of starvation. There was a mountain called frozen killed (*tsoob tuag no*). This mountain had a very rough terrain and snow. It was very cold and many Mong did not survive while crossing this mountain because of frost bites, hypothermia, and starvation. When my grandfather and two great granduncles reached Laos, they married, and they had my father and granduncles [personal communication, San Diego, California].

All the Elders were familiar with this tragic story about the frozen mountain (*tsoob tuag no*). Due to limited research available about the origin of the Mong, I encourage researchers to continue investigating this topic to come to a more conclusive theory.

Mong Oral Cultural Tradition

> Oral cultures indeed produce powerful and beautiful verbal perform-
> ances of high artistic and human worth, which are no longer even possi-
> ble once writing has taken possession of the psyche [Ong, 1982, p. 14].

For thousands of years, the Mong people have lived and developed
within a unique system in an effort to maintain their oral values such as
culture, language, tradition, and religion. Generations have passed down
this oral cultural knowledge for cultural preservation, anchored in a sacred
tradition of harmony to prevent the destruction of that culture by outsiders. Researchers of oral tradition and culture describe the people who
live in an oral society as having different views of interpreting information and having different virtues than those who live in a written society
(Vansina, 1965, 1985; Finnegan, 1967, 1970; Ong, 1982; Dickinson, 1994;
Guss, 1986; Havelock, 1986; Goody, 1987; Sweeney, 1987; Foley, 1988,
1990; Okpewho, 1992; Cajete, 1994; Einhorn, 2000). Oral tradition operates in communal and non-linear structures. The written tradition operates individually and in linear ways. Ong (1980, 1982) states that writing
is only a form of "analysis." Ong declares, "Writing is an absolute neces-
sity for the analytically, sequential, linear organization of thought such as
goes, for example, into an encyclopedia article" (1980, p. 199). Ong (1980)
argues, "In a primary oral culture, education consists in identification,
participation, getting into the act, feeling affinity with a culture's heroes,
getting 'with it'—not in analysis at all" (p. 201). Jan Vansina (1965), a
researcher of oral tradition, contends that:

> As a result, oral tradition in such societies is limited to the exchanges
> that take place in the course of everyday conversation, and consists of
> traditions which are handed down from generation to generation in a
> random fashion, without the aid of any special techniques. Moreover,
> they all serve aesthetic, moral, or didactic purposes. These are by no
> means the purposes common to all types of oral tradition [p. 6].

For people who live in an oral tradition, their transformation of
knowledge is through performance, repetition and memorization. Finnegan
(1970) notes that repetition is one function to help oral people remember.
Oral performances such as poetry, songs, stories, chants, etc., are transmitted in a form of verbal expression. There is no such thing as indirect
translation in the oral tradition. Everything associated with oral tradition
has to do with the metaphysical. Sweeney (1987) states, "In a print culture, however, the given schemata are vastly more numerous or more
'fragmented' than in an orally oriented society" (p. 13). Ruth Finnegan

(1992), who has also done extensive work in the area of oral tradition and oral literature, defines oral tradition as follows:

> The phrase "oral tradition" conceals similar ambiguities, with the apparently more specific "oral" in fact complicating it even further. The addition of "oral" often implies that the tradition in question is in some way 1) verbal or 2) non-written (not necessarily the same thing), sometimes also or alternatively 3) belonging to the "people" or the "folk," usually with the connotation of non-educated, non-élite, and/or 4) fundamental and valued, often supposedly transmitted over generations, perhaps by the community or "folk" rather than conscious individual action [p. 7].

Story-telling is a formality of oral tradition. All types of oral performances, stories, tales, riddles, poems, rituals, and songs are important verbal arts that are passed down from the oral society. Sweeney (1987) conducts research on oral culture versus written culture in the Malay world. The research shows that the Malay people face tremendous tensions in the process of shifting from an oral to a written culture.

Vansina (1985) asserts that oral tradition is a part of the information that helps us to reconstruct our past. Without oral tradition we could not understand what happened in our past history. Finnegan (1992) states clearly that oral tradition, oral literature, oral narrative, oral testimony, and the like are the characteristics of orality. Ong (1982) argues along the same lines that the center of orality must be a person who is totally unfamiliar with writing. Ong (1982) states that oral tradition has no such thing as residue or deposit like written words. According to Ong's argument, a written tradition cannot be achieved without oral tradition. Ong (1977) asserts, "the first age of writing is the age of scribes, writers of more or less orally conceived discourse" (p. 282).

According to research and the Mong legends, the Mong believe strongly in their oral tradition and culture values. They do whatever they can to protect this culture. This is one reason why the Chinese and Mong have had a long history of conflict. The Mong populations heavily opposed assimilation into the Chinese culture, tradition and religion. (Similar issues occur today for the Mong living in the United States, since the elders continue to work to retain their sacred traditions.) The Mong continued their consistent resistance against Chinese Emperors during the Shang, Chou, Han, Tang, Sung, Ming, and Manchu Dynasties. In the early 1800s to the 1900s, Mong populations migrated to Vietnam, Burma, Thailand, and Laos to avoid losing their culture values and being persecuted by the Chinese government (Geddes, 1976; Mottin, 1980; Lewis, 1984; Quincy, 1988; Thao, 1999a). A story told by Elder Tong Yao Her was that his great grandfather had to escape from China because the Chinese captured and killed all the Miao (Mong) men and boys. The Chinese took the Mong women and girls to be their spouses and children. The Mong who were captured by the Chinese and those who cooperated with the Chinese were educated in the Chinese culture. Then, the Chinese used these Mong people to help them locate the Mong who opposed the Chinese.

> In China, the Chinese killed all the Mong males. Boys whose testicles were about the sizes of a bean were all killed. When you had a newborn child and it was a boy then you had to hide him from the Chinese. The Mong went to hide on the mountains where there was rough terrain so the Chinese could not come after them [Elder Tong Yao Her, personal communication, San Diego, California].

Quincy (1988) describes that the Mong were peaceful people. They preferred to live a lifestyle and be independent in their own kingdom. The Mong lived in this peaceful kingdom sometime around 400–900 A.D. in China (Quincy, 1988). Then, the Chinese penetrated into the Mong territory to gain control over the Mong people. He elaborates:

> The final insult was a concerted effort by the civil authorities to sinicize the Hmong, forcing their children to attend Chinese schools, and prohibiting their traditional celebrations. In addition, pressure was brought to bear on Hmong villages to permit Chinese men to take Hmong women for wives [Quincy, 1988, pp. 50–51].

The conflicts between the Mong and the Chinese drove the Mong people out of China. The beauty of the Mong oral cultural tradition was shattered by these historical events.

The oral tradition makes up the Mongs' everyday lives. They have their own method of conserving their traditional values and knowledge from generation to generation. Native American Indian educator Gregory Cajete explains that indigenous education involves all living and non-living things such as people, animals, trees, mountains, lands, rocks, and spirits. Cajete (1994) states, "We learn through our bodies and spirits as much as through our minds" (p. 31). Even though many Mong live in a written society and highly technological countries such as the United States, Canada, and Australia, they still maintain a strong oral tradition. The Elders with whom I dialogued expressed tremendous concern about losing the Mong oral cultural tradition and sacred knowledge. In their families, oral traditional values are woven into their daily activities. Elder Cha Shoua Hang described himself:

> I am a Shaman. I am very busy. I perform my Shaman ritual (*ua neeb*) almost every month. The Mong people who are sick call me to perform a ritual to find out what is wrong with them. I perform Shaman rituals all

over Sacramento, Stockton, Merced, Fresno, Yuba City, Marysville, and Oroville. When they need me, I have to go to help them because the Shaman spirits have chosen me to help people. As long as I am available I never say no to anyone. Usually they come to pick me up. When I perform my rituals, I do not charge them money or place a price to my rituals. Usually, people give me twenty dollars to buy paper money and incense to burn to my Shaman spirits. If I have to perform a difficult ritual (ua neeb nyaav), they pay me based on the cost of the ritual. For example, I get forty to fifty dollars if I perform a difficult ritual. One ritual lasts about three to five hours. Beside rituals, I socialize with other Mong like the way I did on my mountains in Laos. I attend Mong funeral and wedding rites. We perform these ceremonies like we did in our homeland. I say the way we perform our rituals in this country is better than back in our mountains because here we have more older people to participate and to help in the ceremonies [personal communication, Sacramento, California].

Currently, the Elders believe that oral tradition is a positive way to maintain their sacred knowledge, and it serves as a tool to help Mong children keep their language and culture. It is important for the Mong younger generation to preserve the cultural tradition of their parents, grandparents, and ancestors to help them stay balanced in this world and become strong individuals. Einhorn (2000) describes the Native Americans' beliefs that a lack of balance in spiritual harmony can cause sickness and death. "Traditional Native Americans speak about every part of nature as sacred and hallowed" (Einhorn, 2000, p. 22). Nasr (1989) states that the notion of a tradition is to transmit knowledge from the past to the present. The tradition of oral knowledge to the Mong elders is still an everyday learning and processing of information. It keeps them connected and close to the worldview of oral culture. Researcher Vansina (1965) explains her work in oral tradition: "I should like to make it clear that my examination of the topic is primarily based on traditions still alive among peoples without writing, since sources of this kind preserve the essential nature of oral tradition better than traditions found in literate society" (p. 2).

Vansina's statement describes the Mong people and their oral tradition. For example, the Mong do not have a written language, and many important values like stories, legends, chants, rituals, and social skills are passed down primarily orally. The Elders do not support the idea of translating their sacred knowledge, ritualistic secret language, songs and chants into text, because it can create harm to the spirits. Elder Xao Cheng Lee said:

We cannot practice our sacred rituals by reading the chants or secret language from written transcription. If everything were written down then everyone can easily have access to it. Then, they no longer have the same values as the way in oral. The living side (*neej saab*) and dead side (*dlaab saab*) are no longer confidential. The dead side (*dlaab saab*) would pick up the secret power of the Mong chants. Therefore, they would no longer be afraid of the living side (*neej saab*). The creator (*yawm saub*) gave these sacred values for the living side (*neej saab*) to protect them from the dead side (*dlaab saab*). The good spirits and living people are on the living side (*neej saab*) and the evil spirits and dead people are on the dead side (*dlaab saab*). These two sides need to remain in their own boundary in order to balance the living and dead cycle. If a Mong person is sick then possibly his/her spirit was being disturbed by the evil spirits living on the dead side (*dlaab saab*). A ritual must be performed to keep the evil spirits away from bothering this person's spirit. We learned all these ritualistic chants, songs, and secret language by heart. We can perform anytime when someone asks us at any ceremony. There are so many chants and different ceremonies. We have wedding chants, funeral chants, soul honoring chants, soul calling chants, household chants, shaman chants, healing chants, etc. Beside the chants and songs, there are secret ritual languages that go with the ceremonies. There are very few people that know all the different chant categories. The majority know only one, two, or three areas. I know only the wedding chants, funeral chants, and household chants. If I need to have a soul calling ritual done, then I have to call someone who knows to come to perform the ritual. There are so many important things in my oral tradition that we need to keep like the way my people had done for generations [personal communication, Merced, California].

The Elders believe that the non-sacred, legendary stories, folktales, non-ritualistic songs, language and music need to be written down. In this way, the Mong children and other people can learn about the Mong cultural tradition. Musicologist Amy Catlin points out that oral music and song have been part of the Mong traditional culture since they lived in China (Catlin, 1997). Mong music is different than from the music of Chinese and other non–Chinese minorities. The Mong music and songs are related to their tonal language (Catlin, 1997). Lewis (1993) concludes a study on the Mong oral cultural expressions by saying that, "Hmong social pattern is shaped by their sense of identity, transmitted through oral traditions, and a conceptual system marked by flexibility and resilience" (p. 118). Vang and Lewis (1984), Kohler (1986), Livo and Cha (1991), and Johnson (1992) describe that myths, legends, riddles and folktales are part of the Mong oral tradition. They bring entertainment to the Mongs' daily lives. Catlin (1997) also notes that singing songs, sung poetry, and playing musical instruments are important tools in the Mong courtship.

Randall (1985) states that the fascinating things about the Mong culture are their costumes and textiles.

The Mong Elders that I interviewed who converted their religious beliefs said that their traditional rituals, sacred knowledge, and ritual secret language are too complicated to maintain. Therefore, they suggested that the Mong should consider dropping this tradition and convert to other traditions such as Christianity and Catholicism. However, they agreed that the Mong need to keep their culture such as the textiles, costumes, courtship songs, language, and food. The Mong need to eliminate their religion completely because if they believe in God, then God will protect them. These Elders and their families no longer practice the Mong traditional rituals. Now, they go to church. But, they said they still remember the old days when they practiced Mong traditional rituals. They have not yet forgotten some of the chants. When they converted to a different tradition, they stopped using the Mong ritualistic chants, language, and songs. Elder Tong Yao Her said that even though he is a Christian, he still takes on the role of a Mong wedding negotiator (*mejkoob*). When he is a wedding negotiator, he still sings the wedding chants and uses the wedding secret language.

Most of the Elders stated that the Mong must preserve everything that they know and have in their culture. The ritual part is the most important piece of tradition to the Mong culture. The Mong people should not forget it. The Mong perform rituals to keep the good and bad spirits happy so they do not make people ill. These Elders said if the Mong choose not to keep their rituals, then there is no reason for the Mong to preserve their cultural tradition. The Mong should adopt the mainstream culture. This way it allows the Mong people to make an easy transition to the American culture.

Wilson (1995) wrote about a Mong woman called See Lee who lived in Long Beach, California. She tried to understand See Lee's oral history, language, and culture through what she called *"organic" free verse transcription*. Wilson used this term to define the results of her time-consuming task transcribing the tapes that contain hours and hours of See Lee's story. Wilson (1995) concludes in her study, "By using 'organic' free verse transcription, the poetic elements of oral narrative are reclaimed as part of everyday life" (p. 119). She adds that See Lee's oral stories provide consciousness to the American culture regarding the transformation of oral literature to written literature. See Lee has a beautiful oral language and culture. Her needle art works have a special meaning and carry powerful images that portray the Mong people's oral culture and minority people's points of view (Wilson, 1995).

Six Elder women who participated in this study verified that sewing is an important skill in the Mong tradition. They learned how to sew at young ages because they needed to have the skills in order to make outfits for their husband, children and themselves. Elder Jer Thao shared her sewing experience:

> I knew only how to do simple sewing and I never sew a complete outfit until I married. I got married when I was about thirteen or fourteen years old. After I went to live with my husband, I learned to sew outfits from the wives of my husband's brothers (*puj laug*). If you have children and a husband, no one will make clothing for your family. You need to learn how to make them yourself. During this time, we did not have fabric so we had to make our own fabric from hemp. It was very difficult to turn the hemp into fabric (*muab maaj lug ua ntaub*). I do not want to think about it. There were so many steps. First, you cut the hemp. You dried the hemp in the sun. When it was dried then you peeled off the skin. You need only the skin. You smashed the skin (*muab tuav*) until it turned soft. Then you boiled the skin with wood ash until it turns white and very soft. It bleached it. You took it to wash in the river. You used a flat rock to scrub the skins until all the charcoal ash and all the rough spot disappeared. You dried it again. After that, you wove it into string. You spun the string many times until it turned soft. Last, you used the hand made powerloom (*ntus*) to weave it into fabric. When you made it into fabric, you took it to wash again. After that, you dried it in the sun again. Then, you finished. When the fabric dried you could make it into clothing. I remember that I was constantly busy weaving the string so it could turn into soft thread. While I walked to the plantation, collected firewood or got water my hands were busy all the time twisting the string into soft thread. This was a very difficult task [personal communication, Fresno, California].

These six women Elders know how to turn hemp into fabric. All the Elders were proud of the skills they learned. Even though the fabric and all the tools were made only by hand, they were reliable and lasted a long time. These items were almost as good as those made by machines. This tradition continued to be passed down until after the Mandarin Chinese and Laotian traders brought fabric and tools to trade in the Mong villages. Then some families stopped making their own fabric and tools.

Mong Oral Culture Practices

> Culture is a word that has so many meanings already that one more can do it no harm [Hall, 1976, p. 20].

The paradox of culture is that language, the system most frequently used to describe culture, is by nature poorly adapted to this difficult task. It is too linear, not comprehensive enough, too slow, too limited, too constrained, too unnatural, too much a product of its own evolution, and too artificial. This means that the writer must constantly keep in mind the limitations language places upon him. He is aided, however, by one thing which makes all communication possible and on which all communication and all culture depend; namely, that language is not (as is commonly thought) a system for transferring thoughts or meaning from one brain to another, but a system for organizing information and for releasing thoughts and responses in other organisms. The materials for whatever insights there are in this world exist in incipient form, frequently unformulated but nevertheless already there in man. One may help to release them in a variety of ways, but it is impossible to plant them in the minds of others. Experience does that for us instead — particularly overseas experience [Hall, 1976, p. 57].

The Mong people have a very complex oral culture structure. They maintained their information and knowledge only through oral form. When the Mong migrated to Laos, they established villages on the mountains where outsiders could not harm their people and culture and could not restrict them from practicing their sacred traditions. In Laos, the Mong regained their freedom and the peaceful lifestyles they once had in China before the Chinese invaded their land. The freedom and peaceful lifestyles they had on the mountains of Laos allowed them to continue their oral cultural tradition. The Mong Elders whom I interviewed said that the mountains in Laos were unclaimed by the Laotian government. The Laotians lived in the valley (*ntsaag taj*), and they did not pay attention to the lands on the mountains. The jungles in the mountains remained open territory for the Mong and other minority hill tribes.

We, Mong, lived freely on the mountains of Laos (*peb cov Moob nyob ywj sab ywj ntsws tsua sau toj tsoob hauv peg*). There was nobody there to control or to restrict us. On the mountains in Laos, we can farm as many plantations we want, build as many houses as we like to have, cut any trees, and hunt any wild animals and birds. We, all the Mong, lived in villages (*peb Moog nyob tsheej zog*) and the Mien (*Cu*) and Khmu (*puj thawj*) also lived on the mountains. There were no Laotians (*lostsuas*) [personal communication, Boua Tong Yang, Sacramento, California].

Quincy (1988) says no one really knows the early history of Mong cultural practices in China, but the Yangshao Chinese cultural practices are similar to those of the Mong. The Yangshao Chinese performed their traditional rituals, built their houses, raised their livestock, farmed, and had social gatherings like the Mong. It is possible that the Mong are related to this group. The Yangshao were found in China as early as 2500 B.C. Later, a group called the Miao separated from the Yangshao. The term "Miao" was given by the Chinese (Pollard, 1918; Lyman, 1974; Geddes, 1976; Mottin, 1980; Lewis, 1984; Quincy, 1988; Smalley, Vang and Yang; 1990, Smalley, 1994; Thao, 1999a). Thao (1999a) states that to the Chinese this term "Miao" could be loosely translated as barbarian. The term "Miao" means savage to the Chinese (Quincy, 1988). Geddes (1976) adds, "The character for 'Miao' in Chinese writing is generally said to be a compound term composed of one symbol meaning 'plants' and one meaning 'fields'" (p. 13). The Chinese referred to Miao as a kind of plant that shoots out of the soil in the field. This plant is difficult to kill in China. Because the term "Miao" had a negative connotation in the late 1960s to early 1970s, the term "Mong" was used to replace it. Lyman (1974) describes, "The name 'Miao' is derived from Chinese, while the Thai, Yon, and Lao equivalent is 'Meo.' The tribe itself, however, uses the ethnic name Mong to which a descriptive term is added to designate the particular branch of the Mong group" (pp. 9–10).

Elder Nhia Cha Yang, who had lived in Vietnam, Laos, and Thailand, recalled that the Mong people always called themselves Mong. They never used any terms to describe the Mong in a negative way. Elder Nhia Cha said because outsiders such as the Chinese, Vietnamese, Laotian and Thai called the Mong a bad name, they hated the Mong and they did not want the Mong to live in their country. He explained, "In Vietnam, the Vietnamese called the Mong, Miao. They called us the same like the Chinese called the Mong. In Laos, the Laotian called the Mong, Meo. In Thailand, the Thai called the Mong, Meo. I hear only the Americans call us, Mong" (personal communication, Elder Nhai Cha Yang, Banning, California).

Elder Nhia Cha Yang explained the term "Miao" to the Chinese and Vietnamese meant that the Mong were mountain dwellers. The Mong like to live and scatter on the mountains. They like to live by themselves and have independent lifestyles. The term "Meo" to the Laotian and Thai meant the Mong were wild people like the wild cats that live in the jungles. Mottin (1980) asserts,

> The first Chinese writings which mention them date from about the 3rd cent. B.C. They speak the "Sam Miao" that is they say the "3 Miao," but the expression must be understood in a more general plural and translated by "the Miao." Allusion is made there to a relatively precise ethnic group. Nevertheless after that time up to the 10th cent. A.D. no more mention is made of the "Miao" as such. Instead we were told about the

"Man," term which in fact designates all the "non-Chinese" populations. We must wait till the 10th cent, to find again mention of the "Miao," and it first seem to refer really to our "3 Miao" of previous times. But then to complicate things still more, between the 17th and 18th cent. this same Miao word took a broader sense in its turn to include all the non-Chinese populations of the South — West, our Miao being the most well known of them. Sometimes it is true, the two words are found together in expressions such as "Miao — Man" or "Man — Miao." That is to say the Chinese were more or less slow in discovering with whom they were dealing [pp. 16–17].

Quincy (1988) supports this point by saying, "For the consensus among experts is that the Hmong became part of Chinese history no later than 1200 B.C. and perhaps as early as 3000 B.C., which is the date given by ancient Chinese historians" (p. 24). Quincy (1988) states that in the Chinese legends the Miao (Mong) were mentioned during the period around 2700 B.C. According to the Chinese legends, the Chinese Emperor U-Wang and his troops were defeated by the Mong, and a new Chinese warrior by the name of Huan-yuan became the leader. Huan-yuan and his armies defeated the Mong. Huan-yuan's leadership made him become an emperor that the Chinese called the Hoang-ti, the Yellow Emperor (Quincy, 1988).

Cultivation (*kiv ua laj ua teb*), raising livestock (*tu tsaj tu txhuv*), parenting (*ua neej hab tu tub tu kiv*) and conserving rituals (*ua dlaab ua qhua*), and customary traditional values (*coj kwv coj tij, coj neej coj tsaav hab ua noj ua haus*) were deeply rooted in the Mong daily cultural practices on the mountains of Laos. Geddes (1997), Cooper (1998), Lewis (1984), Boyes and Piraban (1990), and Cooper, Tapp, Lee and Schworer-Kohl (1996) who conduct their research about the Mong people who lived on the mountains in northern Thailand, reported that the Mong's daily survival relied on animal raising, rituals, farming, and hunting. These were skills that were passed down generation to generation. Cajete (1994) describes hunting as a form of spiritual learning and teaching in indigenous cultures. Chindarsi (1976) asserts that the Mong believed all things and places had spirits associated with them. When they cleared a place for farming, they honored the spirits of the place first. Chindarsi (1976) states, "During the clearing of the fields, whenever they are about to eat, the spirits must be invited to eat first" (p. 55). Cajete (1994) explains that to the Indian people everything begins and ends with the spirits. "The land was full of spirit" (Cajete, 1994, p. 75). Einhorn (2000) supports this statement: "By living things, Native Americans do not mean just people, trees, and plants. To them everything lives both physically and spiritually. Mountains move.

Winds whirl. Seas swirl. Trees, plants, and other elements in nature live, possess souls, and communicate" (p. 21). The Mong believe in spirits and nature similar to the Native American Indians as described by Cajete and Einhorn. American missionaries Paul and Elaine Lewis (1984) assert the Mong believe that there is a lord of the land. This lord protects the Mong from wild animals, fire, enemies, and evil spirits. Therefore, the Mong make offerings to the lord of the land once a year to help them sustain unity.

The Mong typical lifestyle on the mountains of Laos was associated mainly with farming and raising animals similar to the Mong who live in northern Thailand. Geddes (1976), Cooper (1984), Davidson (1993), and Cooper (1998) point out that in northern Thailand the Mong food resources are rice, corn and vegetables. Mong livestock are chicken, pigs, goats, cows, and water buffalo. Davidson (1993) notes that "chickens and pigs served as the main source of protein in the Hmong diet" (p. 50). O'Connor (1995) has stated "rice is the primary nutrient and the center-piece of the entire diet" (p. 88). The Mong left their animals to scavenge and browse around their village and in the forest. They built fences around their gardens and plantations to keep the animals out (Geddes, 1976; Cooper, 1984; Cooper, Tapp, Lee and Schworer-Kohl, 1996; Cooper, 1998).

FARMING

Cultivation was a formal task that kept the Mong busy from year to year. In Laos, all members in the family were good farmers because they had to know how to produce their own crops. Their crops depended on the weather. They did not use water irrigation, fertilizer and manure. Children were brought at a young age to the plantations to watch the parents, grandparents, older siblings, uncles, and aunts work in the field. The children absorbed farming techniques, and when they were ready, they joined in light work in the field. Children from seven to twelve years old were the primary babysitters, allowing the adults to work in the field. Geddes (1976) states, "Children may play an important part in the economy in other ways, too, such as helping with the planting of padi or maize, or looking after infants and so freeing their parents for more exacting agri-culture work" (p. 137).

The Elders who participated in this study said they learned how to farm by being with their parents. When they were small children they often went to the plantation with their family, because there was no one in the home to watch them. As they grew older they became babysitters for their younger siblings, nieces, and nephews. While they spent times observing the older people work in the plantations, they slowly gained the skills to participate with the work. Elder Jer Thao explained:

> When I was about six or seven years old I baby-sat my older brother Chue's (*Txiv Dlaab Tshuv*) small children and my youngest brother Seng (*Txiv Dlaab Xeev*) while my parents, older brother, and sister-in-law worked in the field. When the children were hungry, I carried them into the field to get breastfed from their mother. Sometime, I had to stay for several days in the plantation to watch my older brother's children, and I missed my mother very much. My mother had to come home to do other chores. There were no diapers for small children in Laos like in America. The small children wet my clothes everyday and it smelled of urine very bad. I had to change my clothes at least three to four times a day. At one time, I ran out of skirts to change and I had to wear the skirts that belonged to my older brother's wife. I watched my older brother's small children all the time and he got me several skirts. When I was old enough to do the work in the field, then I went to work. My brother had his older child watch the youngest. When my mother was getting old and she no longer could work in the field, then she watched her grandchildren [personal communication, Fresno, California].

Farming was a very important tradition to the Mong people. Cultivation was their main occupation and the way to bring food into the family. The larger the plantation the more crops a family produced to obtain more secure resources. Cooper (1998) asserts, "The Hmong have a very full working year. Because they traditionally produce three crops — rice, opium and maize — and since the 1970s, have added or substituted a variety of cash crops, the Hmong are more consistently busy in their fields than the great majority of traditional farmers in Asia, most of whom have a single main crop" (p. 67). However, Geddes (1976) and Cooper (1984, 1996, 1998) add their assumption that the Mong cultivated opium for cash economy. Cooper (1984) states, "Opium is both wealth and poverty to the Hmong" (p. 200). He repeatedly mentioned that opium production served as a larger scale cash crop for the Mong who lived on the mountains of northern Thailand. A similar assumption was made about the Mong people who lived on the mountains of Laos. Research is needed to investigate the history of opium cultivation that first began in China. Michaud and Culas (2000) describe how opium became the Chinese profitable crop in the early 1800s.

> As early as the eighteenth century, though, Chinese leaders were worried by this growing trade and the huge loss in revenue due to the net importation of thousands of tons of raw opium. Inevitably, as a result of such

high stakes, the two main opponents eventually clashed in what were called the Opium Wars (1839–42 and 1856–58), both of which were won by the European colonialists. Following the Opium Wars and the Treaty of Nanking in 1842, China was forced to allow the Europeans, and the Americans too, to install trade posts at a number of locations on the Chinese coast and, subsequently, to allow them to trade almost freely in the huge Chinese market. In order to compete with the intruders and avoid a huge loss in revenue due to the net importation of thousands of tons of raw opium, the only option left to the Chinese was to promote and support the production of opium within its own territory, which the central authorities quickly managed to do. The populations inhabiting the areas suitable for this production, basically the mountains and plateaux of the south, were pressured into growing poppies and producing raw opium for sale to government agents, to be processed and sold in the interior market [pp. 104–105].

Quincy (1988) adds that the Chinese used opium to trade with the Dutch, the Portuguese, and the British from the 1600s until after World War II. In this case, the Mong people who lived in the region where the Chinese promoted opium cultivation learned about the value of this drug. According to Pollard (1919), Geddes (1976), Mottin (1980), Quincy (1988), and Thao (1999a) the Mong people resided in the southern part of China in the Yunnan, Kweichow and Kwangsi Provinces before they migrated to Southeast Asia.

The Mong traditional agricultural practices on the mountains of Laos, Vietnam and Thailand are similar to the way people cultivated around the world before industrialization. They depend on the sun and the rain to help their crops grow. They need an open field to plant their crops so the crops can get good sunlight. Anthropologist Cooper's research about the Mong questions their farming method of slash-and-burn. He said the Mong swidden farming is destructive to the environment on the mountains of Thailand and Laos. Cooper, Tapp, Lee and Schworer-Kohl (1986) and Cooper (1998) state that they flew around northern Thailand and throughout the provinces in Laos and saw everywhere that the mountains had no trees because of the Mong cultivation. They did not mention anything about other ethnic minority hill tribes who also live and practice cultivation similar to the Mong, nor the lumber industry economy in Thailand and Laos. There were Karen, Khmu, Khmer, Lao Lue, Lao Theung, Lue, Mien, Thai Dam, Yunnanese, etc., living on the mountains in northern Thailand and Laos as the Mong neighbors (Lewis and Lewis, 1984; Smalley, 1994). The Mong Elders explained that not only the Mong cleared the jungles for farming. All the many tribes living in the mountains cultivate in that way. Also, they witnessed that the trees on the mountains in Laos were gone because of Laotian logging. Elder Chai Xiong explained:

> The Mong have only axes (*taus*) and long knives (*txuas*) to cut the trees. When we cleared the forest, it took us months. The big trees took about three to five men to bring one tree down. It took them a half to one full day to chop the tree down. The Laotian loggers have saws and machines. They brought down the big trees easily. They used elephants to help them with the logging. The elephants dragged the logs to the road, then they put them onto the logging trucks to take to their cities.

PARENTING

Parenting was an important part of the Mong everyday practice. They took care of their children and spouse in order to have a prosperous and healthy family. The Elders said parenting was the first lesson they received when they were young girls and boys. They were taught to take care of their younger siblings, nieces, and nephews. As they reached puberty they knew that sooner or later they would marry, have children, and start their own family. Therefore, they had to have the knowledge and skills to prepare themselves as a father or mother. Elder Xao Cheng Lee expressed:

> I learned about sexuality secretly. Something I did not know, I asked my older brother, friends, and uncles. My parents did not teach me about sex. They taught me important lessons about how to take care of my wife and my children. My parents said if I do not take good care of my wife and she no longer can have a baby than I will not have a happy life. Especially, after she gave labor. She needs to rest. She cannot eat hard food, drink cold water and perform heavy tasks. These things could cause damage to her uterus while she is healing. Also, children are the most important gift in my culture. They said if one does not have children, then one's life is not complete. When the children are young my wife and I must nurture them and make sure they are healthy, teach them the necessary skills in the Mong customary values (*kiv le kiv cai*) so they can join the work with the family and also pass the customs to their children [personal communication, Merced, California].

The Elders with whom I dialogued explained that the Mong men and women have different roles in terms of parenting. The role of the father is to make sure the children fulfill the obligation to maintain their kinship and family rituals. The mother's role is to make sure the children know how to show respect to the older people, learn basic working skills, and establish solid working habits so they can perform these tasks themselves. Lee (1999) asserts that the Mong men are expected to teach the boys folk songs, poetry, riddles, proverbs, rituals, and secret language in their religion. The Mong women do similar things, but mostly for the girls. Goldstein (1988) adds that the men are responsible for heavy agriculture work such as clearing land for planting, serving as economic producers, maintaining the relationship between the family's clan and outside clans, and bringing subsistence needs into their family. The Mong women are to give birth, supervise children, and teach children to work hard. Elder Phoua Her responded,

> When I was a young girl (*ua hluas nkauj nyob*) my parents always reminded me that after I married I must give my greatest respect to my husband. When people respect my husband than they would have the same respect for me. In order to be a good wife, I need to be sure my children learn all the skills that my parents taught me so once they married they can begin their own life. My mother said to me that as a girl I must not create any problems that would damage the family reputation. I must always watch myself before I do things. This is my role. My husband's role is to pass on the family's rituals, and ritualistic language and songs to my sons. I am Shaman, but I perform only the Shaman ritual and practice herbal medicines. All the family-related rituals I leave to my husband to teach to my children [personal communication, Susan City, California].

Vang (1999) elaborates the roles of men and women in the Mong traditional culture:

> In Hmong culture, the man is considered to be the head of the household. He has the power and authority to make decisions. He is the breadwinner and has responsibility for the family's economic welfare. The Hmong woman is expected through marriage to become a homemaker and mother. These are the primary roles she is to fulfill during her lifetime [p. 223].

RITUALS AND CUSTOMARY TRADITIONAL VALUES

Rituals and customary traditional values are significant to the Mong oral culture practices. Parents must make sure their children continue to carry on these important traditions. The men take seriously their responsibility to teach the males the Mong ritualistic sacred language, chants, and songs. Also, the knowledge about family ancestor ritual performances must be possessed by the males in order to honor the house's spirits and ancestors' spirits. Tapp (1989) states, "The Hmong world is inhabited by a variety of natural, ancestral, and supernatural spirits or gods" (p. 59). Chindarsi (1976) supports this statement saying that the Mong believe in the supernatural and that all men as well as all living things have souls. When they die, their souls return to an afterworld to wait for reincarnation. Lewis (1984) asserts, "Supernatural beings are involved in every aspect of Hmong life" (p. 131). Because of this, the Mong must know the rituals in order to fulfill their spiritual beliefs of the cosmos (Geddes, 1976; Chindarsi, 1976; Mottin, 1980; Lewis and Lewis, 1984; Thao, 1986; Bliatout, 1986; Tapp, 1989; Symonds, 1991; Cooper, Tapp, Lee and Schworer-Kohl, 1986; Ensign, 1994; Cooper, 1998). Within the Mong cosmology, spirits cannot be separated from living and non-living things. Spirits are present to guide, protect and heal individuals. Symonds (1991) describes, "Men must know the Hmong way, the rituals and traditions of the clan and lineage, so that they can honor the ancestors" (p. 118).

The Mong women play a similar role but they are expected to make sure the Mong children maintain their customary traditional values. The women must train their children to learn how to define themselves as good citizens such as being a hard worker, being a good listener to the old people, not questioning the elders, being respectful to others, and being capable of performing tasks around the house and on the plantations. Children must also learn to recognize the roles and status between family and extended family members as well as close relatives. There is a way for the Mong to address one another and everyone must know how to carry out this role and behavior when they become teenagers and adults. Teenage boys and girls were taught by their mother to behave in certain ways. Symonds (1991) finds that the Mong girls were taught to be hard workers and to consistently keep themselves busy even after completing their assigned tasks. When they finish their task, they need to do sewing. Elder Lee Xiong told her story:

> I worked hard all my life. I never got to rest. My older brother who I lived with said to me that if I work and I rest a lot then I force myself to be lazier. I remember after I became an orphan and I went to live with my older brother and his wife, I had to work hard all the time. Whenever I had a free time, I did my sewing. I had to sew for my youngest brother and myself because we had no mother to sew clothing for us. Now, when I think about my life in the past it makes me want to cry. I had a very difficult childhood experience. My parents died when I was a little girl and I lived with my older brother and his wife until I got married [personal communication, Stockton, California].

Girls who do nothing are defined as lazy. Also, young girls must learn to dress themselves appropriately when they go out, so they do not embarrass their parents and family. Symonds (1991) writes, "I was told that to go out without *sev* would cause one to be shame-faced (*txaj muag*)"

(p. 124). The *sev* is a two-piece trouser like an apron that the White Mong women wear to cover their pants on the back and on the front. The Mong Leng or Blue Mong women wear skirts only. They have a one-piece *sev* and it covers the front.

The teenage boys were taught to take on their father's role when the family had guests or go out and do their tasks without the father present. Elder Chong Yer Thao said,

> When I was a young boy my parents showed me how to watch the Shaman perform rituals (*saib neeb*). My father is a Shaman and whenever my older brother was not home then I watched my father perform his rituals. I assisted my father to burn the paper money and incense during his rituals. I hold him to keep him balanced so he does not fall off from the bench while he performs ritual. During his ritual performance, he jumped up to stand on the bench when he guards the spirits so I have to stand behind him to hold him in case he falls. My mother told me that I must be able to accompany our guests if my father and older brothers are not home. Also, I must be a hard worker so as I grew up to be a man people would like my tasks and work habits. Then, I become attractive to young women and their parents with my skills. This is the only way I can get myself a good wife [personal communication, Stockton, California].

In the Mong tradition, when they seek a husband, wife, son-in-law or daughter-in-law, they prefer someone who is a hard worker, respectful to the older people, and has a good reputation.

Summary

The origin and history of the Mong, their oral cultural tradition, and cultural practices examined in this chapter are the fundamentals of culture that defined the Mong people. They relied on this important oral tradition to be passed on to the younger generation. This tradition is still an everyday living experience and memory to the Mong elders.

3

Mong Society and Sociocultural Settings

Mong society centers around a kinship system and operates through communal lifestyles. The Mong people establish strong alliances within the foundation of clan organizations. Clans function to unite, organize, support, and govern family and social positions. In this context, religious doctrine plays a very important role in balancing people's selves with nature both physically and mentally. This chapter describes the kinship system, cultural identity, environment, and social dynamics.

The Mong Kinship System

Kinship regulates relations within a relatively small collective (group) of people; it mediates the individual's position in a system of horizontal ties by superseding the discrete character of different descent groups. Descent regulates relations between different groups and at the same time establishes the individual's membership in a given society as a whole and in specific subdivisions of it; this membership involves both corresponding rights and commitments and sometimes even social positions [Khazanov, 1994, p. 140].

Kinship in Mong society is established to guide cultural tradition, language, and religion within each collective clan group as well as to define social and political positions. Twelve original clans can be found in the Mong society: Chang (*Tsaab*), Hang (*Haam*), Her (*Hawj*), Chue (*Tswb*),

31

Khang (*Khaab*), Lee (*Lis*), Moua (*Muas*), Song (*Ntxhoo*), Thao (*Thoj*), Vang (*Vaaj*), Xiong (*Xyooj*) and Yang (*Yaaj*). In addition to these twelve clans, some believe that other clans such as the Cheng (*Tsheej*), Fang (*Faaj*), Kong (*Koo*), Kue (*Kwm*), Lor (*Lauj*), Phang (*Phab*), Vue (*Vwj*) and others branch off from one of the twelve original clans. These clans do not have signified sacred ritual names. Studies show that there are eighteen clans that have been identified in Western anthropological studies, but in the White Hmong dialect there are names found for more clans (Cooper, 1998).

The Elders said that each clan is attached to a sacred ritual name called "*qhua*." For example, Chang is *qhua nrig*, Hang is *qhua taag*, Her is *qhua dluag*, Chue is *qhua nkug*, Khang is *qhua pluag*, Lee *is qhua cai*, Moua is *qhua zaag*, Song is *qhua koo*, Thao is *qhua dlub*, Vang is *qhua vug*, Xiong is *qhua mob*, and Yang is *qhua yawg*. Thao (1999a) has found that the dynamics of these sets of ritual (*qhua*) are difficult to describe in English.

All the clans existing in the Mong society, according to the Elders have twelve sets of sacred ritual names (*qhua*). The twelve clans that have sacred ritual names are believed to more accurately represent the origin of Mong clans. Thao (1999a) has found supporting evidence for this information provided by the Elders, and he has concluded that "the traditional Mong consisted of twelve clans that corresponded to their rituals. Mong rituals are related to Mong religion directly" (p. 12). To Thao's statement Elder Xao Cheng Lee has replied:

> If an older person does not know his/her sacred ritual name (*qhua*) then this person no longer has the information about his/her kin. There are some clans who do not know their (*qhua*) and these are the clans that are isolated from their original clans. They change (*txa*) to a different clan. Then, they adopted a different dialect and costume. This is a reason why we had Mong Leng and White Hmong. When I asked the White Hmong about their (*qhua*), some no longer know them. They could tell me which clan they belong to but they said they do not have a (*qhua*). For example, some of the Lee members who I came across do not know that we are (*qhua cai*). I am not sure whether they really belong to my clan. They probably converted from other clans because they do not have a sacred ritual name (*qhua*) [personal communication, Merced, California].

The Mong clan system functions to maintain unity and relationships between related clans and clan members and help them to provide spiritual support to one another. Members from the same clan treat one another like one big family even though they do not know one another. Membership in the clan automatically identifies them as related to each other either by religious root or nuclear family.

A person who has a different clan name is considered an outsider to members of other clans. Parents and grandparents often make sure that their children can identify their kin and recognize the members of their patrilineal clan as one large family (*ib cuab*) to continue building their alliances. Lewis (1984) describes the Mong patrilineal clan system as having strong ties with social, political, economic, and religious aspects. It serves as a primary focus for the Mong daily life. The patrilineal clan role is viewed differently from clan to clan. Each clan's priority is to establish a mutual support system for the members of the clan and a person who shares similar kin. They deliver services to support relatives and friends of outside clans after they have taken care of their own clan. The outside clan members are considered *neej tsaa*, meaning relatives. Clan members establish their relationships with other clans through marriage. The *neej tsaa* includes the wife's parents and her side of the family. Members in the same clan are *kwvtij habnkauj muam*, meaning brothers and sisters.

When the women marry they keep their clan, but the children are given the clan of their father. The children automatically become part of the father's patrilineal clan and worship the father's ancestors' spirits. Cooper (1998) states that these people only trace their descendants on the male side of the family and ancestors. Lee (1986) adds that after the men marry and they have two to three children, then they establish their own family. Although they have their own family, they still keep the nuclear family rituals. For this reason, clan members who do not have the same nuclear family rituals cannot die and/or have a funeral in each other's houses. Lee (1986) elaborates on the family-granted funeral ceremony: "Members of a 'ceremonial household' can die and have funerals in one another's houses, as they would share similar ancestral rituals. People merely belonging to a clan or subclan cannot be granted this ceremonial privilege" (p. 58).

The notion of clanship is to determine the religious roots in each clan, how people honor their ancestors' spirits, perform their rituals, and the rules of behavior certain clans forbid. Lewis (1984) asserts, "Each clan has its own way of doing things, such as healing" (p. 124). A clan is prohibited to eat certain food. For instance, the Yang clan does not eat a heart (*plawv*), the Lee clan does not eat a spleen (*po*), the Vang clan does not eat sour fruit with rice, etc. If a member of the clan eats this food by accident, then nothing will happen to them or the members of their family. But, if the food is eaten intentionally then either that person or a member of the family will become blind, ill or die. When preparing food, people are always careful not to mix their food with the items that they are forbidden to eat. For instance, if a family in the Lee clan has a meal and this family is inviting members from the Yang clan to join them, then a spleen and a heart need to be thrown away. The Lee family knows that they cannot cook hearts mixed with the food because the Yang clan members cannot eat it. All clans know what other clans' food taboos are and they respect the taboos. It becomes a part of each clan's religious cult. There has been no research about why certain clans have a taboo about eating certain foods as part of their religion. This topic needs further research.

An important ritual occurs when a person is leaving the family or adding a new member to the family. The family must inform the ancestors' spirits. This is clearly defined at a wedding ritual. The parents must notify the bride's ancestors' spirits that she is no longer living with them. She will no longer worship their ancestors' spirits or need them as her protector and guidance. In this case she can eat a heart (*plawv*) even if she is a member of the Yang clan because she no longer belongs to the family. Her husband and his parents must notify their ancestors' spirits when she joins the family in order that she may receive spiritual guidance and protection. She becomes a member of her husband's family. A house headman must notify the ancestors' spirits when there is a death in the family. A newborn child must also be announced to the spirits through a soul calling ritual (*hu plig*). This way, the ancestors' spirits can protect the child. According to Elder Mai Vang, soul callings vary in the Mong tradition. She described the soul callings for a newborn child:

> When all my babies were three days old my husband and I must perform a soul calling ritual (*hu plig*) to them. Usually, my husband went to call an elder who knows how to perform the soul calling ritual to come perform this ritual. This ritual must be done on the morning in this third day. During this ritual, we gave names to our babies. My husband's parents or grandparents helped us find the names for our children. We named our children after my husband's great grandparents or great uncles who lived long, healthy and had a good life but they are no longer living. My children take my husband's clan. I am a Vang clan. I kept my clan but my husband's ancestor's spirits (*puj yawm txwv txoob*) were my protectors. When my husband and his side of the family call me they go by my husband's name. They never call my last name or clan. If someone asks me which clan I belong to, I say I am a Vang but my husband is a Thao [personal communication, Long Beach, California].

A wife bridges between her clan and her husband's clan. The wife's parents and her side of the family (*neej tsaa*) have the important role of speaking out to the wife's husband's family and his kin when her parents-in-law die, she dies, her husband dies or she has family disputes. The *neej tsaa* must be invited to sit in these events to ensure her wealth and happiness. When there is a family feast such as New Year (*Noj Tsab*), the wife's parents and brothers (*neej tsaa*) must be invited to eat the meal. This custom is true for both sides of the wife's husband's family and her parents' family. Elder Jer Thao shared why her (*neej tsaa*) did not support her after she married.

> My parents and brothers (*neej tsaa*) loved me very much when I lived with them. After I got married, they changed. They did not do that to my sisters who also married. When they had their New Year feast, they invited all my sisters and their husbands except my husband and I. They made me mad so I never visited them. My mother told me that the reason they do not like my husband and me is because my husband's family is disrespectful to my family. They already warned me not to marry my husband because he will never love me. They know my husband's family well. I did not listen to them. I went out with my husband a couple of times and I married him. After I was married to him for a few years, he no longer loved me. He was playing around and talking about marrying a second wife. He broke my heart. I went to my parents and brothers for help. They refused to support me because I did not listen to them when I was single. Because of the conflicts between my husband's family and my family I decided not to share with my parents about the way my husband treated me. I did not want to create another problem to my family. If my parents and brothers know about it then they will follow up the problem. My husband, his family, and my family will have more problems come between each other. I decided not to cause any more problems to my family. I no longer bothered them. After my husband died, I saw my older brother (*dlaab tshuv*), and he told me not to remarry. He said I must listen to my family this time. If I married a man who only loved me but not my children then I would have a harsh life. It was better for me to remain as a widow so my children do not have a hard time. I listened to him. This was the reason why I chose to stay as a widow [personal communication, Fresno, California].

A kinship system has a unique tradition that builds strong mutual assistance between all the families and clans. The Mong believe that to provide and share their resources with extended family, to assist them to perform ritual tasks, attend family feasts, and provide hospitality to other families builds mutual support and trust with different families in a similar clan as well as with other clans. Trueba, Jacobs and Kirton (1990) comment on important kinship relationships:

> Kinship relationships based on patrilineal clans and patrilineage were essential in cultivation and relocation activities which a single nuclear

family could not handle. Kinship ties were critical, both in organizing groups of Hmong and in providing backup resources during relocation [p. 23].

The Mong people referred to these types of mutual services as exchange services (*kiv pauv dlaag zug*). When a family has no food or has other difficulty, other families are there to assist the family. Usually, these services are provided by similar clan members. If there are no similar clan members around, friends and relatives (*neej tsaa*) of different clans step in to help. These services are free, because they generate life-time support to all families, and clans pass on the tradition from one generation to the next. The Elders told that no one knows the path to the future. It is better to follow your customs to help others. They believe that one day all your good deeds will return to you, your children, or grandchildren when they need help. Funeral and wedding rituals are the two major events where people need the most help to perform certain tasks. The people who help with these tasks are not concerned about getting paid. The Elders stated that money does not buy happiness nor provide them the kind of services they receive free from one another from generation to generation. Mutual assistance serves as the principles of lifelong support that maintain the culture and keep society strong and alive. Elder Boua Tong Yang described:

> When I was young, I was a *txwv qeej* (a person who takes on the position to play a sacred *qeej* instrument in the funeral). If a family has funeral rituals, I would go and help them. I learned that if I went to help other *txwv qeej* then when I take on the role of *txwv qeej*, they come to help me too. A *txwj qeej* position in the funeral rite is very difficult. I played the sacred *qeej* instrument for many hours nonstop. I played through the day and night. If I did not have anyone to help me then I can be very exhausted. This never happened because the *txwv qeej* was always willing to help each other when there is a funeral. Usually, a funeral rite lasts for many days, and if I was being selected to be the *txwv qeej*, then I have to carry my duty to the end. I do not get paid for these kinds of services. I do this in hoping that someday they would do the same thing to my family or extended families when we need their help. We do not do like the American professionals where they charge people forty to fifty dollars for one hour. My people do not place price values to things and our services. Also, I am a Shaman. When I perform my ritual to cure the illness, I do not charge them like the way the American doctors do. The American doctors look at your eyes, ears or body and they charge you hundreds of dollars. My people do not do that to other people. I do not charge people money when I perform my services. Sometimes, I perform my Shaman ritual and they give me money. I do not take their money. I think in this country, the Americans

look at mutual support in a different way then the way my people think [personal communication, Sacramento, California].

Cultural Identity

The notion of ethnic identity developed by DeVos includes language, religious, cultural traditions, folklore, lifestyle and art [Trueba, Jacobs and Kirton, p. 22].

This section describes the different Mong dialects, costumes, religious rituals, and culture conflict between the elders and their grandchildren. There are two dialects spoken by the Mong people. One dialect is called the Mong Leng (*Moob Leeg*) and the other is the White Hmong (*Hmoob Dawb*). In American literature one can find the term "Mong Leng" referring to "Blue Hmong" or "Green Hmong." Thao (1999a) states that the term "Green Hmong" has a negative connotation attached to describe the Mong Leng implying that they practiced a cult of cannibalism. "Green Hmong" is offensive to the Mong Leng because they do not practice cannibalism. The concern of culture identity has been a constant issue to both the *Moob Leeg* and the *Hmoob Dawb*, and their dialects and costumes differ. These differences have led to years of tension between the two groups. Each group wants to keep the identity of their dialect, costume and traditional values. Even though there is an identity conflict the two groups have learned to live together peacefully as one society for thousands of years. Thao (1999a) identifies the two dialects:

> The two dialects can be mutually and intelligibly understood by the members of the other group. The two groups can be compared to people who speak American English and British English with approximately thirty percent (30%) difference in ethno-culture and language. The two groups have interwoven their bonds through intermarriage for centuries but, surprisingly, have preserved their linguistic and cultural homogeneity, and have respected each other's differences. Both groups have lived with each other harmoniously for centuries. In fact, their patterns of interaction constitute a system of checks and balances within the Mong society [pp. 3–4].

The Elders indicated that sometimes these two dialects can be very confused when people speak to one another. Some words pronounced differently by the Mong Leng and the White Hmong mean the same thing. The Mong Leng call a firewood carrier (*kiabcuam*), and rice grain (*ntsab*) whereas the White Hmong call a firewood carrier (*Khib*) and rice grain (*txhuv*). If one is not have familiar with these terms, he/she does not know what is meant. Sometime the members of one group may think these differences are used purposely as threats. The Elders described a situation when two best friends (*phooj ywg*) went hunting. One was a White Hmong and one a Mong Leng. The Mong Leng said to his friend who was White Hmong that tonight we would use your rice grain (*ntsab*) to cook dinner and tomorrow they would use my rice (*ntsab*) to cook for breakfast. The White Hmong misinterpreted the word his friend used for rice grain (*ntsab*) and he thought his Mong Leng friend would grab him and cook him for dinner so he ran home. The word *ntsab* to White Hmong means grab.

According to Thao (1999a), the term "Mong Leng" means vein. It refers to the veins that carry the life blood of all Mong. The term "White Hmong" is named after the ceremonial skirts worn by the White Hmong female (Cohen, 1987). The spelling of Hmong is a preferred term in the White Hmong dialect, but the Mong Leng prefer to be called "Mong." Bliatout, Downing, Lewis and Yang (1988) add that the terms Mong and Hmong reflect the dialects spoken. The differences of the two dialects are like British and American English. Lewis (1984) elaborates on the different pronunciation of the terms Hmong and Mong:

> The name "Hmong" (spoken with a slight aspiration through the nostrils as the *m* is enunciated) has become the one more commonly used among English speakers, and is the form we use. It should be remembered, however, that in the Blue Mong dialect the *m* is not aspirated. In both cases the *o* is pronounced as in the English word "roam" [p. 102].

Besides difference in the dialects, each group dresses differently. The females who are Mong Leng wear only skirts and blouses. These skirts are made in thick cross-stitch embroidery, batik designed, and have bright colors (Lewis & Lewis, 1984; Kohler, 1986). The White Hmong are divided into several subdivisions and some females wear skirts, pants, and striped cloths. The pants are solid black and the skirts are solid white. The men's outfits also differ. Lewis (1984) describes the different dress: "Blue Hmong pants are extremely full, having narrow openings for the ankles with the very wide crotch falling mid-way between calves and ankles. White Hmong pants are less full, having a higher crotch" (p. 114). The two groups each have a preference for decorating their outfits. There are many kinds of cross-stitch designs worn by both the Mong Leng and the White Hmong. These different types of stitched artwork on their clothing are based on the tribal and geographical region in which they lived. They also have specially designed costumes for religious celebrations (Chindarsi, 1976; Lewis and Lewis, 1984; Kohler, 1986; Cohen, 1987; Conquergood, 1992). The ornamental designs on some of the Mong outfits are to protect them from the evil spirits. There are burial clothes and clothes that have similar textile designs. These different costume designs represent the diversity of Mong (Kohler, 1986; Cohen, 1987). The Elders said the Mong Leng and the White Hmong often joke and tease about one another's costumes. When they are angry with each other, they use swear words that rhyme to talk about how the others wear their clothes and the things each owns. The words in Mong that are in italics below are rhymes. Elder Ying Yang described the verbal fight in both groups:

> When a Mong Leng person and a White Hmong person have a verbal fight, they often bring up the stereotype of how each wears their outfits. If a White Hmong person is angry at a Mong Leng, he or she calls a Mong Leng person names (*lees txia kua, lees txia ntshav*), meaning the Mong Leng's vein is bleeding liquid and bleeding blood hard; (*Lees taug tsws ntev, ntsaum nab pom ntsawm nab plev*), meaning Mong Leng men wear pants with a long crotch and red ants see it then red ants crawl up from the pants to sting. A Mong Leng says back to a White Hmong (*Zoo le nam qaav tsuam qai*), meaning White Hmong look like a frog sitting on the nest; (*Moob dlawb taug tsws luv ntsaum naab pum ntsaum naab tug*), meaning White Hmong men wear pants with a short crotch, red ants see then red ants bite. Listening to the language a Mong Leng and a White Hmong exchange in their verbal fights makes people want to laugh. They go on and on saying bad things about each other's costume and the items they had such as a Mong Leng called a White Hmong (*Moob Dlawb tsws khawb tawb*), meaning White Hmong carry old baskets. A White Hmong said back to the Mong Leng (*Hmoob Lees ev tawb nees*), meaning Mong Leng carry a horse basket [personal communication, Montclair, California].

Elder Chong Yer Thao stated in his story that when he was a young man, sometimes he had verbal fights with his girlfriends who were White Hmong. They exchanged bad words with one another about the negative stereotypes of each other's culture. If a Mong Leng young man asked a White Hmong young woman out and she did not like him, she would say (*peb tsis nyiam cov nias lees zoo li nej es*), meaning we do not like the veins bleeding like you, whereas a Mong Leng young woman would have said to a White Hmong young man (*peb tsis nyiam cov nam qaav le mej as*), meaning we do not like your frog look.

In addition to the different dialects and costumes, each group has slightly different religious rituals. The Mong have a very complex religious system (Chindarsi, 1976; Geddes, 1976; Mottin, 1980; Lewis and Lewis, 1984; Cohen, 1987; Quincy, 1988; Symonds, 1991; Cooper, 1998; Thao, 1999b, 2002). The Elders said that one example of their differences is observed at the funeral rite when it is time to kill the ox to sacrifice to the dead parents' souls. The Mong Leng have their brothers-in-law (*Txwv*

Dlaab) do the killing whereas the White Hmong have their aunts and their husbands (*Phauj*) kill the animals. Elder Xao Cheng Lee said, "Long time ago, there were more Mong Leng than White Hmong but the Mong Leng who no longer know their religion have converted (*txa ua Moob dlawb*) to become White Hmong" (personal communication, Merced, California). Some of the Elders who speak the White Hmong dialect acknowledge that the Mong Leng were their original ancestors but somehow their great grandparents lost contact with them.

When the Chinese captured and persecuted the Miao (Mong), some families changed their costumes and dialects so that the Chinese could not find them. Other Mong Leng families converted to White Hmong because they lost connection with their nuclear family, and they depended on the White Hmong who had their similar kin as their primary support. Some Mong Leng men married to White Hmong women, who have no nuclear family to support them, begin to speak the White Hmong dialect and adapt to the White Hmong costume with the support and influence of the wife's parents and family. The Elders said that one can find other differences in family rituals because the family has lost their nuclear family's ancestral rituals.

The Elders believe that the purpose of cultural identity is to pass on language, culture, and ritualistic values from their nuclear family to the younger generation. If one does not have a cultural identity, one does not have a strong sense of his/her culture. This is one reason that the Mong fought all their lives to preserve their culture and identity after the Chinese conquered the Miao (Mong). The Elders explained that the Chinese not only destroyed much of the Mong identity and culture, they also destroyed the Mong graves. Some Mong made their grave sites like the Chinese to preserve them. Quincy (1988) comments upon the importance of this historical event:

> Repeated forced migrations meant leaving the graves of ancestors behind, and Hmong legend indicates that the conquering Chinese often desecrated Hmong graveyards, a matter of critical concern for the Hmong since this would anger the ancestors and possibly bring illness, death or misfortune to the family. For this reason many Hmong began to disguise their grave sites or fashion them in the Chinese way so that invading Chinese would not know they belonged to Hmong. Even today there are Hmong in Southeast Asia whose grave sites ape those of the Chinese [p. 97].

The Elders shared that they face new obstacles living in the United States. The younger generation begins to lose its cultural identity and it causes them to abandon the Mong culture (Adler, 2000). Elder Lee Xiong responded to this issue:

I see my grandchildren are losing their culture and identity day by day. They no longer like to eat the food I eat, speak the language I speak and wear the clothes I wear. When it is New Year, I encouraged them to wear Mong clothes and they said to me that the Mong clothes make them look stupid. It is not their style. Also, my grandchildren are no longer polite to their parents and the elders. They call their parents whatever names they like. I heard some of my grandchildren call their parents by their name, others call their parents daddy and mommy. I correct them to call their parents, my dad (*kuv iv*) and my mom (*kuv nam*). They do not know what *kuv iv* and *kuv nam* means. I explained to my grandchildren that your parents are the two most important people in your life. They give you birth and they must be respected. When my grandchildren upset their parents, they called them names that I do not know but I assumed that these are bad names. I never called my parents, grandparents and the elders with bad names. I can tell by the look on my grandchildren's face and their emotion. Now, the young people are very different than the young people on the mountains of Laos [personal communication, Stockton, California].

The Elders elaborated that the way their grandchildren react to the food they eat and the language they speak at home clearly show that they lack cultural identity. Some young people refuse to eat Mong food. The younger generation no longer wants to eat traditional food prepared by their parents, grandparents, and the older people. Researchers state that Mong produce their own food which comes from their livestock and crops (Geddes, 1976; Cooper, 1984, 1998; Davidson, 1993, O'Connor, 1995). Davidson (1993) asserts that chicken and pork serve as protein in the Mong diet. Rice and maize are the Mong's main crops (Geddes, 1976; Cooper, 1984, 1998; O'Connor, 1995). The Elders said rice is the main dish for every meal. They eat vegetables and meat with rice. These dishes are commonly boiled. On certain occasions, they toast their meat over the fire and stir fry them with green mustard or cabbage. They have several special dishes such as blood dessert (*ntshaav teev*), bitter gut (*quav ab*), and beef, pork, or chicken salad (*lav*). These special dishes are prepared only for special feasts and are made from fresh meat, slaughtered by butchers. On their own mountains, the Mong butchered their own animals.

The Elders expressed major concerns about their grandchildren losing their cultural identity. They observed their grandchildren reacting negatively about Mong food, culture, language, and religion. Now the younger generation attends public school and acquires knowledge that leads them to reject their traditional values. The Elders reported that their grandchildren prefer fast food restaurants and food sold at the supermarkets. They feel that their Mong food is not safe, because no health department officer examines the meats and vegetables that their parents and grandparents use to prepare meals at home. The younger generation believes that the meats and vegetables in the grocery stores are examined by the health department and are safe to eat. The Elders believe differently. They said that supermarket foods are over-ripe, unsafe, have no flavor, and are too expensive. They would rather grow their own vegetables and go to the slaughterhouse to get their meats. They save money and have fresher food. The Elders believe that their traditional values and cultural beliefs are no longer important to the younger generation that lives in the United States. The Mong younger generation who live in the United States have less interest in their parents' and grandparents' traditional values, and the Elders fear there is no hope to keep their culture alive. Trueba, Jacobs and Kirton (1990) speak to this concept of culture conflict:

> As grandparents tell and retell stories and tales of the Hmong, they are also passing along their view of the world, their values, traditions and lifestyle. These values have survived through domination in Laos, degrading experiences in refugee camps in Thailand, and are now sometimes in conflict with the new standards of American culture [p. 61].

The Environment

> Ultimately, there is no separation between humans and the environment. Humans affect the environment and the environment affects humans. Indigenous practices were founded on this undeniable reality and sought to perpetuate a sustainable and mutually reciprocal relationship Cajete, 1994, p. 84].

Certain settings are very sacred to the Mong people. This includes locations in the home, in the field, or in the forest. They are always careful about finding a place to live, to farm, and to bury the dead. They believe that everything exists in nature, which is associated with and governed by spirits (Chindarsi, 1976; Bliatout, 1986; Lemoine, 1986; Thao, 1986; Tapp, 1989; Symonds, 1991; Livo and Cha, 1991; Fadiman, 1997; Cooper, 1998; Thao, 2002). Therefore, the spirits must be treated with respect to prevent death or misfortune. If the spirits that live in the environment are not happy, family members may become poor, ill, or die. In order to avoid such curses the family must consult the spirits before they make decisions about moving from one environment to the other. Livo and Cha (1991) assert that Mong believe every place such as ponds, streams, rivers, hills, valleys, trees, rocks, and even wind currents, has individual spirits. If the spirits are harmed they may cause people to become ill.

The Elders stated that it is important for one to recognize and understand that the world is inhabited with a variety of spirits. There are good or "tame" and evil or "wild" spirits. When family members go hunting, gathering, fishing, and farming they must not boast (*khaav theeb*) to the spirits. If they do not keep a low profile of what they do or say about the spirits in the new environment, the spirits will make some kind of strange noise and high wind to frighten them. This frightening scene can cause a person to *poob plig*, meaning lose his/her soul. Then the person may become ill and sometimes die. Livo and Cha (1991) add that, "If the soul fails to return, death results" (p. 3). A person who is no longer in possession of the soul is dead. American journalist Anne Fadiman (1997) misinterpreted the Mong spiritual beliefs in *qaug dab peg* in her book *The Spirit Catches You and You Fall Down*. The spirit catches you means to protect and guide you. Therefore, you never fall down. *Qaug dab peg* means that an evil spirit called *dab peg* enters into your body to cause this *qaug dab peg* phenomenon. This evil spirit is believed to belong to certain animals. The Elders noted that a person who had the *qaug dab peg* illness could be cured by a Shaman. The Shaman could perform a ritual to send this evil spirit (*dab peg*) back to its own place so it would no longer inhabit a person's body to cause illness. The Elders said that one evil spirit they are most afraid of is called a *Phislosvais*. When a *Phislosvais* scares you, it seems like all the trees are falling, the earth is shaking, and your heart is beating fast from the sound made by this creature. Elder Phoua Her described, "The thing we were afraid of most was the *Phislosvais hab xeeb teb xeeb chaw* (a creature that lives in the forest or the spirit of nature). When we went to sleep over in the plantation or jungles we must be careful not to do anything to anger the spirits of nature" (personal communication, Susan City, California). This *Phislosvais* can kill you. Elder Nhia Cha Yang shared an experience when a *Phislosvais* scared him in Laos.

> It was on an afternoon at my plantation; I went into the forest to hunt. When I walked into the forest, suddenly the sky turns black; the wind begins to blow hard. Soon, there was a loud sound like a pig crying. Where I was standing there are lots of trees and some banana trees. I was carrying an M-16 automatic rifle. I got this rifle from joining the army. I had heard my elders talk about this creature (*Phislosvais*). I knew right away that this must be a *Phislosvais*. Everything was happening so quickly, I could not see anything at all. I felt like the earth was shaking from the sound that this creature made. It looked like a tornado (*khaub yig cua kis*). All the trees are spinning and falling. At that time I have a full magazine of ammunition loaded onto my rifle. I started shooting until my rifle was empty. Then I popped out the magazine and reloaded a new magazine. Then, the pig sound stopped and everything was back

to normal. I ran back to the open field on my rice plantation. My wife and children were working on the field. They asked me what do I shoot and why I was running. I told them a *Phislosvais* scared me. I asked them if they heard a pig sound and felt the tornado. They said they hear and feel nothing. They only heard my gun shots. My elders said when a *Phislosvais* scared; only the people who this creature want to bother can hear and feel it. If you do not have anything to help you then this *Phislosvais* can kill and eat you. In this case, I believe my gun saved me. After I finished shooting, the *Phislosvais* stop [personal communication, Banning, California].

The Elders said a person's body is governed by the souls of his/her ancestors and the good spirits keep the evil spirits away. Anytime this person moves to a different environment, it is like crossing a boundary where evil spirits can easily attack. Therefore, it is important to call the ancestors' spirits for protection and consult with the spirits to foretell the future before traveling to a different environment. A common ritual (*siab yiag*) the Mong usually perform before relocating their village, building a home, or finding a place to farm is the sacrifice of two chickens to the spirits. They have an Elder such as the head of the house, grandparent, or uncle say a sacred chant to the two chickens. The chant asks the chickens' help to communicate with the spirits by leaving omens on the chickens' feet, skulls, and tongues for good or bad news about the trip that they are planning or a location they will visit. Then, they kill the chickens and clean them carefully. They boil the whole chickens in a big pot until half cooked (*vum*). They take the chickens out and put them on a bamboo tray (*vaab*). The Elders who know how to read the spirit signs of the chickens' feet, skulls and tongues examine them. If positive signs appear on the chickens' feet, tongues and skulls, they proceed with the plan. If the Elders have concerns about the way the signs read, they change their plan.

The Elders said that when they are looking for a new location to build a house or to relocate the whole village and/or agriculture plantation, even though the omen signs from the chickens are positive, when they get to the place they will also make a offering to the nature spirits. They call for the nature spirits to communicate with them through dreams that night. While they sleep, any negative signs such as high wind, other types of strange sounds, and/or bad dreams indicate that the location is not good. They must find a different place. A location to build a house must be especially carefully chosen. Lewis (1984) elaborates on the nature of searching for a good house location.

The site for a Hmong house is chosen with great care, as it is important that the site be acceptable to their ancestors. The family make a tentative choice, then consults the ancestors through an offering of "paper money" to determine whether the choice is acceptable [p. 122].

The household head must also consult the ground spirits for approval before the construction can begin (Livo and Cha, 1991; Cooper, 1998).

Chindarsi (1976) and Bliatout (1986) assert that there are several types of methods Mong use to communicate with the spirits. When they visit the forest, for every meal they eat, they must call for the nature spirits to eat with them. They place some food on the log, stump or rock to feed the spirits. They read the chicken omen signs to help them determine a future event. It is believed that the chicken omen signs are one way to communicate with the spirits. They also use different objects to communicate with the spirits such as divination horns, joss sticks, eggs, rice grain, beans, spoons, etc. (Chindarsi, 1976; Bliatout, 1986). A Shaman (*neeb*) is a person who can communicate with the spirits directly through his/her power (Chindarsi, 1976; Lewis and Lewis, 1984; Bliatout, 1986; Thao, 1986; Tapp, 1989; Livo and Cha, 1991; Fadiman, 1997; Cooper, 1998; Thao, 2002). Elder Cha Shoua Hang explained to me that when he performs a Shaman ritual, his chanting songs (*nkauj neeb*) are to communicate with the spirits. The Elders agreed that there must be spirits present to help the Shaman chant for hours. If there are no spirits present to help, the Shaman could not keep swinging his/her body, jumping up and down, and shaking his/her entire body for four to five hours. Elder Cha Shoua stated:

> As a Shaman, I always take good care of my Shaman spirits, house spirits, and ancestors' spirits. It is important not to let people disturb the spirits. It is my responsibility to teach my children to learn how important it is not to harm the spirits. The spirits live in a very sacred environment with me in the house. I have many spirits living in the house to guard my family and I. My door spirit (*dlaab tsoog*) lives on the main door entry into the house, a stove spirit (*dlaab qhov txus hab qhov cub*) lives where the stove is located, the Shaman spirits (*dlaab neeb*) live on the big altar facing opposite to the main entrance door to the house, the ancestors' spirits (*dlaab puj yawm txwv txoob hab xwm kaab*) live in the smaller altar hanging on the wall next to the Shaman altar, and my house middle post spirit (*ncij dlaab/ncij tsu*) lives on the middle post. The bed spirit (*dlaab txaag*) lives in the bedroom. This is the reason why the home environment becomes a very sacred place to my family and the spirits who are our protectors [personal communication, Sacramento, California].

The Elders noted that a woman who just gave birth cannot enter the house through the main door. This woman is still bleeding from her uterus and healing her wound. If she walks through the main door it harms the door spirit. A woman who is a member of the family is not allowed to enter through the main door until three to five days after childbirth. She enters the house from the back door or through a window. A woman who is not a member of the family is not allowed to enter through the main door until she is *puv hli*, meaning she has completed her thirty days of recovering from childbirth. All the women must know about this restrictive rule. If a woman does not know and she breaks the rule, a ritual must be performed immediately to *khu qhov tsooj tsaa txaj meej*, meaning to reconstruct the home of a door spirit. This ritual requires a pig to be sacrificed to the door spirit and some dowry paid to the head of the house. People must take serious precautions to protect the environment where the spirits live. Elder Phoua Her shared that the reason her two sons died was because a neighbor chopped a tree, which fell and hit the altar where her Shaman spirits lived. Her husband fixed the altar back and she performed a ritual to try to restore her own Shaman spirits. She said her Shaman spirits were unhappy about the incident. They made her family ill, and her two sons died. After the children died, her husband asked the neighbor to buy animals to sacrifice to her Shaman spirits and repair the altar again. Then Elder Phoua Her and her husband got well. It is important that one must always remember not to disturb the places where the spirits live in the house and/or out in the forest. Chindarsi (1976) elaborates further about the Mong spiritual ecology belief:

> The Hmong believe that there are spirits who resemble ordinary humans everywhere. They have their abodes in the earth, the mountains, forests, and streams. At the same time they believe that there is one spirit of a whole mountain who is more important than the others. If one disturbs the dwelling place of a spirit it may strike back by causing misfortune to oneself, a family member, or one's crops or animals [p. 21].

Peter Gold (1994) describes the Tibetan belief in spirits as

> spiritually attuned Tibetans constantly interact with power beings inhabiting spots of earth on which they live, work, and travel. The sadag, master of the earth, is frequently invoked through prayers and ritual acts. Any significant event that takes place on his localized spot of earth — essentially any human action, ranging from plowing, planting, and home building to outdoor operatic and dance performances, exorcisms, and tantric initiations — requires the permission of the master of the earth. By outwardly asking for his permission, one inwardly reinforces a sense of connection with, and respect for, one's own place on earth [p. 48].

A house is a central universe to the Mong. It must be securely protected to keep the evil spirits, wild animals, or other creatures away. It is a Mong belief that when these creatures enter the house, they bring bad luck or curses (*vij swv vij npug*) to make the members of the family sick and die. The Elders told me that birds, snakes, and other wild animals cannot enter the environment where people and their spirit protectors live unless a member of the family brings them in with him or her. If a wild animal enters their home, it is a warning that a curse will happen to the family soon. It means a demon has invaded the house environment. A Shaman must perform a ritual called *ua neeb thib vij swv vij npug* to get this demon out of the house so that it cannot cause harm to the family. Elder Xao Cheng Lee described a family he had witnessed losing several family members because they had a curse on the house.

> When I was traveling to a village with my older brother to sell his fabric, there was a family that has a death who was an older woman, and an old man who is the head of the house was also very ill. We stayed for several days in this village to help the family mourn their dead. This was the third member who had died in this family in less than a year. The family was devastated. There, people were talking about what caused all these problems. We asked an older man who was the brother to the family to explain to us more in detail. He said first, a tiger killed his brother family's cow. The tiger ate half of the cow and left. Then the family took the leftover meat home to eat. We called this *noj tsuv qub*, meaning eating tiger's leftover food. A few months later, out from nowhere a big snake was in their house. They killed the snake and threw it away. They did not have a Shaman perform a ritual to get the evil spirit that was already living in their house out. This incident did not seem to bother his brother. He encouraged his brother to consult with a Shaman, but his brother did nothing. Now, five years later (*tswb xyoos tom qaab*), the family became very ill. Then, in less than a year, the family lost three people. The head of the house also was very ill. The brother knew about these problems well because he told me that with the death of his brother's children, he called on a Shaman to perform a ritual to diagnose (*ua neeb saib*) what caused the illness. After that Shaman finished performing, he said to the family that in the past this family had eaten something dirty and the ancestors' spirits did not like it. Then, there was a creature that had entered the family house that brought the demon to live with the family. This demon was staying in the house to create all these problems. The Shaman asked the house head man to think back and try to remember if a similar event had occurred to his family. He responded to the Shaman yes. Then, he explained to the Shaman what happened several years ago [personal communication, Merced, California].

Elder Xao Cheng Lee said in order for a Shaman to get the demon out of the house in a case like this, it will cost the family two pigs, three chickens, lot of paper money to sacrifice to the spirits, and one silver bar or dowry (*ib dlaim nyiaj*) given to the Shaman for his services to restore the house spirits. If the family had a Shaman perform the ritual right after the snake entered the house then it would not cost as much. The longer you wait the more difficult for the Shaman to perform rituals to get an evil spirit or demon out of a house or a human body.

The Elders said that a house is a very sacred environment in which the spirits reside. When they build their houses, the location must be carefully chosen and the house plan must be designed the way it was passed down from generation to generation in order to accommodate the ancestors' spirits as well as the people who live in the house. The Elders stated that a house environment is to maintain balance of health, harmony, and prosperity. Cooper (1998) makes reference to this house location selection:

> The location of a house is selected with much care. Ideally, a site should be chosen that harmonises perfectly with the shape of the surrounding mountains. However, the days when land was so plentiful to allow such considerations are long past. Today, village Hmong maintain a notion of the perfect house site but few can remember many of its classical attributes [p. 30–31].

Elder Xai Dang Moua shared that his father once told him having a house in a good location could bring good fortune to the family, and he has been searching for this fortune all his life without success. This is one reason he decided to send his son to Laotian school. He hopes that one day his fortune will come true if his son finishes school. His family bought a house in southern California. The houses in America were designed by American engineers and built by American contractors. These environments do not resemble their houses on the mountains of Laos. The Elders have no other choice because it is not their real house. A few families who could afford to hired American professional contractors to build their houses like Mong houses. The Elders expressed that the dream to live in a house like their real house would not be possible until their grandchildren have good jobs or they return to live on their sacred mountains in Laos.

A burial site is another very important environment to the Mong. Lewis (1984) notes that the Mong believe having a proper funeral and finding a good location to bury the dead makes the souls of the dead happy, able to live debt-free in the next life, and have a prosperous life in the afterworld. When the souls of the dead have prosperity in the next life, the living family members too will receive good fortune with their help. These are the souls of ancestors whom the family worships. If a dead family member was buried in a bad location, then his/her soul could not find a way to reincarnate. The soul of this death becomes a curse to the living family members. In that case, the living family members must have a Shaman perform a ritual to repair the grave site (a home of the dead soul) and send this dead soul to a destiny where it can reincarnate. Conquergood (1992) states, "Disembodied spirits, souls that have not been reincarnated properly, return as ghosts to haunt and menace family and village" (p. 214). Elder Chai Xiong shared that she does not want to die in America. When she dies, there is no way her soul can reincarnate because she knows that her children cannot afford to get her a good grave site and bury her the way she prefers. Also, she does not like the way people bury their dead in this country. She shared her personal feeling:

> There is no way my soul can get out from the grave. I went to see how people buried the dead and the grave was sealed up with concrete (*laag zeb*). My soul would never be able to come out to be reincarnated. When I think about it, I feel bad to myself because I had made the wrong choice to come to America. I already got my U.S. citizenship too. There is no way that I can go back or the Americans would allow my body to be buried on the mountains where I was born [personal communication, Fresno, California].

Social Gatherings

There are many occasions when the Mong people gather. An event that has the highest attendance is the New Year festival. New Year is a time for families, relatives, and friends to gather and visit one another. People who live in the same village and nearby villages come together to celebrate this important event. This celebration is often held in a village with a central location, so that people can travel from far distances. The Elders observed that their New Year celebration is a time to remember the beauty of their traditional culture that has been preserved for many centuries. It is a blessing for families to have good health and good fortune in the coming New Year and to teach and pass on traditional values. This gathering is a time of courtship for the young people. People are busy working every day of the year to provide their family with crops, livestock and other needs. New Year's days are their only days to rest and to seek spouses for their young men and young women. Research indicates that this courting period in the Mong New Year is very special. The old people come together to share information, and the young people dress in beautiful clothing to attract a potential marriage partner and to demonstrate their talents and skills of singing sung-poetry and playing musical instruments (Geddes, 1976; Mottin, 1980; Lewis and Lewis, 1984; Cooper, Tapp, Lee

& Schworer-Kohl, 1986; Catlin, 1986, 1997; Conquergood, 1992; Cooper, 1998; Thao, 2002).

Funerals, weddings and other ritual services are also important gathering occasions. The Elders told me that people attend these ritual services to support one another and bring their young people with them to learn about the important elements of their tradition. They said that friendships and support alliances are reinforced through social gatherings. When they hear that another family who lives in the same village or nearby villages has a funeral rite, they try to attend the services to show support to this family. This family does not have to be related to them. This is their way to maintain strong communal support within all the clans and families. Lewis (1984) adds, "When death seems imminent, close relatives gather around the dying person for mutual comfort, and for sharing the many duties that arise when death occurs" (p. 128). Cooper (1998) elaborates further on the death mourning:

> Male members or relatives of the house will be sent out immediately with whisky to invite guests from the neighboring houses, and a "master of ceremonies," to the funeral; all the locally available male close-kin of the deceased should be present before the funeral rites can begin. Others may come from villages several days away before funeral rites are completed [p. 138].

Nusit Chindarsi (1976), in his writings on the Mong religion in northern Thailand, states that during a funeral ceremony relatives and members of the family will invite any passing people into the home. Some people give money to the family to assist in the ceremony and others give their time to help the family perform the services. When people give money and services to the family, the family members thank them by kneeling on the ground and bowing their bodies to the ground two times. The owner of the house also comes to show his respect to these charitable people in the same way as his family members (Chindarsi, 1976). The Elders told me that usually in all the ritual gatherings people give money or offer other types of support to assist the family's ritual. In the United States, the custom continues. Some families give money, others give food, drink, or their time to help the family.

Beside funeral rites, Mong families usually have social gatherings after supper. The boys gather with their father, grandfather, or uncles for storytelling and to learn ritualistic chants and songs. The girls gather with their mother, grandmother, or aunts for stories, to learn sewing, and sung-poetry, and other types of music. Elder Ying Yang noted:

> The only time my mother, my sisters, and I gather is on the rainy days where we cannot work on the plantation or after dinner. When we

gather, we do sewing, listen to stories or learn how to sing songs. I was shy with my mother so I learn all my songs from my uncle's wife (*puj laug*). I like to play musical instruments so I learned to play the jew's harp (*ncaas*) and bamboo flute (*tsaaj*). My uncle's wife taught me some lessons, I take some lessons from my friends, and my older sisters and I also watched other people play. Then I began to learn the skills myself.

American musicologist Amy Catlin (1997) writes that Mong music relates to the tones of their language. It has many genres. The music texts are primarily focused in two different forms: vocal and instrumental. She elaborates on this interpretive view of Mong music:

> The distinctive timbres and structures of Hmong music help to differentiate the Hmong from the many other minority peoples in their environment. Listeners identify these sounds within the surrounding soundscape of distinctive insects, birds, animals, and human groups. And within the Hmong context, their music functions as a sophisticated communication system for conveying thoughts and feelings, for transmitting traditional texts and framing extemporized verbal art, for ranking and rewarding performances of the musical culture, and for resolving the dilemma of death [p. 80].

Social gathering events are very important for children and young people to observe their cultural practices and to practice daily social skills. Parents encourage their children, and masters encourage their apprentices to attend and/or participate in ceremonies and public gatherings to reinforce their talents and skills.

Summary

Chapter 3 provided the historical overview of Mong lifestyles and their oral tradition maintained through a strong kinship system. The discussion described clan structure, cultural identity, physical environment and social gatherings shared by the Mong Elders. The Elders in this study brought this information from the mountains of Laos to the United States. This chapter captured some of the important cultural and religious values explained by the Mong Elders about their spiritual ecology and beliefs. Also, it described the alliance formed between clans and families and how these roles become an important factor to the communal lifestyles within the Mong society.

4

Oral Tradition as a Source of Knowledge

Oral tradition values and unwritten constructive knowledge serve as everyday living and learning experiences to the Mong people. The Mong lives are embedded with oral information that infuses their customs and religion. These oral culture values are transmitted by word of mouth from generation to generation. This chapter explains how the Mong obtain their oral knowledge through oral literature using traditional stories, songs, sacred chanting songs, funeral and wedding songs, soul calling songs and ritualistic secret language chanting songs.

Traditional Stories

Once there was a time when folk tales were part of communal property and told with original and fantastic insights by gifted storytellers who gave vent to the frustration of the common people and embodied their needs and wishes in the folk narratives. Not only did the tales serve to unite the people of a community and help bridge a gap in their understanding of social problems in a language and narrative mode familiar to the listeners' experiences, but their aura illuminated the possible fulfilment of utopian longings and wishes which did not preclude social integration [Zipes, 1984, p. 4].

This section describes the Mong oral knowledge (I use the term oral literature), which encompasses traditional stories such as epic poems, fables, riddles, folktales, legends and myths. The Elders used oral literature to educate children about their important heritage, life skills and for evening pastimes. In the mountains of Laos, the Mong do not have a written system to record their important oral stories. Therefore, poems, fables, riddles, tales, legends and myths are maintained only in an oral form. Finnegan (1970) states, "The concept of an *oral* literature is an unfamiliar one to most people brought up in cultures which, like those of contemporary Europe, lay stress on the idea of literacy and written tradition" (p. 1). Ong (1982) adds that oral literature has nothing to do with writing at all. He notes "The term or 'oral literature' that is 'oral writing'" (p. 13).

Oral literature plays an active part of Mong everyday life. This literature is used as a teaching tool to educate children about communal living, moral values and historical events. Epic poems, myths, legends, riddles, tales and folk stories are told after supper. Finnegan (1967) has conducted a research in the Limba cultural tradition. She states that the Limba stories are also told in the evening after the sun has set. "Such storytelling sessions do not take place on set occasions but arise spontaneously from the informal groups gathered together in leisure in the evening" (Finnegan, 1967, p. 65). The Elders said children and young people gather with their parents, grandparents, uncles or aunts around the fireplace (*qhov cub*), in the guest bed (*txaj qhua*) or outside on the platforms called (*tsaavlawj*) for stories telling. These platforms (*tsaávlawj*) are built to dry rice grain (*zab nplej*) and for out-of-town visitors to sleep. These stories, myths, legends, poems, riddles and tales continue as long as people can stay awake to listen. Sometimes people stay late into the night to listen to story-telling. They do not have time to tell legends, poems, riddles and stories during the day because they are busy working in the field, taking care of livestock and doing other house chores. The Elders said they do not tell stories during the daytime because it will cause one to have red eyes (*has lug nruag ntsuab nub qhov muag lab*). However, they indicated that no one really had red eyes for telling stories in the daytime. This phrase is only used to warn people. This way people do not create a habit during the day to sit around listening to stories without getting any work done around the house or in the plantation. People tend to be lazy if they rest too long. Therefore, they encourage people not to use the daytime to sit around and tell stories while there is lots of work yet to do in the plantation and/or around the house.

Poems, fables, riddles, tales, legends and myths contained important oral information to help Mong children and young people learn about their cultural values as well as to understand the past. Smith Tuhiwai (1999) notes that these traditional oral stories serve to connect the past with the future and also become an integral part of day-to-day indigenous lives. Mythology provides historical accounts about the Mong people, their heroes, heroines, and magical spells. Faderman (1998) asserts, "Hmong folklore contains a tale that is very much like the Eve story of Genesis" (p. 125). Vang and Lewis (1984) write about how Mong tell stories through legends:

> The legends tell of a time when Hmong lived in a cold land, covered with ice and snow, and where night lasted for half the year. The Hmong were living in Western China before the Han Chinese lived there, but they were always known as outsiders or barbarians, because they spoke a non-Chinese language, and wore special clothes that were not like Chinese. To avoid conflict with the Chinese, the Hmong settled in remote mountain areas, living and supporting themselves with agriculture. When the Chinese attempted to force the Hmong to become Chinese, giving up their language, customs, dress and life-style, many groups of Hmong refused, and the Chinese persecuted them and attempted to kill the leaders. This caused the Hmong to move southward, looking for places where they could live in peace [p. 6].

Quincy (1988) adds that Father Savina used his work on legends and tales to collect information about the Mong origin, creation of the world and human race. They are the only sources of information to provide evidence of Mong early historical accounts. The Elders added that legends help them to understand what happened to the Mong when the Chinese conquered them in China hundreds of years ago.

Vang and Lewis (1984), Livo and Cha (1991) and Johnson (1992) assert that Mong oral folk literature is a moral teaching to young people to learn their traditional stories, culture, custom and religious rituals. The Mong use their oral knowledge to teach children to learn about social experiences and good and bad values. Since the Mong epic poems, myths, legends, riddles, and folk tales are transmitted orally, people do not need much light to see during story circle, unlike reading from the books. The Mong use natural light such as pork oil lanterns, bamboo torches, fire and moonlight to see at night. The Elders shared that they did not learn about electric light until they were at the ages of forty or fifty. Most of them experienced how electric light works when they were living in the United States. The Elders said in America people see better at night with electricity, but it causes people to lose their vision fast. Also, electricity can easily turn on the television, radio, tape player, computer and video game to keep people busy. Children are no longer interested in story-telling. They have these machines and books to entertain them and to teach them the information they need. On the Mong Mountains in Laos, they do not have machines and books so people teach people. The Elders indicated that children pay more attention and learn better from oral teaching when they do not see things to distract them. If there is too much light and children can see other things, then this distracts them from focusing, listening and memorizing the information. The Elders said to live in a primary oral society one learns orally through participation in story-telling, songs and rituals. They decoded information by listening, reciting and rehearsing in an environment where no other distraction is going on. Gregory Cajete (1994) elaborates on the nature of traditional American Indian learning: "As a whole traditional Tribal education revolved around experiential learning (learning by doing or seeing), storytelling (learning by listening and imagining), ritual/ceremony (learning through initiation), dreaming (learning through unconscious imagery), tutoring (learning through apprenticeship), and artistic creation (learning through creative synthesis)" (p. 34). Elder Chong Yer Thao shared a story about his learning experience:

> I learned how to tell stories by listening to my elders (*cov laug*). I liked it when we stayed outside on the platform (*lawj*) and my elder told a scary story. We usually stayed late until midnight to listen to a story when there was a bright full moon. The moon was beautiful. During the story-telling when it comes to a very scary part the elders would point to something like the shadows of trees or stumps and said that looks like ghosts or monsters to make us more frightened. We sat very close to each other. I liked the scary parts most because they helped me to remember the story. If the story became too scary to people then the elders stopped. They told a different story but this story must continue later or on the next night to finish. They never leave a story unfinished because it is not good. The elders said if he/she does not finish a story then he/she will have children without a head (*has lug ntsuag tsis taab xyaa mivnyuas tsis muaj tau hau*). Therefore, people tend to believe it. When they tell a story they have to finish it [personal communication, Stockton, California].

The Elders stated that fables, myths, legends and tales are usually told to younger children between the ages of four and ten. Adolescents and adults like epic poems, riddles and longer stories. The older children and adults tell poems and riddles during courting. Myths, fables, legends and tales help children to develop their language and vocabulary skills, as well as to understand the common values found in the Mong society. The Mong do not have people with credentials as language developmental specialists to help children build their language cognitive skills or a psychologist to evaluate people's behaviors and learning styles, etc. Children develop their cognitive learning skills by listening and observing daily tasks, social events and rituals. Children are encouraged by family members such as older siblings, parents, grandparents, uncles and aunts to get involved with the family story circle and/or work responsibilities at their early age to learn all the necessary skills. The Mong believe older people are more knowledgeable and wiser. Children and younger people always respect the older people because of their wisdom. The Elder Jer Thao said, "If young children are not trained early when they turn to adolescents, they become shy, then they have a more difficult learning."

Traditional stories are very important to children. The Elders said these stories help the Mong children who grow up on the mountains of Laos to mature faster than the Mong children who grow up in the United States. They believe the early exposure children get to oral stories, social skills and family gathering expands children's knowledge. In the United States, television cartoons, books and video games freeze children's oral knowledge. Children are staying home alone with no adult contact and no exposure to daily survival skills and this causes a delay in maturity. The majority of adolescent Mong children living in America still have their childhood experience whereas the majority of adolescent Mong children who live on the mountains of Laos are like adults. Goldstein (1988) elaborates on this point:

> Hmong did not recognize adolescence as a special developmental period — they had had no prolonged or marked period of transition to adulthood. By Hmong standards, teens are adults with adult responsibilities to family for economic support and household maintenance [p. 8].

The Elders stated that the age of adolescence is very important to Mong children. If they do not have the basic adult skills then they will have a difficult time starting their own families. Young children reinforced these skills through listening to stories, doing light work on the farm, helping with house chores and taking care of small children. This way they would understand the primary responsibility of being parents or adults.

This societal difference causes Mong children who live in America to have different views of their elders' oral literature and cultural life. Havelock (1986) asserts that these different views create a culture collision between the oral act and writing act. Marshall McLuhan (1962) states that the revolution of electronic and manuscript culture is overwhelming to the non-literate cultures. This revolution creates different perspectives in how people think, codify and transmit information and knowledge. McLuhan (1962) quotes Ashley Montague, "The more 'literate' people become, the more they tend to become detached from the world in which they live" (p. 76). Walter Ong (1982) uses the folk culture beliefs as an example to contrast between the oral and literate society. He referred to Marshall McLuhan's term "global village" as a way that information has changed in the print world. Information brought a new way for people to communicate and think in literate society. Ong describes the Latin language that had been an oral language but became a school language which moved "too far away from its origins" (Ong, 1982, p. 112). The mother tongue of the Latin language had disappeared because new vernaculars developed to replace it (Ong, 1982). Ong (1980) comments upon this literate society:

> We are so literate in ideology that we think writing comes naturally. We have to remind ourselves from time to time that writing is completely and irremediably artificial, and that what you find in a dictionary are not real words but coded marks for voicing real words, exteriorly or in imagination [p. 199].

The Elders commented that poems, fables, riddles, folktales, legends and myths written in books have only the Americans' values and perspectives. When Mong children learn from books, they get only the American culture and language. If they need to know the Mong culture and language, then they must learn it in an oral fashion. In this case, Mong children do not become interested in learning orally. Elder Phoua Her described the reaction her grandchildren have with Mong oral stories:

> My grandchildren are becoming too American. They no longer understand Mong. They said Mong stories are too boring. They do not know what the story is about because they have lost the Mong language. When I try to teach them about my traditional stories and cultural values they walk away from me. When I ask them to go out to the garden in our backyard to get me lemon grass (*tauj qab*) to put on the food they do not know what *tauj qab* looks like and they bring me green onion, cilantro or other types of vegetables [personal communication, Susan City, California].

The Elders expressed that this modern tradition creates a breakdown in intergeneration communication, relationship and trust. They missed the story circle times and the roles to make sure Mong children can identify their important societal norms.

Songs

Songs are not a special category of tradition. Most songs, however, fall in this category insofar as they are poems or set speech, that is, they are in everyday language but memorized [Vansina, 1985, p. 16].

Musicologist Amy Catlin (1986) asserts that the Mong have many types of *kwv txhiaj* (songs), such as songs of love, separation, war, orphanhood, homesickness, and more. The greatest numbers are love songs. In the Mong society songs are not sung to put children to sleep and/or to consolidate people. Songs release personal hardship, express physical life and beauty, and are used for courtship. Mong children do not study songs until they reach their puberty. Young boys and girls learn to sing songs to each other to engage in romantic relationships. Okpewho (1992) indicates that in the African tradition people express love through songs. The Mong people also sing songs to accompany each other or to himself/herself while working in the plantation, walking to and from their home to the plantation and being with a loved one. Finnegan's (1970) research in the African tradition also stated that young people learn songs, proverbs and poetry while working in the plantation and they sung songs to accompany their hard physical labour. The Elders added that people sing songs to release personal stress (*kiv nyuaj sab*), about being lonely (*kiv khua sab*), to remember their loved one (*kiv sib ncu txug tug hlub, phooj ywg los yog kwvtij*), and to *tau luag*, meaning not being afraid while being alone. Young people learn how to sing songs from family members who know how to sing. The Elders said during rice harvest time (*cai muab nplej*) young people get together with older people who know how to sing songs to learn from them. Young people want to learn songs to be prepared for the New Year. Rice harvest season begins in late October and it ends in the month of December when they celebrate New Year. Young people have about two months to learn some songs to sing at the New Year celebration. Therefore, almost every night, the young people gather after dinner to study songs. Elder Ying Yang described the way she learned how to sing:

Lub caij hlais nplej, meaning during rice harvesting my sisters and I gathered with my brother Vang Chai's (*Vaam Ntxhais*)·wife and my uncle Chong Pao's (*Ntxhoo Pov*) wife to learn singing songs. We called our brothers' wife *dlaisdlaab* and uncles' wife *pujlaug* or *nam ntxawm*. At the plantation, my sisters and I stayed til past midnight (*nyob tseej taag mo*) to learn how to sing songs. *Dlaisdlaab Vaam* (Brother Vang Chai's wife) and *Pujlaug Pov* (Uncle Pao's wife) were the only two people who know how to sing sung poetry in my family. *Dlaisdlaab Vaam* said her mother taught her. *Pujlaug Pov* told us that she learned from her brother's wife. They took turns to teach us their favorite songs. First, we listened to them sing. If we liked the songs then we asked them to teach us. This was how we learned the songs. The instructor sings the whole song for us to listen. Then, the instructor broke down the song into parts (*ib nqais ib nqais*). We learned each part at a time from the beginning to the end. The shortest songs have four parts. The longest songs have eight to ten parts. Most songs are between five to eight parts. The most important thing to know about learning how to sing songs is to capture the meaning of the song. When you know the meaning of each part of the song then you sing into the singing voice. You sing to the instructor part by part. If you have it wrong, the instructor will sing and you repeat after it. You sing over and over again until you get it before you move onto the next part. Some people have good memory (*cim xeeb zoo*) and they listen to the instructor sing a couple of times they can pick up most of the parts in the song on their own. It takes me a couple of nights to learn one song. Some people with good memory, they learn one song per night. When we learn the songs, we practice singing aloud during the day while we harvest rice (*muab nplej*) in the field. If we forget a part then we ask the instructor to sing again to us to listen when we get together after dinner. If you become familiar with the lyric patterns then you can quickly pick a song after listening to other people sing. My brother's wife and uncle's wife teach my sisters and I how to become familiar with these songs [personal communication, Montclair, California].

When young people become familiar with the lyrics, then they begin to recognize the formulas of the songs. After that, they pick up the words and contents of the song much faster. Once they know how to recite the song, it increases their mnemonics of other songs. They learn all these songs by reciting and listening to them over and over again with their instructor as well as on their own. Ong (1982) states that in a primary oral culture if knowledge is not repeated over and over again, then this knowledge will vanish quickly. Mong young people must constantly repeat the songs aloud in order to remember them. The Elders indicated that once you know a song by heart then you can begin to learn different songs. You have to constantly practice singing the one you know. If you leave it for several days by not singing while continuing to learn new songs, then you can lose the songs. Although, even if you lose it, if you keep reciting, soon you will remember it, as long as you do not leave it for several months and you completely forget the lyrics of the song. The Elders said that songs are very popular during the New Year celebration. People tend to gather around a person who is a good singer to listen to him or her sing. This is how they become attractive to people through their singing skills. There is a game called *swb pob* (a competition where boys and girls toss a soft black cloth ball to each other). If one misses the ball while catching, then one has to give up something to the opponent. This something can be a necklace, bracelet, belt, or apron, a piece of clothing they wear over their outfit. By the end of the game, they will use the items they get from the opponent to exchange for their own belongings. If someone was out of items to exchange with their opponent for their own belongings, each item returned will cost a song. The person who needs lost items back has to sing songs to the opponent in order to get them. When this person runs out of songs to sing, the items will be delivered in a private meeting with the person at nightfall. The young man goes to the young woman's house at night to meet her. There, they can discuss how to retrieve the items. This is a way for the young people to meet each other privately and have a chance to build their relationship. Cooper (1998) elaborates on this ball game:

> By accident or design, a ball is dropped. Whoever drops it might give the partner an article of jewellery or clothing. These may be retrieved in exchange for a song. A rapid retrieval or a poor song is a subtle way of indicating that a change of partner might be in order. As the day moves into evening, all but the determined have left the field. Catchers become increasingly maladroit and clothing changes hands and is not immediately retrieved. As darkness halts the game, each couple comes together to retrieve clothing and exchange songs. Not everything is retrieved and if a girl is wearing a man's watch the next day, it is a clear enough sign that she is out of play as far as open courtship is concerned [p. 60].

If the young couple has strong feelings for one another, they could end up getting married. Lewis and Lewis (1984), Kohler (1986), Catlin (1997), Conquergood (1992), Cooper, Tapp, Lee and Schworer-Kohl (1996) and Cooper (1998) state that the Mong New Year festival is for boys and girls to sing to one another. It is a courting period for potential marriage partners. Okpewho (1992) writes that song is part of the African tradition courtship: "The song clearly reveals a young man's excited admiration for his girl friend, moving him to a determination to marry her" (p. 140).

The Elders responded that people sing songs to let others know about personal feelings. Orphaned young people tend to sing songs reflecting their orphanhood. The meanings of the songs are about not having parents to love and support them. The songs describe the orphan's life living with an uncle and his wife. Life was miserable. Elder Lee Xiong said orphan songs touch her heart so much because these songs help cope with the life difficulties she had. She is not a good singer, but she likes to listen to them. Songs teach her many things such as to be a good person, focus on living and maintain strong hope as an orphan. Also, there are songs about missing family members, relatives and friends. Elder Xai Dang mentioned that singing songs is a way to help him through his difficult transition living in America and leaving family members behind in Thailand and Laos. Geddes (1976) adds that many Miao (Mong) songs are about sadness. In short, songs provide comfort for family separation due to war, attract people for potential marriage, educate people about personal hardship and entertain.

SACRED CHANTING SONGS

Our sacred chanting songs are for us to communicate and accompany the souls [Cha Shoua Hang, personal communication, Sacramento, California].

According to the Mong Elders, sacred chanting songs are not permitted at any secular event. These songs can be sung only at religious ceremonies. There are thousands of different chanting songs found in the Mong custom. This section describes the most important chanting songs used by the Mong people, such as the Shaman's chanting songs (*qhua hab nkauj neeb*), funeral songs (*txwv xaiv, nkauj hab kiv nyiav*), wedding songs (*zaaj tshoob*), and soul calling songs (*hu plig*).

The Elders stated that in order to make offering for the spirits, one must know the appropriate sacred song to conduct such rituals. These sacred chanting songs are rigorously hard to learn. People spend months and years to learn them. There are songs that people cannot learn without the spirits' guidance. Elder Boua Tong Yang elaborated on how he learned his Shaman chanting songs:

When I became a Shaman, I learned everything from my shaman spirits. They gave me direction and power to communicate with spirits through songs. First, I went to ask for a master shaman to help me get started. My master taught me some of the basic skills about how to perform a shaman ritual. My master continued to mentor me until I knew all the sequences and how to conduct my own ritual performance. Then, my master shared with me his Shaman practice experience. When I was ready to be on my own, my master and I performed a ceremony at the same time to divide our magic power. This is a way for me to honor my master for his/her mentorship. When I performed a shaman ritual, it is like the shaman spirits put all the words of the song to my mouth. As soon as I begin to perform my ritual, my singing just happened naturally. When I do not perform a ritual, I cannot remember the songs. I believe the shaman spirits guide me with the singing part [personal communication, Sacramento, California].

Other Elders who are Shamans also shared that when they do not perform rituals they could not remember the chanting songs. They said it is difficult to explain the experience of being a Shaman. The only way to know is to become a Shaman but one can only become a Shaman by being chosen by

the shaman spirits. Without the spirits present a Shaman has no power to
cure the illness and perform rituals. Lemoine (1986) describes the way
spirits help the Shaman:

> One cannot be a shaman without a predisposition to get into a trance.
> But a trance is not only achieved through physical training. It is an
> inherited ability that one cannot have at will. It must be provoked by
> spirit helpers. The sounds of the gong, the rattle and the finger bell cer-
> tainly give the tempo and help the shaman to alter his own conscious-
> ness. But they accompany rather than precede the shaman's singing. The
> trance always starts first, for it is, as the shamans themselves explain,
> provoked by spirit helpers [p. 340].

Intensive studies of Shamans state that one goes through a serious
illness before becoming a Shaman. Not everyone can become a shaman.
Shamans are only chosen by the spirits (Chindarsi, 1976; Lemoine, 1986;
Thao, 1986; Tapp, 1989; Ensign, 1994; Cooper, 1998; Thao, 2002). The
spirits give power to the Shaman to fight the evil spirits and to cure illness. Shamans use the sacred chanting songs to communicate with the
spirits in the other world. The sacred chanting songs are the Shamans'
special power to battle with evil spirits. These chanting songs are very
difficult to understand. Tapp (1989) makes reference to this point:

> Many of the words of these chants are as unintelligible to the average
> Hmong as Latin church services are to the average Christian, but add to
> the power and mystery of the occasion in much the same way, for Chi-
> nese words and phrases are used which hark back to the Taoist influences
> upon Hmong shamanism. It is sometimes said that the spirits are
> "frightened" when they hear a man speaking in different tongues, and it
> is the shaman's business to frighten off the spirits which may have
> afflicted the fallen self of his patients [pp. 77–78].

The Elders explained that the Shamans' chants have some Mandarin Chinese words in them, because long ago the Mandarin Chinese and the Mong
were brotherhoods (*kwvtij*). They lived together in China and their religious rituals influenced one another.

According to Thao (1999a), in the Mandarin Chinese vocabulary
there is a compounded word *kwvtij*. *Kwv* means older brother and *tij* means
younger brother. The Mong and the Mandarin Chinese were once *kwvtij*
but somehow they became enemies to each other because of the way the
Chinese Dynasties treated the Mong. Elder Xao Cheng Lee described that
based on Mong legends the creator sent two brothers to teach the Mong
and the Chinese how to conduct their rituals. One brother had a bad
heart (*sab phem*). He taught all the sacred songs that have Chinese words

to the Chinese but not to the Mong. They were supposed to teach both the Mong and the Chinese the same chants. Therefore, the other brother taught the Mong some of the Chinese words so the Mong could understand the Chinese rituals and chants. He did not teach sacred chants in Mong words to the Chinese. This way, if the Chinese evil spirits caused harm to the Mong, then the Mong could communicate with them through the chanting songs. They could make offering to the evil spirits to leave them alone. The Chinese do not know the Mong's rituals and chants. This is why the Chinese do not like the Mong. When the Mong perform rituals for their ancestors' spirits, they cannot speak Chinese or any other foreign language. If they used words other than Mong, it would offend the ancestors' spirits. The ancestors' spirits can punish them by making members of the family ill. But, the songs that are used to perform rituals to keep the evil spirits away can be found in Mong or Chinese. The Mong believe that the evil spirits are sometimes the angry souls of the dead *dlaab Moob, Dlaab Suab, Dlaab Lostsuas, Dlaab Cu, Dlaab Pujthawj, has lug yaam dlaab*, meaning these evil spirits can be Mong, Chinese, Laotian, Mien, Khmu, etc. The Elders indicated that it is necessary to know other cultures' chanting songs just in case the evil spirit does not understand Mong.

FUNERAL AND WEDDING SONGS

The funeral ceremony is very important to the Mong people. The Elders shared that the dead people value life the same way as the living people. Even though a person may be dead, his/her soul is living and the living people must accompany the dead through songs during the period his/her body keeps for the mortuary rite. People need to honor and treat the souls of the dead with extreme care, so the souls can depart to the other world happily. Family members, relatives and friends sing mournful songs (*quaj hab nyiav*) to the corpse as a way to express their grief. These mournful songs are to let the dead know how much he or she will be missed. It also shows their sorrows. Symonds (1991) states that the mournful songs are very emotional. The keen songs sung to the dead by family members and close relatives are about their sadness in losing him or her. They sing these songs to let the dead know how much they love him or her. People who are not related to the dead sing mournful songs as a way of giving messages to pass on to loved ones who have passed away and of expressing how much they miss them.

Beside the mournful songs family members select people who know how to sing the songs called *nkauj* to their dead. The *nkauj* are sung to keep the souls of the dead company and greet the people who attend the funeral. Family members pour wine into a cup and give it to the person who knows how to sing *nkauj* to ask him to sing. If he accepts the family's request, he drinks the wine. After that, he walks to stand at the center facing the corpse to sing. In the Mong traditional funeral rite, family members leave a big space from where the corpse is placed to where the people sit. This space is saved for people to perform ritual activities, for visitors to have more room to get closer to the corpse while they sing mournfully or cry softly, and for people to be able to get closer to the corpse while they come to pay their respects.

Most importantly, this space is for the *txiv qeej* (the person who blows the sacred *qeej* instrument to communicate with the souls of the dead) to have more room for their performance. A *qeej* is a bamboo reed pipe with a wooden windchest made by the Mong people. This is a very special instrument. Cooper (1998) describes the *qeej*:

> The *qeej* is made up of six bamboo pipes, passing through a windchest made of a reddish hardwood, known to the Hmong as *ntoo txiv pem*. The instrument has a long neck (*kav qeej*) which tapers up from the windchest to the brass (sometimes silver) mouthpiece (*ncaug qeej*). Dimensions vary somewhat but a length of 73 cm (29 inches) from the tip of the mouthpiece to the end of the windbox is normal. The inside diameter of the mouthpiece measures 12 mm (half an inch). The mouthpiece is strengthened and protected by a ring, usually of brass, some 2 cm (three-quarters of an inch) wide. The neck and windchest are bound with rings of silver, brass, copper or tin. When the qeej is not in use, the mouthpiece is stopped up with an ornamental hardwood plug called *lub ntsws*. The six pipes of the qeej, known as *ntiv qeej* are of greatly different lengths and diameters. For the short, thick pipe, a type of bamboo called *xyoob tuam tswm* is used; the five other pipes are made from *xyoob qeej*, known for having a long distance between nodes [p. 84].

A *txiv qeej* says all the chants to the souls of the dead. During the performance, a *txiv qeej* may stand still or move around, turning and spinning. Therefore, he does not want himself or the *qeej* to trip anyone.

The Elders said the *qeej* chants are songs but not music songs. They are more like a language because they communicate to the souls. They help the souls to depart to the ancestors' world. Western researchers assert that this sacred *qeej* instrument makes music codes. Catlin (1985, 1986, 1997) and Cooper (1998) state that to the western ears the Mong's songs by the *qeej* are music. Therefore, a *qeej* is a music instrument. Both Elder Boua Tong Yang and Elder Nhia Cha Yang are master *qeej* players. They said the *qeej* chanting songs are only about the dead. When a person dies, a *qeej* chant called *qeej tu sab* (last breath) is the first chant song that is played to the dead person. Then there are thousands of chants that are played during the mortuary rite. There are *qeej tshais* (breakfast chanting songs), *qeej su* (lunch chanting songs), *qeej mo* (dinner chanting songs), *qeej sawv kiv* (chanting songs to lead the souls to the burial site) and *qeej civ neeg* (chanting songs to lead souls to the stretcher). Then the corpse is put onto the stretcher. According to the Elders this stretcher is a ghost horse. The corpse lies on this stretcher in the house during the mortuary rite. People use this stretcher to carry the corpse to the burial site. Then, they transfer the corpse into a coffin to bury. The stretcher is cut into three parts and left on top of the grave. The stretcher must be cut apart in order to kill the ghost horse.

People spend years to learn how to blow the *qeej*. Both Elder Boua Tong and Elder Nhia Cha Yang said learning how to play this instrument is very difficult. This is one reason why very few people know how to blow the instrument. They remembered that they have to stay up every night to learn to play the instrument from their mentor. Sometimes, they practice all day and night blowing the *qeej*. Elder Boua Tong described:

> Every moment I have free I grab my *qeej* and practice blowing. At one time my mother complained to me that it is too noisy and I should stop practicing. I almost quit from learning to blow *qeej*. It was a stressful learning experience. Sometimes, I felt like I do not have time to do anything because I spend so much time practicing my *qeej*. When I played for my mentor to listen, I thought I got the chant right but it was still wrong. It took me several years to be able to understand the *qeej*. The *ntiv* (the basic fingering parts) are the most difficult stage. Most people quit learning *qeej* because they do not make it through this *ntiv* stage. I have to listen carefully to my mentor blow the instrument, look carefully at his fingers to see how they work. It was very frustrating but my mentor was very good. He really wanted me to learn so he spent so much time to teach me. You have to know how to control the air you blow into the *qeej*, using your tongue, lung, breath and fingers. It is like your fingers doing the singing instead of using your mouth. You recite the chanting songs in your head and use your fingers to make the sounds [personal communication, Sacramento, California].

The master *qeej* players receive high respect in the Mong community. They are very important people because without them present to blow the *qeej* in the funeral rite, people would not know what to do to provide funeral services to their dead.

Tub coj xai is a person who sings the *txwv xaiv* or funeral songs similar to prayers to the members of living family. A *tub coj xai* is carefully selected by family members, especially the sons for their mother or father's funeral. People tend to find a person who has a reputation for singing good songs and having a beautiful voice. In a funeral rite, if a well-known *tub coj xai* is singing, the funeral draws in lots of people. People like to come listen to the songs because these songs teach people how to live a happy life. *Txwv xaiv* songs are sung on the very last night before the day of the corpse burial. This night is called *mo has xwm*. A funeral rite for older people requires a *tug coj xai*. Chindarsi (1976) describes the role of a *tug coj xai*:

> The long prayer known as Sersai is also connected with the mortuary rite, in the case of the death of an old person. It is prayed on the night before the burial day. The purpose of this prayer is to teach the descendants how to behave to one another. It is so long that it takes all night to finish [p. 148].

Elder Xao Cheng Lee, one of the well-known *tub coj xai* in the California central valley in the Mong community, said *txwv xaiv* (funeral songs) are sung to help members of the family cope with sadness. The songs are like a lecture. It teaches family members to learn how to love one another, look after one another, not become bad people and not do bad things to him/herself as well as others. If one follows the advice in the *txwv xaiv*, one will have a happy life. No one is able to live by these rules because they are very complicated rules. But if one listens carefully to the songs and takes the meaning for granted, this could help him or her a bit. The songs teach people how to prevent family disputes, to prevent trouble by hurting other people, to avoid affairs with other people's spouses and stealing from other people, etc. They are basically about moral values. Sometimes the songs bring good fortune and prosperity to the family if the family is able to live by the rules. Songs can help people to solve personal problems and make decisions during difficult times. See the detail from Elder Xao Cheng Lee's story about becoming a *tub coj xai*. He explained the need for a *tub coj xai* for every older person's funeral:

> There was an old man who lived with his two sons. The two sons often fought one another. Even though both of them already had wives and children, they still did not respect each other. The father tried everything he knew to help his two sons learn how to get along. The two sons did not listen to him. The father worried that when he died his sons would continue to behave disrespectfully to one another. The father was getting old. One day he became ill and he knew that he was not going

to make it. He told his two sons that after he died, the only wish he had for them was to learn how to love each other. There would be no one there to help them solve the problems they often had with each other. The old man requested that after he died his two sons call an old man who lived down the slope to come to his funeral to give advice to the sons. Soon, the father died and they invited the old man to come on the night before his burial day. When the sons went to call the old man, he answered why him? He did not know anything. Their father was a wise man and they did not even listen to him. How does he know that they will listen to him? He had no advice to give them. The sons said because he was the one chosen by their father before he died. The sons know that the old man will not come because he knows about them all and the problems the brothers had. The old man requested that they go find someone wiser. The sons came back home and they prepared some food and wine. They went back to the old man's house. They set the food and wine on the table. They asked the old man to come sit at the table. Then, they stood on the other side of the table facing the old man. They poured some wine into a cup and gave it to the old man. After that, they bowed with their knees touching the ground two times to the old man. They said to the old man that even though there were many people he was the one that their father had chosen (*txwv xaiv*) before he died. The old man was recognized. Then, the old man drank the wine to accept their request. The sons asked the old man to eat the food. This meal was prepared only to honor and respect the old man for his wisdom. It was *tam hab ua tsaug* (meaning to give thanks and to request for permission). The old man came to the funeral. He did not have much to say to the sons. Here is some advice he gave to the sons. He asked them to remember everything their father had taught them. If they do not get along as a family then how are they going to get along with people who are outside of the family? Also, what they do can be harmful to their children because they observed this behavior everyday. If they did not stop, their children could grow to be like them. As brothers, they need to support, love, protect and look after one another. This way, they can be happy and able to accomplish whatever task or goal they want to reach. After the sons buried their father, they sat down together and thought through all the advice the old man said. Then, they began to change the way they treated one another. The brothers no longer have problems between them. Since then people began to believe that having someone give advice to the members of the family is a very good idea because having a death in the family, especially the father or mother, pulls the family apart. This person helps the family members to cope with one another so they can maintain a stronger family. Having a strong family makes everyone happy and they can accomplish whatever goal they try to reach. A *txwv xaiv* (father chosen) derived from this story. As *txwv xaiv* became recognizable in the funeral rite, instead of giving advice in talking, they put the words into songs to sing to members of the family. These songs became very popular in an older person's funeral because they teach moral values and tell descendents how to live a peaceful life [personal communication, Merced California].

Zaaj tshoob (wedding chanting songs) are another very important piece of oral literature in the Mong tradition. The wedding chanting songs are sung in the wedding by the *Mej Koob* (person who knows the wedding chant songs and rituals). The *Mej Koob* is in charge of the wedding celebration and serves as the wedding negotiator between the bride's family and groom's family. Hayes (1984) adds that the *Mej Koob* negotiated with the girl's and boy's parents through a go-between. "The go-between process is to insure that the customs are followed throughout the wedding celebration" (Hayes, 1984, p. 113). The Mong Leng traditional ceremony only requires two *Mej Koob*. One *Mej Koob* is selected by the bride's family and usually is the bride's uncle or an elder who is a close family member. This *Mej Koob* is called the *Mej Koob huv tsev* or *txum mej* (inside house *Mej Koob* or bride's *Mej Koob*). The other *Mej Koob* is called the *Mej Koob saab ntsau* (outside house *Mej Koob* or groom's *Mej Koob*). This *Mej Koob saab ntsau* also must be related to the groom's family or it can be a clan related member. The White Hmong's traditional wedding ceremony requires four *Mej Koob*, two from the bride's family and two from the groom's family at all times.

Elders said that based on legends, the wedding chanting songs (*zaaj tshoob*) came from *Yawm Zaaj Laug* (great great grand father dragon). The Mong learned wedding songs and how to perform wedding rituals from the grand father dragon. The *Mej Koob* sing these songs during the wedding rite to ask questions and give answers to one another, to bargain the price of the bride, to seek support from the bride's family members such as parents, siblings, uncles, aunts and grandparents to grant the groom's family a fair wedding celebration. Hayes (1984) describes the Mong negotiation process:

This is done through an elaborate process, wherein the go-between arrives at the prospective bride's home and sings a song about the young man's love for her. Also, the go-between brings several gallons of corn or rice whiskey as a symbol of honor for the woman's male cousins, uncles, brothers, and grandfathers [p. 113].

According to researchers, the *Mej Koob* have big responsibilities in the Mong traditional wedding. Their jobs are to ensure both the bride's family and her clan as well that the groom's family and his clan approved the way the wedding ritual was conducted. An agreement of bride price has been reached and a wedding permission has been granted. This way in the future when the two same clans have another wedding they do not bring up the old problems from the previous wedding. They are the people who make sure the wedding goes well, and ensure the welfare of the bride and act as witness to this marriage (Chindarsi, 1976; Geddes, 1976; Lewis and Lewis, 1984; Hayes, 1984; Scott, 1986; Livo and Cha, 1991; Symonds, 1991; Cooper, Tapp, Lee and Schworer-Kohl, 1996; Cooper, 1998; Thao, 2002). Elder Tong Yao Her described that he had taken the role of a *Mej Koob*, but he did not know how to sing the wedding chanting songs. When it was time to sing then he would get someone who knows on the side of the family whom Elder Tong Yao Her represents to sing. The Elders stated that these wedding songs are *puj ua tseg yawm ua cia*, meaning grandma and grandpa perform this method from thousands of years in their tradition. In Laos on the Mong Mountains, hundreds of wedding songs were sung because a wedding celebration goes for three to four days.

The Elders indicated that in America the *Mej Koob* have too many things to worry about and they don't have time to master all the wedding chanting songs. The Elders are not satisfied with how some of the *Mej Koob* in the United States perform their duty in the wedding ceremony. When they requested the *Mej Koob* to sing certain special chanting songs, some of them keep making excuses that they never study or know these songs. Elder Xao Cheng Lee who was also a *Mej Koob* expert stated:

> Today, our *Mej Koob* are taking a short cut. They do not take time to go from detail to detail because it takes too long. The wedding ceremony is being condensed into a one-day ceremony and many things have been cut out. If the *Mej Koob huv tsev* or *txum mej* (inside house Mej Koob) requested the *Mej Koob saab ntsau* (outside Mej Koob) to sing the chanting songs, the *Mej Koob saab ntsau* often apologize to the *Mej Koob huv tsev* or *txum mej* and the bride parents that he does not know the chants. We know that he knows but he's only making excuses so they can keep the ritual rolling on during the ceremony [personal communication, Merced, California].

SOUL CALLING SONGS

Soul calling chanting songs (*hu plig*) are one of the many ritual elements that the Mong commonly use in their daily lives. They perform the soul calling rituals to guide the soul to return to the human body. The Elders explained that there are many types of soul calling rituals such as family souls calling during the New Year, when a child is born, when someone is ill, when a young woman is married, or when someone has witnessed something frightening and is afraid his or her soul has left and could not find its way back to the body. A soul calling is performed to bring the soul back to the body. Cooper (1998) describes the way Mong believe a soul leaves the body:

> Such souls leave the body during sleep and go off to play like children with other souls. Like children, they may wander too far and get lost, or they may fall into the Otherworld through a hole in the Earth, or they may be ambushed and captured by hungry and malevolent dab qus. They may also leave the body at other times, particularly during long and arduous journeys, in case of sudden shock or during grief [p. 116].

The soul calling songs are not as difficult to learn like the wedding and funeral songs. All Shamans know how to perform soul calling songs and almost all the old people know them. People tend to pick up the soul calling songs faster like how people learn folk stories and sung poetry. One can learn how to perform a soul calling ritual by observing another person perform and asking him or her to explain the sequences. The Elder said only the people who are not shy can perform a soul calling ritual. This is a reason why more older people perform the ritual than younger people because they have to sing the songs aloud in pleasant voices so the soul can return to the human body (*plig txhaj lug*). The young people are too shy and they not ready to be good soul callers.

RITUALISTIC SECRET LANGUAGE CHANTING SONGS

There are so many secret language chanting songs used for different purposes. The secret language chanting songs are best known under these two categories: *khawv koob* (healing power) and *laig dlaab hab fiv dlaab* (feeding the spirits and requesting the spirits' help). Elders suggested there are certain songs in the *khawv koob* category that they cannot reveal because they are very secret to the Mong culture. These special chanting songs *khawv koob* work like magic. But, they are not magic or spells. They are miracle power. Westerners or people who do not have *khawv koob* would not believe in them, as though they are magic or illusions. Finnegan (1970) asserts that in the African tradition there is a great variety of religious poetry, which is part of their divination system. The African practices of divination support the Mong ritualistic secret language chanting songs. *Khawv koob* to the Mong is some kind of special healing power. There is no translation for *khawv koob*. They can be taught to an individual who is interested in learning them. These chanting songs are very complicated to learn. Once the person masters all the songs, then they have to have an altar for the spirits of these chanting songs to live. These songs are used to fight against the evil spirits. Also, there are songs that people sing to ask the spirits to protect and to assist them when they face dangerous moments. Elder Phoua Her said she knows many songs. Some of her songs are *khawv koob* and she uses them for herbal medicine treatment. She is a medicine woman.

> Beside my Shaman altar, I have another altar for my medicine spirits (*dlaab tsuaj*) to live. I have to worship the medicine spirits in order to give me the power to prescribe herbal medicine (*tsuaj ntsuab*) to people. People who know the secret language songs to cure for broken bones, stop bleeding and to close wound need to have an altar. We need to *txw* (using an animal such as chicken or pig to make sacrifice) to these spirits once a year. The spirits give power for us to make these secret language chanting songs work [personal communication, Susan City, California].

A Jewish American Lillian Faderman (1998) conducted a comparative study with the Mong and Jewish. She interviewed a Mong Elder named Nao Kao Xiong about his beliefs in *khawv koob,* secret language chanting songs. Elder Nao Kao Xiong responded:

> The reason I believe in *kher kong* is that it worked for me. How can you explain why a person's hands, when they use *kher kong*, cannot be cut by a knife or burnt by steaming water or very red hot iron rods? I have done these things. Because of that, I know there has to be some spirit that is making *kher kong* work [Faderman, 1998, p. 109].

Then, Elder Nao Kao Xiong described his personal experience using *khawv koob* to cure the Mong patient with the American doctors. People called Elder Nao Kao Xiong the Mong doctor. The American doctors who knew him were amazed by Elder Nao Kao Xiong's healing *khawv koob* power. The Elders explained that many of these secret language chanting songs are no longer used in America because people no longer need them in defense of the kinds of evil spirits that live in the mountains of Laos. Elder Tong Yao said he learned a *khawv koob* that can keep a *Phislosvais* (nature spirit) from bothering him when he went hunting and sleeping in the forest. Before he went to sleep, he says the chanting songs to call for the spirits to guard him. He has good sleep because there was nothing bothering him at night. He stated, "I do not even hear a cricket sound during the night."

Elder Nhia Chao Yang said his father recommended he learn a secret language chanting song called *taw kiv* (leading a dead to his/her ancestors' world). This chanting song goes under the category of *liag dlaab*.

Since he did not have the talents to learn other things, he said he only knew how to blow the *qeej*, some wedding songs and a *taw kiv* chanting song. A *tub taw kiv* is a very valuable person because he shows the souls of the dead their way to the afterworld and the Mong believe this place is the ancestors' world. After the corpse is washed and dressed up in new clothes, a *tug taw kiv* begins saying the chanting song to the corpse (Chindarsi, 1976; Symonds, 1991; Cooper, 1998). Chindarsi (1976) states, "The Hmong believe if there is no saying of the Tergee the deceased will not know that he has died" (pp. 82–83). The Elders stated that the most common secret language chanting songs widely used in the rituals are to make an offering to the ancestors' spirits and the house spirits that guard their family. The spirits need to be fed and honored so they can protect people. They called these rituals *kiv ua dlaab ua qhua*, meaning the Mong worship system. The *khawv koob* are not used as often because there are modern medicines and doctors can cure for burns, broken bones, fever, chicken pox, etc. Basically, the *khawv koob* are used to treat for these kinds of culture. There are other things the *khawv koob* are used for but the Elders do not want them to be documented.

Summary

This chapter described the oral constructive knowledge that is maintained through the Mong oral literature, including oral traditional stories such as epic poems, fables, riddles, folktales, legends and myths. The knowledge of songs, sacred chanting songs and ritualistic secret language chanting songs plays an important part of this oral tradition. The Mong obtained an incredibly complex oral knowledge.

5

American Education
and the Transformation
of the Mong Community

The Mong community in the United States does not live like the community in the mountains of Laos. Oral tradition education has been replaced with the concepts of written society. Institutions such as schools have introduced different characteristics of cultural and lifestyle values to the Mong community. The culture of schools builds great tension between the Mong Elders and their grandchildren. It creates a major cultural conflict within the Mong tradition. This chapter describes some of the dilemmas that the Mong Elders encounter living in the United States while the younger Mong generation is educated in American schools. The Mong who are moving into a literate culture are experiencing a loss of oral traditional customs, language and culture, and religion values.

The Loss of the Oral Tradition Custom's Values

Without oral traditions we would know very little about the past of large parts of the world, and we would not know them from the inside. We also could never build up interpretations from the inside [Vansina, 1985, p. 198].

There is a significant change to the traditional customs within the Mong community. The younger generation of Mong who grow up in the

73

United States no longer recognize the values of their parents' and grand-parents' tradition. Research overwhelmingly indicates that Mong young people who live in the United States are resistant to their parents' culture, but are attracted instead to the mainstream, dominant culture. Trueba, Jacobs and Kirton (1990) note that Mong children no longer have loyalty to their family unit and traditional values. Vang (1999) adds, "Hmong children adopt new customs and habits fast, contributing to the concerns of Hmong-American parents who want to retain the cultural standards which are associated with respect for and care of elders, proper socializa-tion of children, and maintenance of family" (p. 224). The Elders stated that these issues of the younger generation devaluing their cultural tradi-tion are becoming everyday concerns to them. The Elders are having a difficult time communicating with their grandchildren because their grand-children are no longer interested in Mong traditional values. Mong chil-dren are becoming detached from their family and extended families due to the schools. Fifth-generation Irish American Donald Hones has writ-ten about the life story of a Mong man who lived in Chicago. Hones (1999) states:

> Parents face much competition in their role as primary educators of chil-dren from mass media, other youths, and the schools. Parents who differ from the dominant society culturally, linguistically or socioeconomically often experience additional difficulties in communicating with children, who believe that to become like other *Americans*, they need to distance themselves from the home. When children turn their backs on these parents, they lose touch with a valuable source of learning and wisdom, and their parents may become further isolated from both their children and the dominant culture [pp. 134–135].

The Elders said their grandchildren want to be individualistic. Timm (1994) adds that Mong children "have interpreted the American culture value of individualism to mean that they can do anything they want" (p. 43). The young Mong no longer want to listen to their parents and this type of behavior can easily get them into legal trouble with the American justice system. Adler (2000) notes that after Mong youth rejected their own culture they face an identity crisis. This lack of belonging to a cul-tural group causes Mong youth to seek gang affiliation. Elder Cha Shoua Hang shared his personal observation of young Mongs' reaction to the older people:

> Today, I see the young Mong children are no longer seeing their parents and grandparents are important people. They are no longer having respect to them as their parents or grandparents. They argue, have verbal

fights and fight their parents. There was a father who got beat up by his sixteen year old son. The son hit his father very hard to knock him out. An ambulance had to take the father to the hospital. The police did not even do anything to the son. The son often went out to play. The father said to him not to go play so much. If he like it then his father will teach him how to play the *qeej*. The son talked back to father using English to say bad words to father and about the Mong tradition. The father and the son exchanged a few words then the son knocked his father out. Once in a while I heard similar cases like this happened in here in Sacramento, Stockton, Fresno, Minnesota, Wisconsin, etc. Every time we bring up about our culture tradition to our young people, they often reject them. They said our culture is too dumb and we should not force them to live like the way we live. We are losing our children into gang violence in this American society [personal communication, Sacramento, California].

The Elders stated that living in the United States is like living in a prison (*nyob huv nkuaj ua tuab neeg tsaug txwm*). They cannot go places without having someone who knows the American system to help them. They always depend on other people such as their children and grandchildren to go shopping, visit friends, and go to the doctors. In America, they have to learn everything from the beginning like when they were small children. Elder Lee Xiong shared that she did not know how to make the video machine work. Her grandchildren have to assist her when she wants to watch a Mong movie. The Elders felt like they are worthless living in this country because they no longer can do the things they love doing on the mountains of Laos. Faderman (1998) elaborates on how the Mong Elders felt living in the United States:

> The elders often feel robbed of their power because they don't know how to maneuver in this strange country. It's hard to present yourself as a wise man if your sons or daughters have to teach you how to cross the street or dial the phone. The elders feel they have been reduced to helpless children, as they so often complain. Nor can grandparents generally serve in their traditional roles as revered old members of the household who share their wisdom with their sons and hand down to their grandchildren the fascinating lore of the past [p. 164].

The Elders responded that people are monitored like prisoners in this country. There is too much control in the United States. The Americans use the social security number and other identification to track people like they are not human. Also, people have to have a permit in order to do things such as building a house, opening a business, cutting firewood, fishing, hunting, etc. In addition, people are no longer recognized by skills without school credentials. In this case illiterate people are no longer important to this literate society. The Elders stated that freedom in the United States has not given them the types of lives they lived on the mountains of Laos. Freedom in America does not apply to people who came from an oral tradition and did not have literate skills. The Elders indicated that their skills and knowledge are not validated in this literate society. A lack of understanding about the important oral traditional values makes the Mong elders feel that they have no support for traditional culture conservation. The Elders expressed that freedom in America is only good for the people who have written knowledge and who are willing to assimilate to the American culture. Thao (1999b, 2003) notes that freedom in America is like a dead end road to the Mong parents. The law in America operates very differently than in the mountains of Laos. Mong parents can no longer raise their children the way they did in their homeland. Law enforcement, child protective services (CPS) and school personnel must understand the Mong traditional perspectives in order for Mong parents to trust the American system (Thao, 1999b, 2003). The Elders made similar comments that support Thao's research. They said the Americans do not understand the Mong values. For this reason, Americans place negative stereotypes on the way the Mong operate their customary traditions.

The Elders felt that the Americans should tolerate the Mong traditional marriage. The Mong need to maintain their traditional wedding ceremony in order for the younger generation to identify the Mong unique custom. Mong children no longer know how to address the Elders, members of their patrilineal clans, relatives and friends. They are losing the kinship structure. The custom of Mong traditional marriage is to keep their kinship ties. Elder Nhia Cha Yang explained how marriage establishes the kinship relationships:

> In my culture, if your son or daughter married then they bridge the two
> clans to become *neej tsaab* (meaning relatives). Every member of the
> bride's side of family or clan become relatives to the groom and his side
> of family. For example, you (the researcher), your mother is a Yang clan.
> Your mother relates to me either as my sister, aunt or niece depending
> on the generation. In this case, without talking to your mother to know
> for sure how we call each other. Your mother is about the same age as
> me so you (the researcher) can call me as your uncle. This same method
> is used in the Mong society to keep our close kin relationships. You (the
> researcher) and my son *Txwj Nruag* (Chou Choua) are *kwv tij* (meaning
> brother) not by clan membership but by your mother's kin. Our children need to know this unique custom so they can recognize their

grandparents' and parents' side of family. This way, they become lost from not knowing who they are [personal communication, Banning, California].

It is important not to misunderstand or misinterpret the custom of Mong marriage in the way the bride's parents collect the *nqe tshoob* (bride price). This bride price (dowry) is like a security deposit. In the United States, some families used cash as bride price because they no longer have the dowries in Laos. It does not mean that the parents sell their daughter to get the money. American money works the same way as dowries on the mountains of Laos. If the bride had a happy marriage then the bride's parents can keep the dowry, or if there is an unresolved family dispute and it's the husband's fault, then the bride's family can take their daughter back and keep the bride price. All the gifts given by the bride's parents and close family members are considered as valuable property which can be collected back by the bride's parents if the husband divorces the bride. Davidson (1993) adds that these household goods the bride received are to help her begin a new life. If the bride divorces her husband then her parents need to return the bride price to the husband's family. The husband is allowed to keep all the gifts. Chindarsi's (1976) research on the Mong in northern Thailand did not look into the deeper meaning and purposes of Mong marriage. He said that Mong buy their wives and sell their daughters, and he discredited the Mong polygamous marriage. Chindarsi (1976) did not have a direct English translation of the Mong phrase *yuav qos puj* (getting married) and he said "buying a wife." "This meaning of this word indicates that a wife is considered a form of property, which can be bought and sold the same as any other property" (Chindarsi, 1976, p. 67). The Elders did not support this concept of buying a wife. They said outsider people do not understand the Mong customs. Geddes (1976) stated, "To persons who are not anthropologists familiar with such systems the high bride-price may give the impression that women are bought and sold like chattels" (p. 58).

The Elders expressed tremendous concern about the Mong younger generation losing the sacred knowledge to perform at the Mong wedding ceremony and the important values of their traditional marriage customs. Traditional marriage customs help the married couple to have a strong marriage because they maintain a tie to families and clans. The Elders said the Mong young people who live in the United States have different attitudes about marriage. These changing marital attitudes cause them to worry about the future of the Mong younger generation to keep a strong family. The Elders began to see an increase in divorce in the community involved with the Mong younger generation because they no longer have

the Mong values. Thao's (1999b, 2003) research in the Mong community
in the California North Coast also has noted that the phenomena of family separation, single parents and divorced parents are on the rise. Traditional wedding customs need to be preserved so the bride's family and
groom's family can continue to help secure the marriage. Elder Xao Cheng
Lee described the Mong traditional marriage:

> Marriage is a life commitment to my people. But, now our young peo-
> ple view marriage like buying a car. If they decide not to keep their mar-
> riage, they just walk away. It's like you buying a new car to drive for a
> few years, when a new model come out and it's better. Then, you trade
> in your old one for a newer model or sell your old car then buy a new
> one. These Mong young people's marriage is like that. Mong marriage is
> not like a game. When you decided to marry that person, you live with
> that person until the day you die. You cannot sell your wife or husband.
> You cannot just walk away to marry another person. The Mong young
> people living in America do not understand the meaning of marriage.
> This is the reason why in this society, Mong begin to have divorce prob-
> lem. In my country, our marriage is very strong and we do not have as
> many divorces as in America. This increase in divorce problems in the
> Mong community in America is very disturbing to me [personal com-
> munication, Merced, California].

It is a shocking experience for the Mong Elders to see these rapid changes
in the Mong marriage within the last three decades. The Elders indicated
that these changes have increasingly become a major interference to the
Mong traditional customs and belief systems. Meredith and Rowe (1986)
concluded a study on how the impact of a new culture affected the Mong
marital relationship:

> The Lao Hmong can anticipate further change in attitudes towards mar-
> riage as their residence in the United States lengthens and they come
> under increasing Western influence through the educational system, the
> media and personal relationships with those of the new culture.

Faderman (1998) notes that there are big changes in the Mong culture
since they have come to live in the Western world. The young people want
to be like Americans but the parents still keep their Mong tradition. These
different cultural values divide their family. Timm (1994) who has studied Mong families in Wisconsin asserts that:

> The clan continues to have a major influence on Hmong social values
> and that the primary ideological conflict between Hmong culture and
> American culture is a focus on the family as compared with an emphasis
> on individual freedom. This issue of the family vis-á-vis the individual is

impacting decision-making, personal activities, marriage choices, and traditional roles of women. The tug between these two value orientations is at the heart of the Hmong dilemma in the United States and is causing problems within families, across generations, and in the Hmong community [p. 37].

Faderman writes a Mong college student's story about dating in America:

> But even then I would not have anything like an American date with her. To you — to Americans — to date is to get to know each other on the first date. But in our culture, we have to have the girl's parents' permission, and then we can get to know her in her house. There is just not such a thing as a real American-style "date" like going out alone together. And even if we can go to her house, we are almost never alone with her. If the mother cannot sit there, she will have one of the brothers or sisters sit with us. So you can see that privacy for us dating couples is definitely not the same as for Americans [p. 136].

Western researchers Chindarsi (1976), Cooper (1984), Scott (1986), Davidson (1993), Faderman (1998) and Cooper (1998) state that Mong marriage custom is done by force such as kidnapping and stealing. The Elders said researchers do not understand the Mong method of marriage. There are two types of marriage arrangements that the Mong use in their marriage custom. *Nqeg tsev yuav*, meaning the groom and his family enter the bride's home to bargain for the marriage arrangement with her parents. Through this method the groom and his family give to the bride and her side of family the highest respect. The bride who marries through a *nqej tsev yuav* has the greatest honor. Her parents, grandparents, siblings, uncles and aunts are treated nicely and this makes them have good faith in the bride's marriage life. Also, this method does not make the bride and her side of the family lose face. The other method is *yuav ntsau los yog qaab ki pob*, meaning the bride goes with the groom secretly without letting her parents know. Often researchers misinterpret this method of *yuav ntsau los yog qaab kiv pob* as the groom kidnaps the bride. The Elders who are women said even if the bride is willing to marry, she has to pretend that she is not during the wedding arrangement. If she did not pretend to make it difficult for the groom and his family then rumors would start going around that she is a whore. Therefore, she can easily lose face as well as her parents. Also, there are lesser dowries paid for the bride price when the marriage was arranged through *yuav ntsau los yog qaab kiv pob* and/or a simple arrangement. People tend to go for a wedding arrangement that costs fewer dowries. The Elders said mostly people want to maintain their good reputation. The bride and groom must have some kind of discussion about how they are going to get married without breaking each other's reputation. If the marriage arrangement does not work out, then both can lose face as well as have a bad reputation. The young people whose marriages fail or have a divorce history often end up marrying a person who is older or who has a previous marriage. It is more difficult for the women than men to find a partner if they have a bad reputation. In this case, sometimes the women become a wife to an older man who is a widower or become a second wife.

Chindarsi (1976), Geddes (1976), Cooper (1984), Scott (1986), Davidson (1993), Fadiman (1997), Faderman (1989) and Cooper (1998) note that the Mong have a polygamous marriage when the men take two or more wives. There is a lack of understanding of the values and reasons why some Mong men had more then one wife. Geddes (1976) defines Mong polygamy as "additional wives are gained by economic success which in turn they facilitate" (p. 128). However, the Elders explained that some Mong men married more than one wife because their first wife did not have children or did not give birth to sons. In the Mong tradition, the sons' roles are to look after and take care of the parents and carry on the family sacred tradition and rituals. Also, Mong need a larger family so they can produce more resources for the family and extended family. The more family members, the more people who can work in the plantation and do chores around the house. Also, the men have no choice but to take their older brothers' wives as second wives so the family does not lose the children. Fadiman (1997) quotes Yang Dao who is a Mong scholar about the practice of polygamy:

> The institution of levirate marriage, in which a widow was expected to wed her dead husband's younger brother, was also revived. This practice kept the children and their inheritance in their father's clan but often saddled the new husband, who might well be fifteen years old or have ten children already, with crushing responsibilities [p. 135].

Elder Ying Yang shared that she had to marry her husband's brother after her husband died. She had no choice because her husband's side of family does not want to lose her and the children. If her brother-in-law was not willing to accept the responsibility to be the stepfather of Elder Ying Yang's children, as a widow, she could have married any man she wanted and could have taken the children with her. If she married a man outside the family, then all her children were no longer part of the family. The Elder contested that according to the American culture this is polygamy. However, polygamy does not bother the Elders because they believe that keeping the family and the children in their biological father's clan is more important than having one wife. Elder Ying Yang described the ritual her brother-in-law has to go through in order to take her as his second wife:

The night before my husband's burial, my brother-in-law bowed and paid respect to my husband and said that he would look after my children and I. My brother-in-law also stand in front of all the elders, his family and my family to make promise that he will provide shelter, love, food and take good care of my children and I. I did not really want to marry my own brother-in-law because he already had a wife and children. During this time I did not know what to do because after my husband died was like the roof of my house falling down. I no longer have a house. My children are too small. My oldest child was about thirteen years old. My two sons are eight and five years old. They are not ready to help me. My side of family and my husband's side of family encourage me to accept this marriage because I need a man to look after my family. I do not have a husband then people will not respect my children and I. My life will be very difficult. I married to my brother-in-law but we do not have a strong love. I was too old for him. I lived with him and his family for a few years. When my sons grow up and they are able to help me then my children and I moved out to live in a different house. My oldest son got married when he was about fourteen or fifteen. I pushed him to get a wife so he can become the head of the house. In Laos, on my mountains fourteen and fifteen year old boys are fully mature like a young adult. They were not like the boys who grew up in America. When my sons and daughters were in their teens they could do adult tasks whereas in America my grandchildren who are fourteen or fifteen years old still have the young children's attitudes [personal communication, Montclair, California].

The Elders argued that it is not only the Mong who have two or more wives. People in other cultures also married more than one wife. Finnegan (1967) asserts that in the Limba society people take two or more wives because that is a wish of the culture for the men.

The Elders expressed great concerns about losing their traditional customs in the Mong community to the American culture. They said customary values are to maintain family, clan members and outside clan relationships. The Mong children have the Western culture influence through school and they begin to rebel against their own culture. A well-known Brazilian researcher Paulo Freire (1993) states, "The invaders impose their own view of the world upon those they invaded and inhibit the creativity of the invaded by curbing their expression" (p. 133). Those that are invaded are the objects of the dominators. The oppressed are swallowed up in the world of the oppressor, or at least, the world that they have created for them. Freire (1993) adds, "For cultural invasion to succeed, it is essential that those invaded become convinced of their intrinsic inferiority" (p. 134). Cultural revolution is the antithesis of cultural invasion. It is the effort at *conscientizacao*, to raise people to a critical consciousness of their reality. He notes, "Cultural revolution develops the practice of permanent dialogue between leaders and people, and consolidates the participation of the people of power" (p. 141). It is through dialogue and communication that a true revolution can succeed. Paulo Freire's comments fit the predicament faced by the Mong Elders and their grandchildren.

The Mong younger generation no longer believe their customs. Therefore, it is very difficult for the older and younger generations to engage into a level of conversation that can help the young people to understand their traditional custom values. Elder Mai Vang shared her feelings about the changes of behaviors of her grandchildren:

> My grandchildren no longer believe me. They said I lied. When I began to talk to them about my customs they started to walk away. Sometimes, they told me to stop preaching about my culture to them. They said they really tired to hear me keep telling them about how important my culture is. They yelled to me using English words. I did not know what they said, but probably they were bad words. I could tell by the look of their expression and their reaction. Also, they have the same attitudes to their parents when their parents ask them to learn the Mong culture. My grandchildren no longer like to eat Mong food, listen to Mong songs, to watch Mong movies, to wear Mong cloths and to speak Mong. I felt very sad about the way our grandchildren behave in this country. On my mountains in Laos, children listened to their parents, grandparents, older siblings, uncles and aunts. They respected what the elders told them. In America, if you do not listen to the children they will call the police on you. Living in America is very difficult especially for an old person like myself [personal communication, Long Beach, California].

The Elders made a strong statement that if the Mong younger generation lose their traditional custom values, then they are cultureless in this country. They no longer have a cultural integrity to define their identity, roots and tradition. Therefore, they will no longer identify as *peb yog ib tsob Moob,* meaning us united as Mong, whereas they will become *mej yog leejtwg,* meaning who are you? they or them.

Language and Culture Loss

> The phenomenon is a familiar one in the United States. It is the story of countless American immigrants and native children and adults who have lost their ethnic languages in the process of becoming linguistically

assimilated into the English-speaking world of the school and society [Wong-Fillmore, 1991, p. 324].

This section describes the issue of language and culture loss faced by Mong children from the perspective of the Mong Elders. The issue of language and culture discontinuity is increasingly becoming another major concern to the Mong Elders. This is an important theme the Elders and I dialogue about — the phenomenon that caused the Mong children to lose their primary language and culture. The Elders told me that the Mong children living in America lose a whole lot of the Mong language and culture. Now, the majority of Mong children no longer can carry a Mong conversation with their parents or grandparents. The Elders say that when they speak Mong to their grandchildren, most common responses are either a smile back, a shake of the head or shoulder or *Kuv tsis puab* (I don't know). These reactions tell the Elders that most Mong children no longer know the Mong language and they no longer understand it. Lee (1999) has conducted a statistical study on second-generation Mong teenagers' language maintenance and language shift in Stanislaus County, California. He has concluded that the Mong teenagers have a major language shift to English rather than maintaining the Mong language because they need to acquire English to survive in an English-dominated society. English has been a frequently spoken language by the second-generation Mong teenagers and they do not have the proficiency in their native language (Lee, 1999). Young and Tran (1999) found that the Vietnamese in America face a similar language shift. They state "The longer a family lived in the United States, the greater the shift toward English use (from all Vietnamese, to bilingualism, to English only)" (Young and Tran, 1999, p. 80).

Elder Xao Cheng Lee described that the biggest problem for Mong children unable to maintain their language and culture is that they do not understand the real values behind the Mong cultural tradition. Mong children are put into school at a very young age and it creates an early separation between the language and culture of their parents. As these children grow older they have mixed messages about their parents' language and culture as being educated in schools. The schools' culture values are not similar to the Mong. Morrow (1989) did a study on the Southeast Asian communities in the United States, which supports the idea that Southeast Asian communities have different culture values, behaviors and beliefs from most of the Americans. Morrow (1989) also has noted "many Southeast-Asian cultural values differ from American values. In almost every area, including child-rearing, family relationships, interpersonal communication, and even basic philosophy of life, there are often vast differences" (p. 291). Elder Xao Cheng Lee said:

Once the Mong children reach their ages of thirty or forty then they will begin to realize what happened to them. Now, I try to explain to my grandchildren about the importance of Mong language and culture but they do not listen to me. When there are Mong traditional ceremonies I encourage my grandchildren to go watch so they can understand what is happening. They do not want to go. I see that my grandchildren are no longer interested in speaking Mong because they are being pushed to learn English too soon and they lose the Mong mother tongue quickly. When they speak Mong, they do have the right vocabulary so they do not even force themselves to try it. One day, they will feel guilty for not being able to speak Mong. Right now, as an elder, the Mong children think what I tell them is not true [personal communication, Merced, California].

Elder Cha Shoua Hang expressed similar concerns:

My children and grandchildren often communicate to each other in English. When I speak to them in Mong they respond to me using Mong mixed with English. If I don't listen to it carefully I do not know what they mean. I ask them to speak Mong with me. They told me that Mong is too hard and it is no longer important to them. When I question them why they said Mong is no longer important, they do not give any answer and they just stare at me. As I keep talking to them they walk away from me. It is hard to establish a conversation with my grandchildren because once I begin to talk to them they begin to walk away [personal communication, Sacramento, California].

Elder Nhia Cha Yang says that when he took his grandchildren to be his interpreter he noticed they do not understand Mong. Elder Nhia Cha Yang's grandchildren cannot translate English into Mong and also Mong to English. He said, "The Mong children do not know the Mong words so as they speak they cannot determine the right way to say" (personal communication, Banning, California). Elder Nhia Cha Yang stated that he would rather have a Mong person who came to the United States during his young adulthood or an older age to be his interpreter. This person may not have a strong English skill, but he/she is still able to understand Mong language. Thao (1999b) has argued that being a translator is not an easy task:

It is not that you are bilingual and you can be an effective interpreter. An interpreter must know what is right and what is wrong in the message in which needs to be translated to both parties. The most important role for a translator is to build trust with the Mong parents and let them know that he/she is there to help them. An effective Mong interpreter must maintain a good conversation between the Mong parents and teachers without having one getting angry with another or turning them off because the translation gets lost [p. 63].

Trueba, Jacobs and Kirton (1990) assert that using Mong children as interpreters creates a major problem because they do not have the language skills to understand the terminology doctors or professional people use. Therefore, it causes more difficulties not only for the parents but the children as well.

Elder Phoua Her stated that when she is cooking and she asks her grandchildren to go get a lemon grass plant out of a garden in their backyard to put into the food, her grandchildren do not know what a lemon grass plant is. They go out to the garden and bring her green onion. Mong called lemon grass plant "*Tauj Qab*." She said she had taken her grandchildren outside and shown them the plant. A few days later, when she asked them to go get the plant again, they forgot the name. Elder Phoua Her thinks that Mong children are losing the Mong language because they have little time to be around their elders and parents. Also, the Mong children do not practice speaking Mong often at home. Lee (1999) finds that Mong teenagers speak English more than speaking Mong at home. Elder Phoua Her described that her grandchildren use English all the time at home such as reading books, doing homework, playing games, watching television or going outside to play with friends. When she tries to teach them Mong they show no strong feeling to learn the Mong language from her. Elder Phoua Her expressed, "I think the teachers train our children to focus only in English so they can do well in school but schools do not help the Mong children much when they come back to the Mong community. They no longer know how to speak and understand Mong" (personal communication, Susan City, California). Crawford (1993) has argued:

> The foundation of the current American education program is based on the assimilation theory. This theory has resulted in the rejection of home communities and ways of responding by generations of learners from culturally diverse populations in order to gain educational access [p. 3].

Elder Tong Yao Her responded that when a guest comes to his house his grandchildren no longer know how to greet them. When it is time to eat, his grandchildren no longer know how to call their guest to come eat with them. He said the Mong children are afraid of the Mong Elders because they cannot speak with them. When Mong children see the Elders such as their uncles, aunts and grandparents coming into the house they run to hide. Elder Tong Yao Her described:

When I go to visit my oldest son Boua Xue (*Npuag Xub*), his children are afraid of me and they do not stay around to talk to me or when I call his house and my grandchildren answer the phone. I said in Mong, your parents home? Then the phone just goes silent and I repeat myself several times "*Koj puav nov, Koj puav nov,*" meaning you hear me, you hear me. If my son or daughter-in-law is home then they come to the phone. If they are not home then I heard a voice say "No," then the phone hangs up. When I see my grandchildren I remind them that if people call and they want to talk to your parents and if they are not home you do not say "No." You need to say, "*Kuv nam hab kuv txiv tsis nyob lawm os, puab moog tsua nuav tsua nuav lawm,*" meaning my mother and father are not home. They went to this place or to that place [personal communication, San Diego, California].

Elder Lee Xiong added that her grandchildren no longer called her and their parents in Mong. She constantly reminds them to call their father, "*Kuv Iv,*" mother, "*Kuv Nam*" and grand mom, "*Kuv Puj.*" It is hard for her grandchildren to remember these words because they are so used to the English words "Daddy," "Mommy" and "Grand Mom."

The conversations with the Elders about their concerns and perspectives of the Mong children's language loss help us to understand the deeper meaning of this issue: it creates a cultural discontinuity in the Mong society. The Elders are the only generation that knows how to conduct Mong rituals, knows the Mong sacred chants, values the Mong traditional customs and speaks fluently in Mong. During the conversations, the Elders expressed their sadness to see the Mong children abandon their cultural values and beliefs system. The Elders worry about losing all the sacred knowledge that Mong have to know in order to honor their own souls, the souls of their ancestors and the souls inside their home and the souls of nature since the children are no longer proficient in Mong. The Elders told me that when the Mong language is lost then their knowledge is also lost. Again, the Elders are losing communication power to their grandchildren. They do not speak English and they are not recognized in the English-only speaking communities and institutions. In this case, their children or grandchildren are taking over the role of the Mong parents and grandparents. The Elders felt that they are becoming worthless people to their grandchildren and the Americans. Davidson (1993) states: "Because of this situation within their homes, Hmong teenagers sometimes perceive themselves to be very important because usually they are the only ones who are able to read, write and speak English. They see themselves as the link to the outside world" (p. 151).

Tollefson (1991) has conducted research on Southeast Asian refugees.

He said that Southeast Asian children face serious communication problems with their adults because they adopt new behaviors and values while being in school and learning English. Tollefson (1991) asserts, "Thus, children gain exceptional power through their ability to speak English, while adults lose authority and resent the changes they see taking place within families increasingly out of their control" (p. 109). Trueba, Jacobs and Kirton (1990) did a study about the Mong refugees in Southern California using a fictitious Hmong community called La Playa. They added to this notion that:

> The stress and difficulties associated with adapting to city life in a new country are common to all the refugee families in La Playa who have to acquire not only a new language and new skills, but a radically different perception of the world. This perceptual change is necessary in order for the Hmong to understand life from a new cultural perspective. Many circumstances influence Hmong families' ability to cope with the change in values, the new experiences, and the pace of acculturation. Undoubtedly the school plays a key role in the socialization of Hmong families to an American lifestyle and English literacy [Trueba, Jacobs and Kirton, 1990, p. 74].

Trueba, Jacobs and Kirton's (1990) research has stated that Mong children face the greatest cultural conflict in school and at home. Mong children feel isolated in school because the school culture is extremely different from that of their home. They feel the same pressure at home because they do not fully have the Mong traditional culture in place.

According to Soto (1997): "Elements of power can be viewed as intervening within community contexts that value or devalue home languages and cultures. Coercive power is capable of imposing oppression, abuse, inequity, and totalitarianism, and of violating human rights and freedoms" (p. 84). Darder (1991), whose work focuses on language, culture, critical pedagogy, and democratic schooling, notes that "in order to understand the relationship between culture and power we must also comprehend the dynamics that exist between what is considered truth (or knowledge) and power" (p. 27). Delgado-Gaitan (1990) has conducted a longitudinal study of Mexican families' involvement and literacy empowerment in American schools. Her research found that American school policies apply differently to Mexican and immigrant families who do not have formal schooling background: "School rules and norms regarding the parents' role comprise a cultural expectation that is different from the experience of many Mexican parents. This was especially true for those parents who are immigrants from rural areas, where schooling was not accessible to them" (Delgado-Gaitan, 1990, p. 122).

The statements described by Soto, Darder and Delgado-Gaitan relate the obstacles the Mong Elders shared in their stories about their struggles with living in America. The Mong Elders explained that since they do not read, write and speak in English or read and write in their own language, they are hoping the Mong children will help them to find a way to preserve the Mong language and culture which are passed down orally. When Mong children become literate in this written society they oppress the Elders. Elder Lee Xiong explained how her grandchildren react to her when she encourages them to use Mong in the house: "When I tell them to speak Mong, they scold at me to not continuously tell them what to speak. They do not want to hear me" (personal communication, Stockton, California).

Wong-Fillmore has conducted research focused on the language and culture loss that minority children experience when learning English. She argues children as young as three to four years old begin to drop their primary language once they are enrolled in school to learn English. Wong-Fillmore (1991) states, "Language minority children encounter powerful forces for assimilation as soon as they enter the English-speaking world of the classroom in the society's school" (p. 324). Wong-Fillmore (1991) has noted that since children are losing their primary language, the parents who are not bilingual have a very difficult time carrying on a conversation with their children, whereas the parents who are bilingual do not have this problem because they are able to switch their understanding while the children switch their language. In the case of these Mong Elders, if the Mong children use a combination of Mong and English, then the communication quickly breaks down. The Elders do not speak and understand English.

Wong-Fillmore (1991) has stated that when the families experience conversation breakdown it becomes a tragedy. The parents begin to lose their authority over their children. Liu (1995) adds that since Mong parents do not understand the American systems or speak English the Mong teenagers gain control and authority over the family. The Elders indicated that their grandchildren have no respect for them. Wong-Fillmore (1991) notes that it is important for teachers to be aware of the consequences of actions such as teachers encouraging parents and students to speak English at home, because this will destroy the students' family relationship. Losing the primary language can be harmful to students and parents, so teachers need to encourage them to speak their native language at home. Lisa Delpit (1995) elaborates what teachers should do to help the students whose cultures are different from the school: "First, they should recognize that the linguistic form a student brings to school is intimately connected with loved ones, community, and personal identity" (p. 53).

The Mong Elders said Mong children's language changes rapidly and they believe that the children learn this from schools. Schools provide the information that changes Mong children's views of the Mong language and culture beliefs. Children no longer want to listen to their parents. Parents cannot get them to help with house chores or to assist them to do work that relates to the Mong culture. The Elders stated that Mong children have bizarre attitudes toward their culture. Sometime children requested their parents to pay them for their services. If the parents do not pay them, then they will not complete the tasks. Also, the Elders indicated Mong children begin to refuse to eat their traditional food. Children like to eat out and no longer want to cook their own food. They also no longer want to wear Mong costume during traditional social functions. Elder Xao Cheng Lee described that when Mong children use pigs, chickens and cows for ritual purpose or went to get fresh meats such as to *tua npua* (butcher pigs) and *tua nyooj* (butcher cows) at the *chaw tua* (butcher house), Mong children said what Mong eat is too gross. They do not want to eat the meats. They would rather buy food at the stores or restaurants where doctors had checked the meats to be sure there are no diseases. Vang's (1999) research supports the Elder Xao Cheng Lee's comments: "Some young Hmong children tend to favor English over Hmong and prefer hamburgers, tacos, and hot dogs to traditional food. Young Hmong children, in adopting American culture, become more expressive" (Vang, 1999, p. 225).

The Elders said the majority of Mong children rebel against anything that involves values of Mong traditional culture. When the Elders teach their grandchildren about Mong culture, the children no longer believe them. The Elders expressed that it does not matter how hard the Mong Elders and Mong parents try to encourage, Mong children will not be convinced to come back and learn the Mong language and culture. The Mong children place greater value on their schoolwork and the American culture because they are completely surrounded by American values. In the home, they listen to American songs, watch television programs that speak English, access information on the computer only in English. At school, they learn only about American culture and language.

Hayes's (1984) research stated that the older Mong parents are depressed because the children going to school to learn the American way has made Mong children respect the parents less. The Elders said the brains of Mong children are clouded with all the schools' information. They no longer understand why it is important to maintain the Mong tradition in order to continue receiving guidance and protection from the souls of their ancestors. The Mong children living in this country do not

know anything about how important the spirits can be to help them or
to hurt them. These children tend to think in linear ways and believe in
the things they learn from schools. Hayes (1984) contends, "Since schools
are now taking care of the children's education, they feel less in control of
their family. In essence, the fact that the children rely more heavily on
school has reduced their influence" (p. 93).

Religious Conflict

> Religion, too, played an important role in traditional Hmong life.
> Unlike other ethnic minority groups that incorporated the Buddhist
> beliefs of the lowland Lao during their residence in Laos, the Hmong
> (until Christianity was introduced) retained a traditional belief system
> based on animism and ancestor worship ... Ritual ceremonies were asso-
> ciated with daily and calendrical activities, life-cycle critical events and
> crises [Trueba, Jacobs and Kirton, 1990, p. 24].

The Mong living in the United States face a major religious conflict
within the Mong community and outside community. A lack of understanding Mong traditional religion practices by the Americans, Mong children and the Mong family who converted to Christianity creates negative
criticism about the Mong religion. The Elders stated that it has been very
difficult for the Mong to practice their traditional religious rituals in the
United States, because their religious leaders such as the Shaman, Medicine Women or Men, Wedding Negotiator (*Mej Koob*) and other spiritual
healers do not have credentials like the Americans. Therefore, they cannot practice their religion in public. They are always careful during their
religious ritual not to disturb the neighbors. They are becoming vulnerable when someone calls the police on them while they have their religion
rituals. Elder Cha Shoua said he had to obtain a permit in order to practice his Shaman ritual. He paid two hundred dollars to an organization
for a piece of paper to prove that he is a Shaman. He explained:

> If someone call the police on me while I perform my ritual then I can
> show the police officers my paper. I do not know whether this paper is
> a legal permit or not. The people who work in the organization said this
> paper is a legal permit. Now, the Shamans are getting this permit. The
> organization is located in Fresno, the people who work in this organization
> are Mong. They told me that their organization works with the American
> Civil Liberties Union (ALCU) organization. They got this permit
> approved from the city of Fresno and are working on it to get approved by
> the state of California [personal communication, Sacramento, California].

American John Ensign (1994) has written a doctoral dissertation on the Mong traditional healing of nine Shamans who live in Fresno, California. He described that the American neighbors often created problems for the Mong over their traditional healing practice. Neighbors harassed the Mong by calling the police while the family has a ceremony. Ensign has stated that most of his participants move frequently because of the problem they encounter with Shamanic ceremonies. Ensign (1994) asserts, "Several described conflicts with the majority society regarding traditional healing and cited past harassment by police and neighbors as the reason they routinely pulled the curtains and locked the door prior to ceremonies" (p. 125). The Shaman who lives in a predominantly Mong neighborhood does not have this problem (Ensign, 1994). Elder Boua Tong spoke about this issue of neighbor complaints:

> When I lived in an apartment my next door neighbors were not Mong. It was very hard for me to perform my Shaman ritual. At one time, one of the neighbors called the police to come to my house. The policemen said my family is making too much noise. Also, my neighbor saw people bring in live pigs to kill in my house. I did not speak English but my nephew translated it for me. I said to the police officers, it is not that I like to make noise or like to bring live animals to kill in the house. It is my culture, my religion, which I must do. I do not do this every day or every month. I have this ceremony only once in a while. Also, I did not kill the animal in a brutal way. I respect the animal and its spirit the same way as people. Before the animal is killed, I burn paper money to the animal's spirit and also apologize for taking the animal's life to sacrifice for my ancestors' spirits or for the evil spirits. My neighbor does not understand my culture and they assumed that I tortured the animals. The police officers gave me a warning and also suggested that next time I was going to do something noisy make sure I let my neighbors know. Then, they left. A few months after this incident, I told my son Choua Xue (*Ntsuab Xwm*) that we need to find a different place to live. Then, we found this place. It was a house and these neighbors were very nice. I lived here for over nine years and no one has called the police on me [personal communication, Sacramento, California].

A journalist, Kie Relyea (1994) has written a newspaper article about Mong's religious sacrifice of animals in Eureka, California. She has quoted Thao who is a Mong advocate:

> When animals are sacrificed during Hmong religious ceremonies, the rituals are preformed humanely and with the deepest respect ... The Hmong, refugees from Laos, believe all living things have spirits. When an animal's life is taken, the gift must be acknowledged [p. A1].

Ensign (1994) asserts that the Mong Shamans have great concern over the restrictions of the laws in the United States to use animal sacrifice for traditional healing practice. This is an issue that causes the disappearance of Mong traditional healing practice in the United States.

Mong religion also suffers under the consequence of the Western health care system and religious belief. The Elders stated that in the nature of illness, there are many possible things that can cause a person to get sick, such as by the spirits, diseases or organic matter. When the spirits cause a symptom, then medicines cannot cure it. In this case, physicians are not able to treat the patient and only a Shaman or other spiritual leaders can. Fadiman's (1997) research has stated that cultural beliefs, misunderstanding and miscommunication between the Mong's tradition and U.S. modern society has created a major conflict over health issues. She has described a controversial issue that involved a Mong child called Lia in Merced, California, who had a serious illness. Lia's medical doctors said she had epilepsy. Lia needed to have brain surgery and to be treated with modern medicine. Lia's parents and the Mong Elders believed that her symptom was *qaug dlaab peg*, which means an evil spirit had inhabited her body. Every time Lia fell down and was knocked unconscious, it was believed that an evil spirit had entered her body to harm her soul. Lia's illness exemplified a serious culture clash between Mong traditional beliefs and Western beliefs related to the cause of illness (Fadiman, 1997).

Researchers Bliatout (1986), Lemoine (1986), Thao (1986), O'Connor (1995) and Thao (2002) also note that the Mong's perception of illness is very different from the Western societies where an influence of medical treatment can result in problems. A belief in Western health care treatment sometimes causes conflict with the Mong traditional healing arts (Bliatout, 1986). The Elders stated that the American health care providers are good, but they have to recognize the Mong spiritual beliefs too. In this way when the American doctors cannot diagnose what causes the illness, a Mong Shaman or spiritual practitioner can be called in to perform the Mong traditional religious healing ceremony to determine whether it is the spirits that are making the person ill. The Elders indicated that sometimes a person is very ill but has no temperature; then the American doctors cannot determine what causes the illness, especially for small children. A sickness like this one needs a Shaman or spiritual healer to come in to help find out what caused the problem. Elder Cha Shoua described his Shaman spirits who guide him to understand how to diagnose a sick person:

> When I felt the person's pulse on their wrist or felt their temperature by touching the ears sometime the spirits tell me what is wrong with this person. Usually, when a person is sick and you feel the lower part of the

ears are cold then this person is *ceeb* (a major frightening moment caused disturbance to the spirit to make the person sick). When I cannot determine the symptom then I have to *ua neeb saib*, meaning to perform a Shaman ritual to find out the cause of illness [personal communication, Sacramento, California].

The Elders stated that if a sickness is not caused by the body or diseases then a Shaman or spiritual healers can almost be certain about what kinds of spirits caused the illness by looking, touching or performing a Shamanic session called *ua neeb saib* to see the patient. Tapp (1989) added "*ua neeb saib*," for his diagnosis, which requires no sacrifice and can be performed at anytime" (p. 76). A Shaman's *ua neeb saib* dose not require a sacrifice of an animal — only the *ua neeg khu*, meaning healing ritual does. The Elders said the spirits that make people ill could be the *dlaab vaaj dlaab tsev puj yawm txwv txoob los dlaab qus* (the house spirits, ancestors' spirits or the evil spirits).

The Elders also said the surgery procedures performed by the Western doctors are sometimes harmful to the spirits. According to O'Connor (1995) the soul of the person will not able to reincarnate if a part of the body is missing. In the Mong cosmology, they have a religious myth that a body and a soul cannot be separated. If something harms the spirit then it causes sickness to the human body (Chindarsi, 1976; Geddes, 1976; Bliatout, 1986; Lemoine, 1986; Thao, 1986; Symonds, 1991; Cooper, 1998; Thao, 2002). The Elders stated that if a dead body is missing a body part, it is very difficult for the soul to depart to the ancestors' world. Therefore, this dead person's soul becomes a demon and returns to make members of the living family sick and possibly die. If a member of the family dies, then his or her soul is taking over the place of the soul of a recently dead family member who has a missing body part. This soul will continue to cause a family curse. A Shaman ritual must be performed to help guide the soul that cannot depart to the ancestors' world. The spirits of Shaman help this demon soul to find its way to the after world so it can be reincarnated. O'Connor (1995) adds that if a body part of a dead person is missing, then the person's ghost may return after death to look for its original parts as well as to cause illness or misfortune to the living family members. Elder Chai Xiong said she does not like what doctors do to the dead body. She explained:

I do not like it when doctors take out the dead people's brain, eyes and intestines. They should leave the dead bodies alone. I do not know what will happen to my body after I die. If they took everything out from my body then I do not know whether my soul would be able to be reincarnated. I do not like what the Americans do to the dead body at all.

This is really disturbing to me. I want to die in my country so my soul can leave this planet happily [personal communication, Elder Fresno, California].

Elder Ying Yang shared what had happened to her oldest son:

My oldest son Pang died because the doctors cut his right foot off. He was very ill because his foot was swelling. He had a pain of *mob taw vwm* (crazy foot pain or gout). The doctors said if they do not cut his foot off then he will die. His foot was causing him too much pain. They cut his foot. He stayed in the hospital for nine days then he died. We asked the doctors to put his foot back on after he died. We do not want him to leave this planet with a missing part of his body. If we know that the doctors could not be able to save him we would not let the doctor cut his foot. Some of my sons and daughters do not want it to be cut but it is our only hope that he will live. For now on, if there is a person really sick and the doctors ask to do any surgery, make sure the doctors are certain about what they are doing before given them the permission. Sometimes, the doctors just want to have experience so everyone needs to be careful and not to fully trust the doctors. When I think about my son's case, I wonder if his leg is not cut maybe he would not have died [personal communication, Montclair, California].

O'Connor (1995) has stated that the Mong are not confident about biomedical system views replacing their traditional views. He quoted two Mong educators, "There is a shared suspicion and fear among many Hmong that Western physicians will use Hmong patients for purposes of experimentation, or for practicing techniques actually uncalled for in their particular medical circumstances" (p. 89). The Elders indicated that the Western physician needs to understand the Mong culture and their world-view of cosmos, that illness may sometimes be caused by the spirits. This way there is no conflict between the medical and spiritual care givers. They said it is really difficult for the Mong to bring a Shaman or spiritual healer into the hospital that does not know about the Mong traditional beliefs to do their traditional spiritual healing. There are some hospitals and doctors that are beginning to allow the Mong to do their traditional spiritual healing but others still do not. Chindarsi (1976), Geddes (1976), Mottin (1980), Bliatout (1986), Lemoine (1986), Thao (1986), Symonds (1991), Cooper (1998) and Thao (2002) note that Mong traditional religious rituals play a central part of their everyday life. Therefore, Mong indigenous practices of spiritual worship are ways to protect the cause of illness and/or misfortune.

An increase of Mong conversion to Christianity brings another controversial issue to the Mong traditional religion within their community in the United States. An American, Jack Davidson (1993), has conducted a historical study of the Mong culture and its implications for the ministry. He found the influence of education is changing Mong beliefs from traditional religion to Christianity. The other reason some families converted to Christianity was because they had bad experience of the cause of sickness, misfortune and even death by the spirits. Therefore, these families believe the power of Jesus will help them to heal their problem. Davidson (1993) states:

> Some Hmong are exchanging their allegiance to spirits for Jesus. Most do this as a result of a crisis experience of sickness or misfortune in which they believe they receive healing and power through the God of the Bible. Thus, conversion occurs, baptism is administered, and they begin to attend church [pp. 175–176].

Some of the Elders expressed that converting to another religion (*ntseeg luag le dlaab*) is like giving up your religion, culture and tradition. It was like you divorced yourself from your cultural tradition. They referred to this as *ntsauj dlaab ntsauj qhua*, meaning isolated, separated or divorced from your cultural roots, kinships and customs. The Elders stated that it is really difficult for both groups — the traditional religion beliefs people and the religion conversion people — to engage in a conversation about religion. Each time they have a conversation about traditional and conversion religions, the religion conversion people often criticize the people who believe the traditional religion that if they do not believe in Jesus then the only life they have after death is to go to hell. If they believe Jesus then he will take them to heaven. The people who still practice traditional religion are eating *dlaab qub* (spirits' left over food or drink) and this is dirty. The Elders who still follow their traditional religion stated that the Mong who converted to Christianity should not use language that threatens the people who still keep their traditional religion. This is not the way to persuade people to convert to a different religion by saying negative things about another's religion.

Some Elders said it is very difficult for them to practice their traditional religion because the Americans and younger Mong people do not understand Mong religion. Therefore, it always creates a conflict between them. The Mong no longer can keep up with traditional religion because of the tensions coming from the younger Mong and their surrounding American neighbors. Elder Phoua Her described:

> My grandchildren keep questioning me about why we don't go to church like their friends. I keep doing *ua neeb* (Shamanism) that they do not understand. We keep doing things that are not of interest to them. They

do not like it. When my grandchildren asked me questions I always explained the important values of our tradition and told them I was a Shaman. I need to do what the spirits had chosen me to do: to help cure sick people. At one time I sat down with my son and we talked about what is the best way for my grandchildren in terms of keeping our traditional religion or covert to *kiv cai tshab* (a new religion). My son said he does not like the idea of religion conversion. He will make sure his children understand our culture and religion. If we stop practicing our tradition then his children have no exposure to our culture. He also said he does not want his dad's spirit to *ua dlaab tu caaj tug ceg*, meaning has no one to worship and then this spirit becomes homeless. Also, when I died, he does not want my spirit to be like that either [personal communication, Susan City, California].

The Elders stated that sometimes people converted to another religion because they no longer know how to conduct the religious rituals. They made mistakes in their rituals. This is why the spirits caused sickness or misfortune to them. Elder Tong Yao Her explained that the reason he converted to Christianity was because he no longer knows all the family rituals. This makes it very difficult so he decided to go to church instead of keeping his traditional religion. Even though he goes to church, he is still very active in the Mong community such as attending traditional wedding, funeral and other events.

Elder Xai Dang Moua had converted to Christianity almost forty years ago. He said he no longer participates in the events that are involved with Mong traditional religion beliefs. He stated that if you want Jesus to protect and trust you, then you must not get involved in events that are associated with the *coj dlaab* (spiritual worship), which he referred to as the Mong traditional religion. The Elders argued that this religion conversion may work for some families but not for all families. There were many families who converted to Christianity and these families had returned to *coj dlaab* (ancestors' worship). They said it does not matter whether a person is a Christian if the ancestors' spirits *lug ntshav yuav noj yuav haus* (come looking for you because the ancestors' spirits need to eat and drink), then no one can escape from them. If you do not perform rituals to make offering to the ancestors' spirits, then the spirits will make you ill and possibly die. These ancestors' spirits sometimes can be your grandparents, uncles or parents. Chindarsi (1976) asserts that these are the spirits of deceased family members who are demanding sacrifices of animals such as oxen to them. Elder Chong Yer Thao explained his experience of being a Christian for over 30 years and he came back to believe in his traditional religion to worship his ancestors' spirits:

In the mid 1950s, the Christian missionary came to recruit in my village. My wife and I converted to Christianity. In the late 1980s, my wife was very ill. I prayed for God's help, but she did not get well at all. My cousins, grandchildren and relatives who still practiced the Mong traditional religion told me to go back to my old religion. I had done everything I could to cure my wife but her illness was getting worse each day. I decided to go back to practice my old religion. I called a Shaman to cure my wife. I performed *nyooj dlaab* (the son performs a sacred ritual for his parents' spirits by sacrificing a bull) and other rituals. My wife got well and she lived with me a few years. She died in 1994. I went back to being a Shaman [personal communication, Stockton, California].

Scott (1986), Bliatout, Downing, Lewis and Yang (1988), Trueba, Jacobs and Kirton (1990), Davidson (1993), Hones (1999), and Thao (1999b, 2003) state that the changes in Mong religion and tradition beliefs create a generation gap within the Mong community. The Mong children who are born and grow up in the United States are being educated in the American schools. They learn the American culture and religion. These Mong children no longer have the capacity to maintain their profound culture and religion beliefs that their parents and grandparents have. Hones (1999) describes Shou Cha's life story that he too has to go to school part time to be educated in the American culture such as speaking, reading and writing in English and working full time in order to survive in the United States. This leaves him little time to keep up with his traditional culture. Shou Cha and his family became Christian and through church he had more chance to practice and to learn his English-language skills and teach his children in Mong literacy to promote the Mong language. Hones (1999) refers to this transition that religion is the word of literacy. However, Trueba, Jacobs and Kirton (1990) argue that a change in religion will change the Mong traditional values and this will cause more of a culture gap among the Mong younger generation. The Elders expressed that it is literacy which makes it so difficult for them to persuade their grandchildren to maintain the Mong religion and tradition. All the sacred chanting songs and secret language chants need to be recited orally in ritual ceremonies. The Elders said the younger generation has difficulty in memorizing information. They have to write everything down on paper. They cannot perform rituals by reading from the text. The spirits do not like it. Elder Xao Cheng Lee expressed his view about the literate culture:

In my oral tradition, we stored all the information in our head, not on a piece of paper or in books. The Mong children who live in this new society no longer want to memorize information. They trust the print system more than anything and this makes our children want to stop learning what is in the oral tradition. I see that as our children are becoming educated in the print culture they begin to *ntsauj dlaab ntsauj nqua* (divorce their culture, language, religions and customs.) I think in our future living in America, soon our children will become *ntsauj dlaab ntsauj qhua, ntsauj neej ntsauj tsaa, ntsauj kw ntsauj tij* (disconnected to their culture, religious, language, relatives and family) [personal communication, Merced, California].

Sweeney (1987) found similar changes to Malay oral traditional values when Western patterns of print literacy were introduced to the Malaysians. He has concluded that Malaysian children who have a strong oral orientation are doing so well in Malaysian education through the knowledge they have with the oral milieu. Children who classified their knowledge in a new way such as in Western print have detached themselves from the Malaysian spoken words and they process their information in a restricted style. Then they have more difficulty connecting into the past because they have the Western thinking modes (Sweeney, 1987). According to Sweeney's comments, if the Mong parents who live in the United States have the capacities to reinforce their children with traditional values in schools or communities, this will help Mong children to develop a greater knowledge in both the oral and print culture.

Summary

This chapter described the profound issues that the Mong Elders encounter in everyday living in the United States. It explained the conceptual information from schools that is deteriorating the Mong oral traditional customs, language, culture and religion values. In the Mong community they are losing their strong kinship ties, communal lifestyles and traditional religion because of the tensions built among the American general population, institutions and the Mong younger generation and Mong religion conversion group. These factors cause serious concern among the Mong Elders about conservation of their oral tradition.

6

The Stories
of Mong Elders

This chapter contains the autobiographical stories of thirteen Mong Elders. The stories present in this chapter were collected through face-to-face, tape-recorded conversations in Mong, which were then interpreted and transcribed into English. Even though I am a native Mong speaker, there is no possible word-for-word translation from Mong to English. As Finnegan states:

Translation is not an absolute process, and differs according to aim and interpretation. No one of its manifestations, not even the often-assumed word-for-word "correspondence" model, is self-evidently the most "accurate" one and translators have to make up their own minds about appropriate models for their own purpose [Finnegan, 1992, p. 190].

Furthermore, transcribing from oral form to written text may not reflect the main points made by the Mong Elders. In fact, these written transcriptions may not be representative of the oral versions. Finnegan (1992) has written:

The challenges of transcribing from a totally-unwritten language seldom arise nowadays. But writing conventions are themselves part of the subject, so it is important to explore not only your own expectations but also local perceptions of the relation between written and spoken language [p. 195].

Riessman (1993) argues the same points:

By transcribing at this level, interpretive categories emerge, ambiguities in language are heard on the tape, and the oral record — the way the story is told — provides clues about meaning. Insights from these various sources shape the difficult decision about how to represent oral discourse as a written text [p. 58].

The Mong speak in a tonal language; Smalley has elaborated on the sounds of the Mong language:

The complexities of the Hmong sound system lie primarily in the consonants. As with the vowels and tones, there are both simple and complex consonants, but there are many more consonants than vowels, and more kinds of complexity. Hmong spoken consonants are, however, a marvel of symmetry, forming an intricate structure [Smalley, 1990, p. 45].

Bliatout, Downing, Lewis and Yang (1988) add that the Mong do not pronounce the final consonants like English. For example, *I kick a ball*. If this sentence is read in Mong, the letter *k* on the end of the word *kick* is silent. In terms of tenses, the Mong do not have past tense. They refer to the time to indicate the past tense such as *Yesterday, I went to the store*. "Yesterday" initiates the time of action, so the verb "went" remains as "go." *Yesterday, I washed my car*, the verb "washed" remains as "wash." The *ed* is not added because the word "Yesterday" signals that it happened in the past. A native Mong speaker would have said *Yesterday, I go to the store or Yesterday, I wash my car*. Thao (1999a) has described the speech of his kin as:

Though Mong language does not take on any inflections in the past tense forms as in American English, this does not mean that the Mong do not have tenses. They express their tenses through adverbial phrases, such as today, yesterday, tomorrow, etc. [p. 123].

Hence, the translations of the Elders' stories may not follow accepted English grammatical conversations. There is no manual of style to guide the translations into written English from the oral Mong language.

Elder Boua Tong Yang

This is an interpretation of a story by Elder Boua Tong Yang, who lives with his son in Sacramento, California. He came to the United States in July 1982. His age on his immigration papers is eighty-nine years, but he insists that this is wrong. He explained that the American man who gave him papers to enter into the United States just put down his own age. He said that his real age probably is in the nineties or close to a

Yawm Npuag Tooj Yaaj (Elder Boua Tong Yang), holding a *qeej*, a sacred instrument played at Mong funeral services. Sacramento, California, March 2001.

hundred years old. His calculations are based on the fact that his siblings are dead and that he is the second oldest child in the family. In Laos, he lived in Xaignabouri Province. Below is my written version of his story.

I have five brothers and three sisters. One of my sisters passed away when she was a young girl. I have only two sisters. I have a total of ten people in my family. There are eight children in my family. I am the second oldest child and the smallest person in the family. All my siblings have died. I have large extended families, including my brothers' and sisters' children. I married a woman from the Thao clan. My wife's name was Blia Thao, *Nplas Thoj*. She passed away thirty years ago.

I did not get married early like my brothers. Even though I am the second oldest my parents never bothered to find me a wife. Anyway, I did not fall in love early like my brothers, so I stayed single until I was in my twenties. As an old single young man, *ntsaug laug*, it was really difficult to find a wife. I was a *ntsaug laug*, meaning a man who stayed single past his teenage years. In my culture, people usually married when they were in their teens, between ages twelve and eighteen.

This is how I got married to my wife. The reason she married me was because my mother-in-law persuaded her. My wife's mother knew that I was a hard worker and I had a good heart. She knew that I was old for her daughter but she wanted me to be her son-in-law. Also, my grandfather Xai Cha, *Yawm Xaiv Tshaaj*, was a well-known elder in my village. People respected him because of his wisdom and talents. He knew a lot of things about Mong tradition. People often asked my grandfather to help them in funerals, wedding ceremonies, and other rituals. My grandfather was a blacksmith. He made shovels and knives for the people. I remember as a young boy, I spent much time with my grandpa in his forge. I pulled the air blower tube similar to a menthol called *Hub*, which was to blow air to keep the charcoal hot to burn the steel. My wife told me that her mom talked to her about me. Her mother told her that she should get a husband like me so she would not have to worry about depending on others to make tools for farming and other crafts. Farming tools were very important to the Mong because we used them every day in the field.

I was born on the Mong's mountain in a village called *Zog Xam Kaim*. This village was near to the Mekong River. It was a day's walk from my village to the Mekong River. When I was growing up my people never went to the low land where only the Laotians lived, because every time someone went there and came back that person got sick and sometimes died. So we were afraid to go to the low land. We began to not be afraid to go into Lao town or low land when I was in my forties.

In all my life, I was not a good hunter but I was a good trapper. I trapped seven bears and one tiger. As far as hunting, my people did not get automatic rifles until later when we had a war with the Communists. Before that, we only had Mong rifles, *Phom Moob*. I first learned to shoot with a Mong rifle. The Mong Elders made the Mong rifles. Only a very few people who were good at iron making could make these rifles. These rifles used gun powder, *tshuaj phom*. Using a Mong rifle I got only one squirrel, one pheasant and one pigeon. Besides my skill of trapping, I was also good at fishing and frog catching. I remember at night, I used a bamboo torch for light and went to catch fresh water frogs, snails and fishes. At night these animals were very docile. I often went places by myself and I left my wife at home.

When my brothers went to places they often took their children with them. My children were not big enough to be able to go with me. I had bad fortune with children. I had only five children. My two oldest children died at a very young age. Then my wife and I did not have any more children until many years later. We then had three children. Then one of my sons died. Now, I have one daughter living in Thailand. She is married to a member of the Xiong clan. I am living with my youngest son. He is my baby, *tub ntxawg*.

I am a Shaman. I became a Shaman when I was in my thirties. I was very ill for a period of time and my family did everything they could to cure my sickness, but I still did not get well. My family called a Shaman to perform a ritual and he found that a Shaman spirit had chosen me to become a Shaman. He said if I did not become a Shaman then there was nothing that could cure me. I became a Shaman and I got well. I also know a few healing chants, *khawv koob*, folktales, *lug ntsuag*, and play *qeej*, *tshuab qeej*. I learned the chants from my father and uncles. I learned folktales from my elders. During my childhood, my friends and I often got together after dinner to listen to stories. We asked our elders to tell us stories. I learned to tell stories by listening to the elders. The stories that I liked, I learned fast by only listening a few times. I learned to build houses, sheds, and animals' coops and to perform rituals by watching my father and uncles. I learned to work in the field and took care of house chores by observing my parents while I was growing up.

I studied to play *qeej* from my father-in-law Tong Kao, *Tooj Kaub*. Later, I took a few lessons from my two brothers-in-law Chou Mang, *Tsuj Maab*, and Cher Thong, *Txawg Toog*, to complete my *qeej* knowledge and talents. I am a *qeej* master, *txwv qeej*. When I was young, people often called me to be a *qeej* player, *txwv qeej*, in the funeral rites. Now, I am too old and I am no longer able to be a *qeej* player, *txwv qeej*, anymore. I don't play *qeej* as often and I am losing my *qeej* knowledge and skills. Besides knowing and having the skills and knowledge I mentioned earlier, I don't know anything else except the daily skills to work in the farm, *ua laj ua teb, ua noj ua haus*.

I learned about schools when I was already an old man. I did not see printed text until I was already living in America. My grandchildren go to school, and they teach me how to write my name. In Laos, when I was in my fifties I moved to live in a Mong village that was close to a big city. There, I went with my friends to the city and I saw cars and children go to school for the first time. My friends pointed to a long house and said this long house was a school. I never went inside the school so I did not know how it looked from the inside. It was weird when I first saw cars, *tsheb*. Cars looked like a little house that moved and people rode in them. My elders mentioned to me that in the city people have cars so I knew about cars, but I never saw them until I went to the city. It was very strange.

As far as seeing eagle metal, *dlaab hlau*, I saw it fly in the sky for the first time when I was a young boy. During this time, I loved to play seesaw on the log, *tsaaj caav*, on the farm field. I helped my parents farm a while and as I became tired I went to sit on the log and began to swing the log to do a seesaw. When I saw this eagle metal for the first time I asked my parents and they said this belonged to the *Fuablaab*, meaning French. After I saw this eagle metal come by, once in a while eagle metals came until we had the war in Laos.

The most frightening moment I had in Laos was when I went to sleep in my cornfield by myself. I took my horse and donkey with me. I tied them under the corn storage shed and I then went to sleep. A tiger came to attack my donkey. I knew right away that it was a tiger because it was at night. I grabbed my long knife, *maum txuas*, and pounded my metal pot very hard, and yelled very loud. The tiger got scared and ran away. I went out and saw my donkey was lying down. He was bleeding. The tiger took a bite on my donkey's hip and wrestled him to the ground. I made the noise and the tiger heard me, so the tiger left. I was so scared. I built a big fire and stood up all night. In the morning my neighbor whose cornfield was on the other side of the hill came to tell me that a tiger killed his horse that night. The tiger ate half of his horse. I assumed that this tiger must be the same one that attacked my donkey. The tiger could not make a kill, so it went over to the other side of the hill to kill my neighbor's horse. I went over to see my neighbor's horse. We made traps around the dead horse but this tiger was very smart and the tiger did not return to eat the horse. I went to a Mien village, Zog Cu, nearby to find herb medicine for my donkey. I used herb medicine to cure my donkey and it took a month for my donkey to recover from his wound.

Living in Laos, life was not as difficult as living in America. In Laos, I did not have to worry about someone kicking me out of their house or taking my belongings away if I could not afford to pay my debts. The one thing I worried about in Laos was if I got a farm plantation that had lots of weeds, *dlaim teb muaj nroj*. Then, I would have to work hard to keep the weeds out so my crops could grow. Other than that, I did not have to worry about bills like living in America. In Laos, I used firewood to heat my house and cook my food. I got water from the stream. I used a pork oil lantern to light the house at night. I did not pay anyone in order to get these resources. If I ran out of firewood, I went to collect some more in the forest. If I ran out of oil, I killed my pig and used the pig's fat to make more oil. I did not have a flash-light, match, lighter and gasoline lantern until I was in my forties or fifties.

My worldview is very different from the American worldview. In America I became like a small child again, because I did not know anything. My skills and the things I knew did not apply to this country. Living in the United States is difficult because I do not read and write. I have to wait for my grandchildren to assist me all the time.

Elder Lee Xiong

Elder Lee Xiong lives with her youngest son Nhia Pao Yang (*Nyiaj Pov Yaaj*) in Stockton, California. She has eight sons and three daughters. Her oldest son and one daughter live in Thailand. The rest of her children live in Stockton. According to Elder Lee Xiong's immigration document, she is seventy-eight years old. She said her age is probably eighty or near to ninety. Her second oldest son Chue Blong Yang, *Tswv Nplooj Yaaj* told me that his mother's age was not right. She should be around ninety years old. She was born in a Mong village called *Naj Neeb*, pronounced Nai Neng. Elder Lee Xiong's husband was called *Num Kim Yaaj* (Nou Key Yang). He passed away in 1990 in the Ban Vinai refugee camp in Thailand. Elder Lee Xiong came to the United States

Puj Lig Xyooj (Elder Lee Xiong). Stockton, California, June 2001.

in June 1993. She came directly from the refugee camp in Thailand to Stockton, California. In Laos, she lived in Xiagnabouri Province. Below is a narrative interpretation of her story.

I am too old to remember everything that I want to tell you. I remember when I first became conscious about my own life on this earth. I was living with my Uncle *Txaj Kuam Xyooj* (Cha Koua Xiong) and his wife. We lived in a village where mostly the *Moob Vaaj* (Vang Clan) lived. My family was very poor, so my older brother *Nruab Xwm* (Chou Sue) encouraged me and comforted me. I remember these lessons even today. He said since we were the poorest family in the village, I needed to be very careful not to get into any trouble, so we wouldn't embarrass our uncles. My brother told me not to *ua nkauj nyaab* (play dolls) and not to *kov aav* (play in the dirt). If I did not listen to him and I played with dirt, then my clothes got dirty. I had no new clothes to change. Also, the dirt would bite me, and we did not know the medicine to cure it. My brother said that playing with dolls was childish and made children lazy. So, I listened to my brother and I became an obedient child. I respected my brother and my uncles very much, because my parents died when I was a young girl. I looked up to them as my parents. My oldest brother is like my father. I obeyed his rules.

I have three brothers and one sister. I was the youngest child. I remember when I was about seven years old my youngest brother who was a couple of years older than me was very naughty. He had a very short temper. He caused one accident that made my oldest brother and uncles very angry with him. This was how the accident happened. He made the ladder fall and broke my nose. The ladder knocked me unconscious. I was bleeding very badly at that time. It happened on a very cold morning. There were four of us sitting next to a fireplace in the living room to keep warm. My brother *Tswb* (Chue) was bothering my youngest brother *Xyum* (You) and hit him. Then, Chue ran to the ladder standing next to the fireplace. We used this ladder to get up to the storage, *nthaab*. Chue climbed the ladder up to the storage area to escape from my brother You, who chased after him. When my brother Chue climbed to the storage, he tilted the ladder so my brother You could not go up. The ladder fell and my brother You jumped off. Then the ladder hit me on the face and broke my nose. The ladder missed my sister. I sat next to my oldest sister. At that time, I did not remember. My brothers and sister went to call my uncle *Txaj Kuam Xyooj* (Cha Koua Xiong) because my oldest brother Chou Sue was not home. Uncle Cha Koua did a healing chant *Khawv Koob* to stop the bleeding. He was a medicine man so he took care of me. He did healing chants and used herbal medicines to treat my wound. I was lucky to have an uncle who knew many things, because my family would have lost lots of money to pay other people to get medicines and perform a healing chant to cure me. During this time, if we had a hospital like in America, then my family would have taken me there. But, in the Mong mountains, *toj sab* there were no hospitals. We did not know what a hospital looked like until later when I was already an old lady. My husband and I went to the city. My husband pointed to a big building and told me that this building was a Lao hospital, *Lostsuas le tsev khu mob*. I did not know how it looks inside the hospital until I came to the Thai refugee camp in Thailand. I went to get my shots in the hospital. I saw a doctor for the first time in Thailand. In Laos, I heard about medical doctors but never received any treatment from them until we got to Thailand.

My oldest brother told me that my father died when I was very young. My mother died a few years later. Since then, my siblings and I lived with my uncle. My oldest brother took care of all of us most of the time. We worked hard on the plantation everyday to grow crops for the family. Before I was old enough to know how to farm, I babysat the small children. I remember I had to carry the babies one by one out to field for their mother to breast-feed them when they were hungry. Sometimes, I carried the baby to watch the people farming. An old man I called Grandpa *Yawm Xeev Kaub* (Seng Kao) was a very wealthy man in the village. When my family ran out of food, I went to work for Grandpa Seng Kao to pound his rice, grind his corn, and weed his farm to get food, *ua zug*. I remember one year we did not produce enough rice for us to eat for the whole year and we had to eat *mov kuam* (corn meal). Corn meal tasted very different and it never made me full. I always felt hungry. I had to go to work with other people to get some rice so we could mix it with the corn meal to give it a better flavor. My family learned that we needed to work on a bigger field so we could produce enough rice to last for the whole year. The bigger the plantation, the more work we had. But, my sisters-in-law, my brothers, my sister and I learned a great lesson from the previous year eating corn meal so we did not mind the amount of work. The following year, we were able to collect a lot of rice. We had enough to eat and extra to sell. We used the money to buy clothes.

My sister and I were very busy working in the field and taking care of things around the house year to year. When all my brothers married, their wives joined the family. We had more people to work so my sister and I got more rest. The only thing I worried about back in my home was that we produced enough food for the family. The life I had back in my homeland was very different from my life in America. We worked at our own pace. If you wanted to get more crops and money you just needed to work harder. Everybody could work, but in America if you do not go to school and/or have the special experience that people are looking for, then you cannot find work. My children told me that working in America requires an American education degree. They have difficulty getting a good job because they do not have what the Americans look for, and the Americans think my children cannot work.

My oldest brother Chou Sue taught me every skill I needed in order to work in the plantation, take care of house chores, and to be who I am. He never called me by my name. He called me a sweet name Mai, *Maiv*, meaning baby sister. Even when I was a grownup, he still called me Mai. I remember my brothers and sisters-in-law always want me to stay home to watch the house while they went to work in the plantation. My brothers often reminded me not to forget to bring water into the house, to sweep the house floor, to feed the chickens and pigs. My oldest brother Chou Sue constantly said to me that stealing from people and hurting other people, animals, and crops was not nice. He was afraid that I would grow up to be a thief or a bad person, so he always reminded me not to forgot all the lessons he taught me. He said if I listened to him and followed his advice, then one day I would get a good husband and parents-in-law. Men tend to marry the women who have a good reputation of being a hard worker and respecting the elders. Women do the same thing too. Rumors about a disobedient young woman or young man can spread very quickly, so my brother did not want me to create any bad rumors. My brother said to me that we did not have parents and we looked to our uncles as our parents so we needed to work hard and be respectful.

When I was working in the field, he told me to keep my head down and focus on my work. If I kept looking ahead to what I would be working on next then it would make me get tired fast and I never would finish my work. He said, "*Ua teb tsis txhob tsaa tsaa taub hau saib luag teb, luag teb tswv dle dle ua tsis txawj txug,*" meaning that while working in the field I should not pay too much attention to my finishing point, and then I would soon realize that I had already reached my finishing point. Then I would get to rest quicker. If I always looked to see how far to my finish point then it would take a longer time to finish my work. When I worked in the field, I did like my brother told me and I had a good reputation around people that I was a fast and hard worker. I was so busy working in the farm and taking care of the work around the house. I did not have free time to play, learn how to sing sung poetry, see guys, and do other activities like some of the Mong girls. I knew that my oldest brother did not like it when I played around. My special skills were to work in the plantation, do the house chores, and sew. I began sewing when I was a young girl. I sewed my brothers' and my clothing. I learned to sew from my aunts.

My good reputation created a huge controversy about my marriage. My family was poor and my husband's family was rich. My brother Chou Sue did not want me to marry my husband because he thought that we would never have a relationship. My husband's family learned about my reputation and they want me to be their daughter-in-law. My husband's parents came to my house to bargain with my brother for me to marry their son. My brother refused to accept their offer and my husband's family was very upset. They threatened to bring my brother to the Mong justice because he would not allow me to marry their son. My brother said to me that my husband's family was rich and he did not know whether their son would love me. He was not reassuring about me marrying into a wealthy family. A few months later, my husband's family came back to inform my brother that his refusal to establish my marriage arrangement would not stop them. They would steal me from the outside of the house. In the Mong marriage, if the bride is stolen by the groom, then the cost of dowry on the bride is less than if the groom's family comes to bargain in the house with the bride's family: *Nqeg Tsev Yuav*, means to enter inside the bride's parents' home to bargain for the marriage arrangement. *Yuav Ntsau Los Yog Qaab Ki Pob* means the bride leaves the house with the groom without notifying her family before the marriage arrangement. My husband's family wanted me to marry their son, but they knew that my oldest brother would not give them permission. They secretly took me to marry their son and my oldest brother was angry. My husband's family paid some money to the village Elders to help them talk to my brother so a wedding arrangement could be set. When the Elders came to talk to my brother, he said to the Elders that he only accepted the wedding arrangement with one condition because the way my husband's family treated him was disrespectful. First, they came to bargain in the house and later they stole me from the outside. My brother would not lower the cost of the dowry. He requested extra dowry for the damage they did to my brother and my family. Also, my husband's family needed to give an extra dowry to apologize to him and his family for their disrespect. My husband's family wanted to marry me to my husband badly, so they do not mind about losing all the dowries. I had no love relationship with my

husband before our marriage. After our marriage he loved me very
much. We did not have any problem. I think my husband knew the
reason my oldest brother did not want me to marry him was because of
their wealth. He did not want to hurt my feelings or my brother's feelings. Also, the Elders in the village were the witnesses to our marriage
settlement, so my husband and parents-in-law were cautious about how
they treated me.

I never saw cars until all my children were grown up. My family
moved to live closer to a city. My husband and I went to the city to sell
Mong mustard green *zaub ntsuab* and vegetable *zaub*; I saw cars for the
first time. At one time, my husband, my children and I went to the city
and saw a machine that crushes rice, *loos xwm*. This machine crushes
the rice kernel and peels out the skins. In the Mong mountains we did
not have this machine and we used a rice pounder to do it. I looked at
the machine and it was amazing. It does require much energy to crush
rice. Since I learned how to pound rice as a young girl, I used the rice
pounder to crush the rice and it was very hard work. The machine
made the work so easy. I wanted the machine very badly. I asked my
husband and my sons to buy the machine. I said to them that if we get
this machine, we would never have to pound rice from the rice pounder
again. I was wondering to myself why the Laotian *Lostsuas* knew how to
make such a unique machine to do their work for them, when the
Mong, *Peb Moob*, had to use their hands and feet to do all the work. I
felt sad and began to cry. My husband said to me that they would not
sell him this machine but he would buy one for the family if he found
one for sale. We asked the owner of the machine to see how much it
cost to purchase the machine. The owner said it was lots of money. The
machine cost one million, *Ib laab*. My husband said we did not have
this much money to buy the machine. He promised me that whenever
we had the money and he found a machine, then he would buy one for
me. A few years later, we moved to Thailand. We had to leave our
homeland because the Communist soldiers came to harass us and took
our livestock. The Communist soldiers chased us out of Laos, *Nyiablaaj
lawv peb tawm*. If we had not moved, my husband would probably
already have gotten the family a machine.

I do not want to think about my life in the past, because it is very
difficult for me to bring it back to my memory. Every time I think
about it, my tears fall because my life-story as an orphan child makes
me feel sad. Also, I miss my old life in the Mong mountains very much.
I cannot say much about the things I miss, but I want to say that I will
never forget my life in the past until the day I die. Here in America, my

son Nhia Pao and his wife go to work everyday. My nieces and nephews go to school. I am home by myself most of the time. My younger niece comes home from school early. When she gets home I ask her to play the Mong movies for me to watch. Some images in the video are about the Mong villages in Laos, and the video about Mong singing sung poetry reminds me so much of my country. When I am home alone, I am lonely, but then I watch these videos to make my day go by faster. In the Mong mountains, I heard all kinds of birds singing, and monkeys and other wild animals calling. The forest was green and beautiful. It brought me peace and joy. When I went places I did not have to worry, like living in America. In America, I hear different sounds, such as cars, airplanes, people voices and other sounds that I cannot explain. Even though my life in Laos was considered poor to the Americans, I preferred to live that life. I do not like life in a rich country such as the United States, because there are so many things to worry about.

Last year, I went back to Thailand to visit my daughter Cha, *Txab,* my oldest son Chang Her, *Tsaav Hawj,* and my husband's grave. It was very hard. My second oldest son, youngest son, my nephews, and I went together to visit Thailand and our old place in Ban Vinai refugee camp. When I got there, things looked very different. The Ban Vinai camp was closed when we came to America, and it had grown into a forest. My sons had to look hard to find my husband's grave. My sons recognized my husband's grave, because when we buried him they put lots of rocks on it to mark as a head stone *ntxaa* for my husband. I remember it took my children a few days to carry the rocks from the river to my husband's grave and to build his head stone. As we got to the place, my second oldest son Chue Blong, *Tswv Nplooj,* decided not to let me go see my husband's grave, because he was afraid I would pass out if I cried too much. He let me stay with my daughter Cha. Chue Blong took the camcorder to take the picture and let me see it afterward. I got to spend some time with my daughter Cha. My daughter was crying for me and she said she missed me very much. She missed her father, her grandfather Pang Mai, *Paaj Mais,* and all the family members. She said I was the only person who was still alive. When she saw me it seemed like she saw her father and her grandparents. She said all the people she knew that were about my age were all dead. When she saw me, I reminded her of her in-laws and her uncles and aunts.

I remember the very first time I saw a metal bird when I was a young girl. Metal bird is how we refer to airplanes, *dlaav hlau.* This metal bird flew very high in the clouds and it made a very strange noise. I ran to my brother Chue Sue to ask him what it was. He told me that my people called this thing metal bird. It belonged to the *Fuablaab*, meaning French. I did not remember being scared at all. I enjoyed watching it. My brother said there are people inside this metal bird. I asked him how did they get inside? He said this thing knew how to land and when it landed people got in. He was not sure, because he only heard this story from the Elders. He did not actually see it himself. During that time, I was wondering how it looked inside this metal bird and I hoped that one day I would get to ride it.

When we came to America we rode on this metal bird. The metal bird we rode to America was very big, bigger than a house. I was very nervous and scared because it was my first experience riding it. I did not pay much of attention to the metal bird. But, last year when I went back to Thailand, I was not nervous and my sons got me a window seat. I sat by the window and I saw everything. I said to myself how can the Americans make a machine like this to take people in the sky like birds.

I learned about school when my husband sent my second oldest son Chue Blong to Lao school. Chue Blong was already a young man, *hluas laug*, meaning a man who already passed his teens. He went to school for a few years in the city. My husband only visited him. I did not visit him, so I did not know how his school looked. My husband was a very smart man. He sent my son to school because he learned about it from going into the city often to buy stuff for the family. He knew that school was important, so he wanted one of our sons to go to school. Chue Blong was the first person in my family that went to school. He went to school for a while, then we found a wife for him, and he did not return to school. My husband did not want to send all my children to school, because he said children who attended school tended to be lazy. They no longer wanted to work in the plantation or work around the house. He only allowed one child to go to school. My oldest son that lives in Thailand did not attend school. Chue Blong is my second oldest son. He is the oldest of all my sons living in America. My sons and two daughters all live in Stockton. All of them have their own family. Now I have many grandchildren.

Lives in America are not easy to the people like me because I am worthless here. Also, I see that living in America is difficult for everyone. I see that my grandchildren are losing the Mong language and culture. For example, they no longer called their parents in the Mong way. They called their parents "daddy and mommy." They do not know the Mong word for daddy and mommy. In Mong, *Iv* means dad and *Nam* means mom. When it was New Year time, I asked them to dress in the

Mong outfit. They told me that they were too embarrassed to put on the Mong's clothing. I kept reminding them to call their dad, *kuv iv* my dad and their mom, *kuv nam* my mom. I said to my grandchildren that it was important for them to keep my culture and my language. They did not say anything to me. When they responded to me, they said that speaking Mong was too hard for them, and also their friends did not understand them. I told them that if they did not speak our language and wear our clothes, then it was like we were throwing our culture and language away. We picked a language and culture that does not identify us. Now, my grandchildren do not know how to greet the elders and friends that come to visit us. When you speak Mong to them, they just stay silent and you are not sure whether they understand or not.

I want to say that it is very important for our children to maintain the Mong culture and language, especially the Mong tradition. We need to hold onto our beautiful culture so we know where we came from. I constantly remind my children not to speak English to my grandchildren. They go to school to learn English. My children do not have to worry. My grandchildren will learn to speak English. We need to speak Mong to them often and teach them the Mong tradition. I told my children that now I am too old and I will not live long enough to see my grandchildren's future. I want them to pass on my culture to my grandchildren so they can remember me the same way I remember my grandparents and parents.

Elder Nhia Cha Yang

Elder Nhia Cha Yang lives with his son in Banning, California. He has five siblings. He is the oldest. He has two brothers and three sisters. All his brothers and sisters live in Vietnam. According to Elder Nhia Cha Yang's immigration document, he is eighty-nine years old. His parents did not keep a record of his birthday, but he believes his age is about right or he said he could be older. He came to the United States in 1980. In Laos, he lived in Xiangkhoang Province. Below is his personal story.

My parents told me that I was born during the *Rog Phem Npab* (Crazy War) in a Mong village called Zog Vaaj Pheej, Vietnam. The first time we saw airplanes flying in the sky, I was about ten or eleven years old. My friends and I were playing outside when this white *tsheb* (airplane) came by. It made a sound and we could not tell where it came from. It sounded like it came from the ground, from the bushes, or the

Yawm Nyiaj Tsom Yaaj (Elder Nhia Cha Yang), with *qeej*. Banning, California, July 2001.

sky. Then my grandfather came out from the house and he asked us what kind of sound that was. We told him we did not know. He looked up in the sky, and he saw an airplane. He said this sound could come from this strange machine flying on the sky. When this *tsheb* went further and further away, the sound also went away. As this *tsheb* disappeared we no longer heard the sound anymore. My grandfather told us that this machine was called *tsheb*. It belonged to the *Faabkis* (French). My grandfather told us that he had heard a story about flying *tsheb*. When *Teb chaw yuav muaj xwm txheej dlaab tsi, Faabkis txhaj le caij tsheb tuaj* (When this airplane comes, then something will happen in this world). A few years later, we began to see more *tsheb* (airplanes) on the sky. Then, the Elders told us that those *tsheb* were the *Faabkis* (French) riding to war, somewhere in a country on another part of the world.

In Vietnam, I lived close to the China border. When I was growing up, I remember seeing only Mong and sometimes I saw the *Suav Tuam Tshoj* (Mandarin Chinese) who brought fabrics and herbal medicines to trade with my people. They liked to trade for opium. When I was about fourteen or fifteen years old, I began to see *Ncuav* (another minority tribe called Tai Dam) who are not Mong. They established a village near our mountains and lived similar lifestyles as the Mong people. My family grew rice from *ua laj* (wet rice field). We dug an irrigation ditch from the river to bring water to our rice field. We grew corn and vegetables in the mountain. We cleared the forest to grow corn and vegetables. In Vietnam, my people grew rice in open wet fields. All the people did similar agriculture whereas when I came to Laos, the Mong in Laos did not grow rice from the wet rice field. When I came to Laos, we grew rice in the mountains.

When I was young, I loved to dig for mud crab and catch fish. I did not like hunting as much because I was not a good hunter. Everyday, I went to the wet rice field to catch fish, crab, and fresh water snail. I liked to listen to stories and my grandfather often told me stories. I was not good at memorizing things, so my grandfather recommended that I study the Mong sacred chant *taw kiv* (leading a dead person to his/her ancestors' world). My grandfather said this was a very important chant. Once I mastered it, I would become a very important person. Besides that I also learned to play *qeej* (sacred instrument played for Mong funeral), and I learned how to *hu plig* (soul calling ritual). These are the things I know. I did not master all these rituals until after I got married. I did not know how to play a Mong musical instrument or sing sung poetry. I knew some folktales, but I have not told stories for a

long time so I forgot them all. I encouraged my son *Txwj Nruag* (Chou
Doua) to learn the Mong wedding ritual, *qeej*, funeral ritual, and other
rituals. Now, he is the best in Banning and Southern California. *Txwj
Nruag* is almost sixty years old. He is the son I live with now. I learned
all the rituals from my grandfather and my dad. My mother taught me
other things, such as how to be a good husband and work in the plantation. My father taught me how to rototill the land and dig a water
channel to our rice plantation. We used water buffalos to help us rototill
the rice field. We did not have machines or watches. We used animals to
help us transport heavy things. We depended on animals and insects to
help us tell time.

As far as the name of the month we learned it by looking at the
moon. *Xab ib* (first of the month), the moon is big and round. *Lub hli
taag* (end of the month) we knew because the moon disappeared from
the sky at night. Farming was a way to help us know the different seasons. For example, after the New Year celebration, which is December,
we needed to sharpen our tools to get ready to clear a new field for
farming. This was in January. In February we began to *luaj teb* (clear
out the place to farm). Then in March we *laij laj* (rototilled the rice
field). In April, we planted corn and began to grow rice plants in the
nursery. In June, we transplanted the rice plants to the wet rice field.
After that, we went back to weed the cornfield and started more vegetable fields. We began to harvest in October and November. December
was just to finish up harvesting. We were busy from year to year and
never got to rest. Sometimes we decided to take a few days off to go
fishing and hunting. Our real time off was during the New Year celebration. In the month of December, we took a few weeks off to celebrate
New Year and honor our house and ancestors' spirits for protecting and
helping us during the year. The New Year brought good fortune to the
family. We called for our house and ancestors' spirits to continue to
protect us and help us for the upcoming New Year. This tradition had
been passed to us from generation to generation. It taught us many
things. Also, we could tell the different season by the way the plants
change.

I taught my son everything I know. I raised my son with his
mother when I was married to her in Laos. I have other children with
my new wife but they were girls and they all got married. My son
learned other chants and rituals that I did not know from other elders.
Txwj Nruag is the only son I had, my other sons still live in Vietnam. In
1993, I went to visit my family in Vietnam. My wife got remarried. My
sons now have their own family. During my visit, I saw my brothers

and sisters, and they were very old. Both my sisters passed away a few years after I visited them.

In Vietnam, after I was married and already had four children, my people went to war with the Vietnamese. The Mong and *Ncuav* got together to fight against the Vietnamese. Then, later we fought on the French side against the Vietnamese. I was wounded in the war. Then, I was taken to the hospital in Hanoi, Vietnam. During this time, I was probably forty-five years old. I stayed in Hanoi for two weeks, then I was transferred to a hospital in SamNeua, Vietnam. I stayed there for a month until I recovered. After I got out from the hospital, the French were defeated by the Vietnamese in Diê Biên Phuo, Vietnam. Since the French were defeated, they left and the Vietnamese gained control of my mountain. I could not return home. During this time, there were still French in Laos, so they sent me to Laos. My family in Vietnam thought I was dead. When I came to Laos, I started my family all over again. I remarried a widow. Later, when the French left Laos, I joined General Vang Pao's soldiers. This time the Americans supported us. We fought in the war until we lost in 1975. Then, we escaped to Thailand. After that, I lived in the refugee camp for three years, then I came to the United States.

The first time I learned about school is when I was brought to stay in the hospital. My village in Vietnam had no schools. We traded for supplies that we did not have with the Mandarin Chinese. Writing meant nothing to us. When I went to stay in the hospital, I did not know my bed number. I saw the bed number, but I did not know how to read it and understand what it was for until a nurse told me about it. In Vietnam, people did not refer to the patient's name, they only referred to your bed number. I had to know my bed number to ask for food and pain medicine. I was like an idiot and the nurses showed me everything. They showed me how to use the bathroom, turn off the light switch, etc. While I was in the hospital, the nurses taught me to read some basic Vietnamese. They told me that they learned to read and write from schools. When we came to the United States, I had a similar experience and the Americans had to show me everything.

In America, my grandchildren went to school and I learned about the importance of school from them. My son brought us to the United States. He was the head of the family so he knew the basic living skills in the United States. He went to school a few months in Thailand and for several years in the United States. He said school was too difficult for him so he quit. I never got to attend school. The life I lived in the Mong mountains was very different from my life in America. In the

Mong mountains, children were not put into schools. Children spent most of their time helping their family farming and taking care of chores in the house. We had an independent life in the Mong mountains, where no one would force us to go to school, go to work, pay rent, pay tax, and other bills like we have to in the United States. The reason we went to war with the Vietnamese in our mountains was because we were afraid that the Vietnamese would take away our properties and rights. This was why the Mong and *Ncuav* organized an army to keep the Vietnamese away from our territory. Later, the French said they would protect my people by forcing us to pay tax to them. Later, we learned that the reason the Vietnamese kicked the French out of Vietnam was because they did not like the French tax and other policies.

Elder Jer Thao

Elder Jer Thao lives with her oldest son in Fresno, California. She came to the United States in 1988. In her immigration papers, Elder Jer is eighty-three years old. However, she said her real age is probably older than that. All her siblings have passed away except one sister. In Laos, she lived in both Louangphrabang and Xaignabouri Provinces. Below is her story.

I think I am close to one hundred years old. All the people I know who are in my same age group are no longer living. Now, I do not remember much. Sometimes in my conversation I *has tom ntej has tom qaab* (I lose my memory and speak back and forth words that may have no meaning) to you. I got married when I was about fourteen years old. My husband's name was *Laj Maas Vaaj* (La Mang Vang). His *npe hluas* (youth name) was called Mang. His *npe laug* (elder name) was La. Vang was his clan. My parents-in-law gave him an elder name when we got our first child. There is a ceremony called *dlaws npe laug* (given elder name). We did not have an elder name for the wife but the wife always was called after her husband. My brothers-in-law and their wives called me *Ntxawm Laj Maas* or *Puj Laug Laj Maas* (sister-in-law) and my parents-in-law called me *Nyaab Laj Maas* (daughter-in-law). My husband's younger brothers and their wives called me *Puj Laug Laj Maas,* because my husband and I were older than them. My husband's older brothers and their wives called me *Ntxawm Laj Maas* because we were younger.

Puj Ntxawm Thoj (Elder Jer Thao). Fresno, California, May 2001.

I did not listen to my parents and I got married very young. I did not get to stay long with my parents. I rushed to get married, and the life I had after my marriage was miserable. My husband was a player. After we were married for a few years, he completely changed to a different person. He no longer loved me. He dated other women, even though he already had a wife and children. He fooled around with many single women. He dated my niece and he wanted to marry her. My uncle did not allow him to marry my niece. My uncle did not allow my niece to marry him. My uncle said this was not respectful to me as aunt. Did she still want to share the same husband with her aunt? My husband and niece could not marry each other so they *haus ntshaab teg* (drank drops of blood from each other's palm to promise that whoever died first would remember to wait at the place where they drank each other's blood, this way they could get married after life). A few years after they drunk the blood, my niece died. Then a year later, my husband died. I believe that my niece came to get my husband so they could be together after life in heaven.

I did not listen to my parents and I married so young. My parents and brothers were very upset with me. They did not love my husband and me the way they loved my sisters and their husbands. When they *noj tshab* (New Year Feast), they did not invite my husband and me. When they had other festivities, they ignored us. I felt bad because it was all my fault. I was married to my husband for about fifteen years and we had eleven children. I have six boys and five girls. I lost two daughters in Laos. They died when they were about six or seven years old. I have one son and one daughter who live in France. They were all married. My other children live here in America. There are three children here in Fresno. I have a large family and I was also married into a large family. I have seven brothers and six sisters. I am the second youngest in the family.

I remember my oldest sisters all got married, and there were no big girls in the house for me to play with and to help my parents with work around the house. I had to help my mother to do house chores and work in the farm. Of course, I had brothers and sisters-in-law, but they were different. My sisters-in-law never wanted to get up early to cook breakfast. I always woke up with my mother to cook breakfast. I was my youngest brother's baby sitter. I baby-sat my youngest brother and my oldest brother's children. When I was a *miv nyuas ntxhais* (young girl age 7 to 12) I watched my baby brother, my nieces, and nephews while my parents, brothers and sisters-in-law worked on the plantation. I was very busy and did not have time to learn other things such as sing sung poetry, play a musical instrument and tell folk stories.

The person in my family that I was attached to most was my mother. I remember the time I went to stay for several months in the plantation to baby-sit my nieces and nephews so my brothers and sisters-in-law could work on the farm. I missed my mother so much. I cried and my brother Cher Ying asked me why. I told him that I wanted to go home because I missed my mother. He took me to stay home a few days with my mother. Then I returned to the plantation.

My mother was my true mentor. She taught me how to work around the house, work on the farm and to sew. She never taught me how to sing or play a musical instrument, so I did not have any of these skills. I spent time only with my mother so my father did not teach me anything. In my culture, the girls often are with their mother, and the boys get to be with both father and mother. I did not learn how to turn hemp into fabric until after I was married. My mother never taught me. When I married I had to find my own fabric to sew clothing for me and my husband, so I learned it from my *puj laug* (husband's brothers' wives). There were several steps and it took so much time to turn the hemp into fabric. Now, I do not want to think about these difficult tasks. When my husband and I moved from a village called Naj Neeb to a village called Phwv Huaj, we lived closer to a city called Npov Teeb. There, my people could go to the city to buy fabric so we stopped making our own fabric.

I remember when I went to live with my husband and his family. Their rice pounder was very heavy. When it was my turn, I worked the pounder to crush the rice that I would cook for the next day. My husband never stayed home to help. I had to do all the work by myself. His brothers did not do that to their wives. They helped their wives to do all the heavy work before they went somewhere. One time, my husband was about to leave and my mother-in-law knew that he did not help me to do work around the house. My mother-in-law asked him to help me pound the rice before he left. He stayed and helped me finish pounding the rice. This was the only time that he actually helped me to do work in the house.

When my husband died, my children were still very small. He died almost fifty years ago. I chose to remain a widow, and I did not remarry. A short time after my husband passed away I went to visit my brothers and parents. They *qhuab kuv* (gave me advice not to remarry). They said if I got a husband who liked my children then they will have a happy life, but if I got a husband who did not like my children, then they will have a difficult life. I needed to listen to them, because I did not listen to them when I was single. This was the reason why I got a husband who did not love me. I must listen to them this time, and I did. This was the reason I remained as a widow. I let myself be one side as my children's mother and one side as my children's father. I raised them and lived with them.

My oldest daughter got married in Phwv Huaj village. Her husband *Vauv Fwm Yiam* (Son-in-law, Fue Yia) lived in the city. His father was a businessman. During the New Year celebration my son-in-law met my daughter. His family told me that they heard a lot about my daughter's reputation, *nquag heev* (person who is a hard worker). My son-in-law's family came to ask me for permission to let them marry my daughter to be their son's wife. I refused to let them take my daughter. During this time I had no husband and I depended on my *laug* (my husband's older brothers) to help me. I went to ask them to help me talk to my son-in-law's family. While I was talking to my brother-in-law, my son-in-law's family overheard our conversations, because my brother-in-law told me that as long as they promised that they will love my daughter then just let them marry her to their son. My daughter's husband was of the Lee clan. My brother-in-law said my son-in-law's family is a good family. They knew this Lee clan well. If my daughter liked him too, then I should not say anything against the Lee clan. I needed to leave them alone. So I returned to my house and my son-in-law's family told me that they heard my family was happy for their son to marry my daughter. I told them that it was only my brother-in-law, but not me. After we ate dinner, they just abducted my daughter to marry to their son. I could not say anything because I was only a woman. When I went to the city to visit my daughter and son-in-law, I saw cars for the first time. Also, I learned that the Laotians have a school for their children. My son-in-law's brother attended school.

I saw an airplane when I was about seven or eight years old. My mother and I were in the field working, and we saw this strange thing flying in the sky. We were very scared. We ran to hide. When we told this to my father, he said this thing is the French machine. There were stories that the French had machines that can fly in the sky. There were people in this machine. I was wondering what it was like inside this machine. A few years later, there were more airplanes flying in the sky. Suddenly, we heard people saying that the French and Japanese had gone to war. The French used these airplanes to fight the Japanese. When I came to America, I got to ride in this airplane for the very first time. I was very nervous but my son told me not to be afraid so I was not too scared.

My youngest son came to America in 1979. He was the sponsor for my other son's family and me. The Americans sponsored my youngest son. Even though most of my sons and daughters live here in America, I still have a piece of my heart missing: my children who died in Laos, my son and daughter who live in France, and the life I used to have in my homeland. These separations of family and new information I had to learn in this country have caused a great stress to me. I wish that I could return to live in the way I used to have in the mountains. I miss the childhood experience I had with my mother and the activities we often did together.

Now, I am very old and I know nothing. My life is close to over. I do not know what will happen to me tomorrow or the next day. Even though I think so much in my head, I no longer can do anything to make it happen or to make any changes. My grandchildren no longer know my language and culture. They are no longer interested about what I know or in what I have to offer to them. My grandchildren who live in France are worse than my grandchildren who live here in the United States. I can still communicate with my grandchildren here. When I went to visit my daughter and son in France, my grandchildren were no longer able to communicate with me. When I talked to them, they shook their heads at me. My language and culture will be lost forever, because I begin to see our children resist what my sons, daughters, and I try to teach them about our values and our culture.

In my mountains, we did not use money like in America in order to get the things that we wanted. We owned most of the things we wanted, so we did not have to worry about buying food and paying bills. I used the dowries that I collected from my daughters' bride price to pay for my sons' brides. My husband's brothers were the ones who went to help my sons get their wives, but I was the one who paid with the bride price. If I did not have my daughters' bride price to sit on the places of my sons' brides, my sons would never get wives unless they could find ways to pay for their brides. In this country, people work and earn their own income. They have their own money. They do not have to worry about the bride price. The ways that the Mong young people have their own money cause them to think differently than the way we older people think.

Elder Xai Dang Moua

This is an interpretation of a story by Elder Xai Dang Moua who lives in Santa Ana, California. He lives with his oldest son, daughter-in-law and grandchildren. Elder Xai Dang is now over eighty years old. According to his immigrant document he was born in April 1921. He said his age is not a hundred percent certain because he did not have a record. He came directly from the Thai refugee camp to Santa Ana in July 1976. He moved

Yawm Xaiv Ntaaj Muas (Elder Xai Dang Moua). Santa Ana, California, August 2001.

to Merced, California, for a few years, then moved back to Santa Ana. He said the weather in Santa Ana is better for him. In Laos, he lived in both Xiangkhoang and Louangphrabang Provinces.

My parents told me that I was born during the *rog vwm* (crazy war) in the season to plant corn. Probably, I was born in 1919 or 1920. I was born in a Mong village called Phwv Num. My village was near the Xiangkhonag Province area of Laos. My parents told me that the *rog vwm* was fought very heavy in the area near our village for seven months. Then the French and Lao soldiers captured some of the Mong leaders who fought against them. This caused the crazy war to slow down. When I grew up there was no crazy war but I still heard people talk about it.

I was the second generation in my family that was born in Laos. My grandmother had my father four months in her stomach, then my grandfather died. She remarried my granduncle called *Nchaiv Kuam Muas* (Chai Koua Moua). Then they escaped to Laos. My grandmother told us that she had to run away from the Chinese. The Chinese came to the Mong villages in China to kidnap Mong children, and killed all the men and took their wives. The Chinese were mean to the Mong people. They even dug out the Mong's graves. My grandmother said they were called *Miao* by Chinese. My father was born in Laos.

I was the oldest and dumbest child in the family. When I was young I often got teased by people that I was short and funny. I had five brothers and two sisters. Two of my brothers have passed away. I have one brother in France. The other two brothers live in the United States. I have one sister in Laos and one in the United States. When I was young I did not like to study the Mong chants and rituals, so I did not know them. I was a shy person and this caused me to have a difficult time learning all these chants and rituals. I could sing some sung poetry but I had a terrible voice so I did not sing a lot. My father was a thin man. He knew almost everything in the Mong culture. He could play the *qeej* (Mong sacred instrument). He was a wedding and funeral chant master. He knew lots of chants and rituals. He could speak Mandarin Chinese. He was a trader. When the Mandarin Chinese traders saw him, they said he was Chinese. My brother *Txawj Chai* (Cher Chai) was the only person who studied the skills that my father knew, but he passed away in Thailand a few years ago.

I learned some important skills from my father, such as farming, hunting, and doing house chores. I was a very slow person so I did not hunt much, but I was a good trapper. I trapped squirrels, monkeys, porcupine, opossum, wild pigs, deer, etc. I did not like fishing. I was only a *tub qoob tub loo* (a farmer). My parents taught me that as a human being I must not hurt anyone, cause any trouble to another and must not steal. My father said that if I could keep myself away from these things then I would live a longer life. If I caused a lot of troubles, stole, was bad, etc., then I would have a shorter life. The nicer I can be, the better people would respect me. I took my parents' word seriously and in all my life I never got into trouble.

In my mountains, if you put all the efforts you got into your work, then you would produce enough crops for your family. The second year following the year I got married my family ran out of rice. Our rice did not last for us throughout the year. My family starved for about three months. We had to use corn to make *movkuam* (corn meal) to eat in that year. After that we learned a great lesson so we worked harder and we never ran out of rice. Rice was a very important diet in my culture. We eat rice in every meal. Rice was our main dish. In Laos, if one did not produce enough rice, then there is a chance that one might run out of rice in the months of September and October. In November, the *nplej caug* (fast bloom or fast grown rice plant) is ready to harvest. The *nplej taag* (late/slow bloom or slow grown rice plant) will be ready to harvest toward the end of November into December.

In 1953, we could no longer live in *Phwv Num* because of the Vietnam War. Before I moved to Xeev (Xiangkhoang) my hair was long. I had to cut my hair. In Pwn Num I still wore my hair the way my elders' generation did. In my father's generation, every man had long hair that he put in a braid. We moved to live in Xeev (the province of Xiangkhoang). There, I put my oldest son *Nom Tsu* (Na Chou) into school. The reason I sent my son to school was because the children in Xeev were all in school. When we came to live in Xeev, only the people who could read and write got selected to be village chief and clan leader. In this province the Laotian government officials worked closely with the Mong, so if you knew how to read and write in Laotian then they made you a leader. I searched for good fortune all my life. I wanted one of my children to become a leader and a rich man. I decided to put my son into school and maybe if he finished school, my fortune would come true. My father told me that when I build a house or find a house to live I must *saib qua tsev kuam zoo* (find a nice location that could bring you good fortune). When my son passed high school and was ready to enter into college, then the country of Laos became Communist. We moved out of the country. My son went to a Bible school in the Philippines for a few years. When he returned we came to America. Now, he is working as a minister in a Mong church in Santa Ana. My family converted to Christianity in the mid 1950s.

I never attended school. I went to school for the first time in the United States. I attended adult English as Second Language (ESL) classes. School was very difficult for me. I did not do well in school. I could count in Mong, Laotian, and Vietnamese but learning to count in English was harder. My son told me that English has only twenty-six letters. They use them in their writing and speaking. I had a hard time remembering these twenty-six letters and to say the sound of each letter.

Nom Tsu was the household who brought us to the United States. When I first came to the United States it was very difficult for me to adjust to the U.S. time zone. When it was day in Thailand, then it was night in the U.S. It took me several months to get used to this time difference. In addition, I missed my home back in my mountains very much and I asked my wife that we sing sung poetry so I could cool down my heart. She said I was crazy. It was very difficult for me to adjust to the culture, food and lifestyle in this country. There were no Mong in Santa Ana when I first got here. There were Vietnamese, but we were totally different from each other.

In the United States, we have had to adjust to so many things. For example, our children no longer wear our Mong clothes and speak our language. We have to learn how to pay bills, defend our rights, etc. When you go hunting or fishing you have to have a license. When you run a business, cut a tree or build a house you need to have a permit, whereas in my mountains we did not need any license. In the United States, they said we have freedom but our freedom caused our children to go against us. *Tuab neeg muaj kiv ywjpheej yog tuab neeg tawv ncauj* (People who have freedom are people who do not want to listen to others). The Mong children have too much freedom in this country and they challenge their parents' authority. The negative behaviors the Mong children have are creating lots of problem for the Mong parents, especially those who do not speak, read, and write English.

Here in the United States we have good things and bad things. In Laos, we also had good things and bad things. I want to say that money is the main source of destruction. When people have money they forget about the valuable things that they have such as themselves, their land, home, culture, and personal items. In Laos, the Americans used money to buy the Mong into the war. For instance, they paid the Mong soldiers money and these Mong soldiers used the money that they earned to marry a second wife, play with other Mong young girls and buy illegal stuff. As Mong we needed to be a little extra cautious about how we use money. Money is a most powerful source to buy others. Also, it creates enemies for ourselves and our families.

Elder Phoua Her

Elder Phoua Her lives with her youngest son in Susan City, California. She came to the United States in October 1979. She is now eighty-three years old. She is a Shaman and a medicine woman. She had two brothers. Both her parents passed away when she was a young girl. She lived with her uncle and his wife until she married her husband. Her husband is a Thao clan member. All the children kept her husband's clan. In Laos, she lived in Xiangkhoang Province.

I was born in a Mong village called Naj Xaab in Laos. This village is located in the middle of a big jungle. When I was a younger girl, I remember walking with my parents to our plantations. I saw all kinds of birds, pheasants, squirrels, and monkeys that were calling and playing along the side of the road. These animals were very bold. Our mountains were so beautiful. There were many edible wild berries and plants. The streams were very fresh and the water tasted delicious. There were lots of fishes. The fishes that lived in the water stream tasted so good.

My parents died when I was about nine to ten years old. My father died one year early, then my mother died. My father was called *Nuam Suav Hawj* (Nou Shoua Her), and my mother was called *Nub Muas*

Puj Phuab Hawj (Elder Phoua Her). Susan City, California, May 2001.

(Nou Moua). My mother had a very strange illness. She was very crazy before she died. The people said the tiger's evil spirit had gotten into her. She made tiger sounds and acted like a tiger when she got crazy. People said when she died she would become a tiger. I was very afraid of her. We actually believed that when some people died they became tigers. These tigers were not real wild animal tigers. They were ghost tigers. They look like tigers, but were much bigger and more powerful. After the person died, the ghost tigers used a rotten log or banana tree trunk to substitute for the real human body. Then, the ghost tigers took the real human and the spirit with them. The ghost tigers had the power to transform a human to a tiger. When the ghost tigers used a rotten log or banana tree trunk to exchange the human body, the tiger made the rotten log or banana tree truck look exactly like the person. When the dead person was kept in the house a few days for the funeral ceremony, his or her corpse changed so much that people believed the story might be true.

My mother was a Shaman. She named me Phoua after her Shaman spirits. She had one set of *qhua neeb* (Shaman spirits) called *nkauj phuab hau le pho*. She used *phuab* for my name. After she died, I was very ill for several years. Shaman who perform rituals to trace my souls found that the Shaman spirits had chosen me to be a Shaman. I did not know whether these Shaman spirits were my mother's Shaman spirits. I was only a young girl so I refused to become a Shaman. My illness was on and off for many years. In my dream when I fell asleep, the Shaman and medicine spirits kept talking to me. These spirits showed me the methods of how to cure the sick and how to prescribe herbal medicines. After a few years of marriage, I became very ill again. This time it was really serious, so I became a Shaman and medicine woman. I probably would have died if I did not become a Shaman.

When both of my parents passed away, my brothers and I went to live with my father's brother *Tsuj Kuam Hawj* (Chou Koua Her) and his wife. He was my uncle. I had two brothers. When we were little, my parents taught us the skills how to farm and take care of the chores around the house. When we came to live with my uncle and his family they taught us more. My grandmother also taught me many things. Usually, I learned how to farm, sew, play musical instruments, and to sing sung-poetry by watching other people doing these things. When I had questions, then I asked them to show me. While I was growing up I was exposed to everything that my family did so I just knew how.

I had four boys and one girl. My two oldest boys died. When they passed away one was about ten years old and the other one was about six years old. My husband passed away twenty-four years ago. After my two oldest sons died I did not have children until several years later. My two sons and I were very ill. The reason my family got very sick and my two sons died was because my neighbor chopped a big tree and it fell onto my house. When the tree hit my house, it was all damaged. The altars for my Shaman spirits, medicine spirits, and house spirits were all destroyed. They flew into pieces. The house and the altars were fixed back, but the spirits were not happy. The spirits made the family very sick, then my children died. After their death, my husband asked the neighbor to help him buy animals to *khu dlaab qhuas* (restore religious spirits by sacrificing animals to the spirits of house, my Shaman spirits and medicine spirits). After the rituals to restore my Shaman, medicine, and house spirits, I began to get well. A few years later, I had my son *Tswv Nplooj* (Chue Blong), my daughter *Maiv* (Mai) and my youngest son *Txooj Cib* (Chong Chee). Then, I did not have any more children.

Now, I am getting old and becoming senile. I cannot remember everything to share with you (the researcher). I wanted to say that in my mountains, there was nothing like living in America. There, we used hemp to make our clothes, we grew our own food, had our own animals, and owned our houses and plantations. Our spoons, bowls, and pots were made from bamboo and wood. The cooking pots were make from *aav* (special dirt/clay) and metal pots were made by craftsmiths and gunsmiths. We used pork oil lanterns to see at night and firewood to cook our food. Many years later, the Chinese and Laotian traders brought pots, sewing needles, fabrics, flash lights, gas lanterns and other goods to trade with my people for crops, animals, and opium.

There were no schools in the mountains. I did not know that people had writing until my husband, children, and I moved to live near a city called Xiêng. There, people talked about sending their children to Laotian schools. Then my husband sent my sons to school. While my children were in school there was no one to help around the house or in the fields so I was busy working in the fields. I never held a pen or pencil until I came to the United States. I had to learn to write my name to cash a check or sign documents, and I am not good at it.

Furthermore, we had no watches and calendar to keep track of times, days, months, and years in our mountains. We depended on the sun, moon, plants, animals, and insects for season changes, to tell time, etc. There are certain kinds of insects that make sounds when it is night or day. When the night insects make sounds then we knew that it will get dark soon. When the morning insects or animals make sounds then we knew it is morning. I usually got up before the rooster crowed to fix breakfast and prepare lunch for my family. Then my husband and children got up when the rooster crowed. We ate breakfast, then went to the plantations.

When it was near New Year, we knew it from harvesting and there were some plants that bloomed during this time. Rice harvesting always started in November to December. After rice harvesting, we knew it was January because during the months of January and February there were certain kinds of insect sounds. My people's lives in the mountains depended on nature to help for hundreds of years.

Even though where we lived was surrounded with jungles, I do not remember being afraid of wild animals or people who might be bad. The Elders told us stories that there were ghosts on the cemetery, and when I passed by the cemetery it was creepy. But, I never saw a ghost. The only thing we were afraid of most was a *phislosvais hab xeeb teb xeeb chaw* (a creature that lives in the jungle or the spirit of nature). When we went to sleep over in the plantations or jungles we have to be careful not to do anything to anger this spirit of nature. For example, when we went to gather firewood we must only carry the wood. We could not drag it. We could not put cooked crab on a log or firewood, we could not sleep crossing our legs and we could not say things that might offend the spirit of nature. If one did not follow these rules, then this spirit of nature would frighten you. This spirit of nature made you feel like everything that surrounded you was falling. It made a very loud and strange sound, which you could feel in your heart, like there was a very heavy wind and the ground was shaking. In my mountains, even on the mountains here in the United States, my people were scared of this spirit of nature more than anything else. We believed that this spirit of nature lived in every mountain where there was a forest or jungle. They were there to protect the mountains.

I had witnessed this scene myself when my uncle, his wife, children, and I slept over on our plantation. We did not know who broke the rules. After we ate dinner and it was getting dark, a strange sound began to come from the jungle. Then, the sound got closer and closer to us. The wind started to blow harder. In a few minutes, the sound came so close to the shed where we stayed. I could feel the vibration of the sound in my heart. It felt like the earth was shaking and the roof of the shed would be blown away. Everyone was very scared. Then, my uncle quickly got a spoonful of rice and meat. He held the spoon on his hand and he apologized for any mistakes someone in his family had made. He pleaded with the spirit of nature to forgive him and he said it could be that one of his children had done something wrong, but it was not purposely done. It was the children who did not know. It was not the adults who broke the rules. My uncle went outside and left the food out. He came back into the shed. Then a few minutes later the sound stopped and everything went back to normal.

In my mountains, we lived a small communal life where everyone knows each other. People were nice to one another. It was not like living in America where you can find some people who are bad and who rob, murder, rape, and kidnap other people. Besides that in America, we have all kinds of problems within our own family. In some families, the husband and wife kill their children, they kill one another or their children kill them. In my mountains, we hardly heard any tragedy like this happen. After General Vang Pao's War occurred in Laos, many things changed in the Mong society. We began to see many single young women pregnant and lots of divorced people. Crimes, drugs, youth pregnancy, divorce, children and family abuse are getting worse in the Mong community here in America. If I knew that the United States would be a difficult country to live in, I would not have come in the first place. Now, it is too late. I see a lot of change to the Mong children in America. As a living elder, it is really sad for me to see our children killing each other in the street, going to prison and leaving their parents, family, and culture. We have lost everything in this country. I came to the United States twenty years ago, but I never attended the Mong New Year celebration, because it was very difficult for me to cope with the loss of my traditional culture and past memories. I do not go to the Mong gathering so I do not see the change of my culture that causes pain to me.

Elder Chong Yer Thao

This is an interpretation of a story by Elder Chong Yer Thao who lives with his wife in Stockton, California. He is seventy-eight years old. He came to the United States in 1979. He first came to Portland, Oregon. In 1982, he moved to Stockton. He has lived there for twenty years. He had only one child. She died when she was about age twelve. His wife passed away seven years ago. He is remarried to a widow. This is the wife who lives with him now. Elder Chong Yer Thao is a Shaman. He became a Shaman in his early twenties.

I was born in a Mong village called Haav Txiv Cuab Thoj (Village of Guava Fruit). There were lots of Guava fruit. When I grew up my family and I moved to a village called Naj Neeb (named after the river Na Neng) not too far from Haav Txiv Cuab Thoj. A few years later we moved to a village called Laam Theeb (Beauty Village), and I got married there. I met my wife in a village called Tsoob Tob Pov near a big Mong village called Pam Kaam. I was about thirteen or fourteen years old when I married. My parents wanted someone to help the family so they found a wife for me early. My wife and I did not have children until many years later when we were in our forties. We had no luck. We had only one child. If we had had children early, then our children would probably be in their fifties or sixties now. We had only one girl and she died when she was about twelve years old.

I had two brothers and two sisters. I was the youngest. My oldest brother was called *Laj Yob* (La Yao), the second oldest was called *Txwj Pov* (Chue Pao), one sister was called *Lug* (Lue) and one sister was called *Xeev* (Xeng). *Txwj Pov* and I had moved to a Mong village called Phuaj Xaab. We lived there about four or five years. My mother died in Phuaj Xaab. A few years after my mother passed away my father was very ill. My brother and I moved to Haav Loj Faab where my other brother, all my uncles, cousins, and relatives lived. We took my father there and a few months later he died. He was called *Ntsum Kaws Thoj* (Chue Ker Thoj).

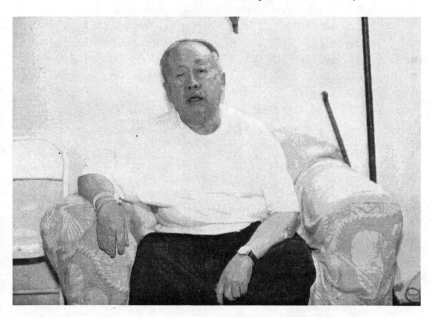

Yawm Ntxhoo Ntxawg Thoj (Elder Chong Yer Thao). Stockton, California, July 2001.

After my father passed away, I did not have any children so I learned to *ua luam* (a person who trades or a person who buys goods to sell to make profit). I decided not to become a farmer. My first trip to *ua luam* I bought a *phaws twm* (water buffalo bull) for *ob dlaim* (two silver bars) in the Mong village and took it to sell in the city. I sold the water buffalo bull for six silver bars. I made four silver bars as profit. Then, I bought more animals from the Mong villages and took them to sell in the cities. I bought fabrics, sewing materials, cooking pots, salt, etc., to sell in the Mong villages. Sometimes I made lots of profit but sometimes I did not. I had to know the thing people wanted in order to make a good profit from it. *Ua luam* took a lot of knowledge, because I needed to carefully find the items that would sell. If my items did not get sold, then I lost money.

I saw cars the first time I took a water buffalo to sell in the city. I was walking on a dirt road. It was getting dark. Suddenly, a big car came toward us. It made a very loud noise and the headlight shone at my face and the buffalo. My buffalo got very scared and he tried to run away from me. I held tight onto the latch. When I got home, I asked the Elders and they said the object I saw was a car. The Laotians had cars. I saw an airplane for the first time when I lived in the Mong village called Tsoob Toj Pob. On a clear day, I saw an airplane flying in the sky. I told my brother *Txwj Pov* that there is a huge bird in the sky. *Txwj Pov* said this thing was an airplane. It belonged to the *Faabkis* (French). I asked him why it was so noisy. He said the *hlau* (steel/metal fly sounds like that). We called this *dlaab hlau* (steel/metal bird). When I went to ask the Elders what they thought of the airplane, some Elders said that we probably will all die because this was a sign that the French will come to destroy our country. When people fly in the airplane they can see everything on the ground. We would have no place to hide and the French will kill us all. I was scared after listening to some of these Elders' stories.

I had only one child so *ua luam* was a good way for me to make a living. When I became more involved in the *ua luam* business I moved to live in a Mong village that was closer to a city. This village had a school. I sent my daughter *Ab* (Ah) to school because everyone placed their children into school. There, I learned about the importance of schooling. My daughter went to school a few years. She was a very smart child. She told me that her teacher did not like her at all. I asked her why, and she said because her teacher did not check her work. Every time she submitted her work, she always got no mark, whereas the teacher marked her friends' work with red ink all over the paper. She said her teacher did not like her work, that was why she did not make any marks on her paper. Because of that she did not want to go to school. I did not go to school but I assumed that a student who got lots of red marks is not a smart student. I encouraged her to stay in school. At this time I did not even know how to go talk to her teacher to find out why. I respected the teachers and I felt that talking to the teacher was rude. I never talked to my daughter's teacher.

Hunting was my favorite hobby. When I was a young boy my father made me a cross-bow for hunting birds and squirrels. My father taught me how to hunt and to weave *kawm* (Mong carry basket) and basket. My brother Txwj Pov taught me to *ua luam*. After I got married, I got a Mong rifle. When I had nothing to do I went hunting. I went hunting with my brothers, cousins, and friends. We went to hunt for deer, wild pigs, monkey, wild chicken, etc. I went a few times to hunt for wild buffalo, but I never got one. Wild buffalo were smart animals and you never found them. They also were very dangerous animals. We had heard stories that wild buffalo killed some hunters, so I did not do buffalo hunting as much. Many years later, we got the good rifles but there were no more of these big animals to hunt. They all disappeared. We got the automatic rifles by joining the army. I was in the army for several years. I was wounded in the war. Then, I got sent home and I never returned. I got shot on my right knee. It was not that bad. We were in the *xov tus* (Vang Pao or Royal Lao Army) side.

I was a good musician. I played the *raaj nplaim* (free-reed bamboo flute). Young girls liked me a lot. One time, I went to celebrate Mong New Year in a different village. At night, I went to visit a young woman. I was playing music to her and she told me that she had never heard anyone who could play music that touched her heart like me. I loved chasing girls when I was young. I could play the Laotians' musical Khene instrument. I learned from my Laotian friends. When I was young, my father and older brothers taught me some *qeej* (Mong sacred instrument) lessons but I did not like it so I did not know how to play until I was already in my forties. I became bored and I went back to take *qeej* lessons from my older brother. I was not a master *qeej* player. I can play but am not an expert like my older brother *Txwj Pov* and my father.

I remember when my friends and I went to play with the girls, they often asked us to play the karate game with them. This is how the game is played. All the boys stayed on one side and the girls stayed on the other side. A line was drawn in the middle. Anyone who stood near the line or crossed over the line got kicked by the opponents. If you got hurt then you called out to quit the game. The group that had more people left in the game won. When my friends and I went to play with the girls, they told us to challenge them in a karate game and if they lost to us then they will play with us. If they won the game then they will not play with us. The girls were bigger, and my friends and I often lost to the girls. We brought some bigger boys, then the girls refused to play the game. When I grew older the girls became more afraid of me because they liked to play with younger boys who do not know anything about love. Once the girls found out that the boys knew about romance then they stopped. In my mountains, Mong girls liked young boys but when they knew that these young boys became serious with them, then they were scared of the boys. First, boys and girls played as friends but as time went by they became boyfriends and girlfriends. After I played with the girls until it got late into the middle of the night then we began to talk about love. This was part of our courtship beside the New Year.

I could tell when it got closer to midnight because it got cold. When it got very cold then it would be morning soon. In my mountains, we only visited girls at night after everyone went to sleep. After I ate dinner and my parents went to sleep then I went to visit my girlfriend. I waited until her parents went to sleep then I called her out. We stayed out until the rooster crowed, then she went back into the house and I came home. Sometimes, I sneaked into my girlfriend's house and stayed in her bed. Boys and girls saw each other only at night. We were always careful not to let our parents know. When your girl's parents caught you in bed or hanging out together outside of the house, then usually you had to marry your girl. This was the only solution. Boys and girls did not date like the people in the United States. We never held hands or kissed in front of our parents, elders, or other people like the young people in the United States. Our relationship was kept as a secret. In our mountains, we did not have soap to wash ourselves or a toothbrush to brush our teeth, and no perfume or cologne to wear, but I do not remember smelling bad when I visited my girl. We did not have a strong smell and bad breath like the people who live in this country. In this country, I can smell all kinds of things from other people.

I became a Shaman after I got married. My father was my master. When I was about eleven or twelve years old I was very ill. My illness was on and off throughout my teens. After I got married, I became more ill. My father was a Shaman and he performed several rituals to find out what was happening to me. He found that the *Neeb Fwj Saam*

(Buddhist Shaman Spirits) had chosen me to be a Shaman. I would die if I refused to become a Shaman. My father told me that the reason I got so sick was because these Buddhist Shaman Spirits were so mean, and they would not leave me alone if I did not become a Shaman. My father helped me to get started on my Shaman practice. I became a Shaman for about twenty years, then I stopped practicing Shamanism. I moved very often and I traveled to places to *ua luam*. In the mid 1950s, the Christian missionary came to recruit in my village. My wife and I converted to Christianity. In the late 1980s, my wife was very ill. I prayed for God's help, but she did not get well at all. My cousins, grandchildren, and relatives who still practiced the Mong traditional religion told me to go back to my old religion. I had done everything I could to cure my wife, but her illness was getting worse each day. I decided to go back to practice my old religion. I called a Shaman to cure my wife. I performed *nyooj dlaab* (the son performs a sacred ritual for his parents' spirits by sacrificing a bull) and other rituals. My wife got well and she lived with me a few years. She died in 1994. I went back to being a Shaman. I did not know the funeral chants, wedding chants, and other chants. I knew only the Shaman chants and rituals. When I was young, I was too lazy to study all these chants. I only liked to chase girls. After I got married and I knew how to *ua luam* then I was never home. I was doing my own thing. This was why I did not know lots of things like my father and my brothers. My brother *Txwj Pov* passed away about fifteen years ago in the Ban Vinai Refugee camp, Thailand. His family did not come to the United States. My oldest brother died many years ago in Laos. He drowned on the Mekong River. His grandson lives here in Stockton.

I want you to know that in my life I had no luck of having children. As you see, now I am very old and I do not know when I will die. I feel sad that I do not have any children or grandchildren. I depend on my siblings' grandchildren. I do not know what will happen when the time comes for me to close my eyes forever. I am thinking every day about my life. When I think too much sometimes I make myself sick.

Elder Mai Vang

Elder Mai Vang lives in Long Beach, California, with her youngest son, her daughter-in-law and grandchildren. She came to the United States in 1993. According to her immigrant document, she was born in

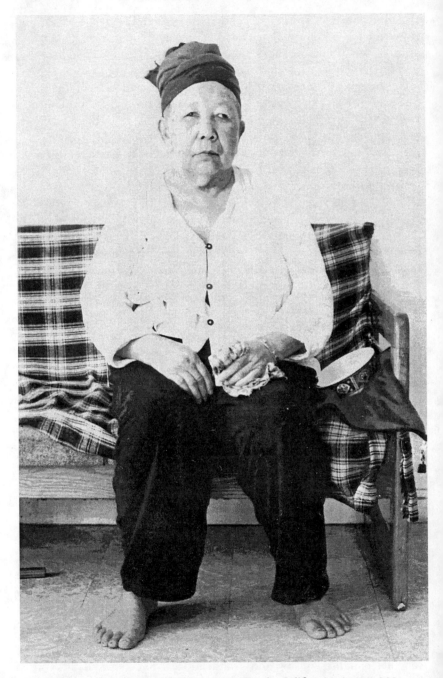

Puj Mais Vaaj (Elder Mai Vang). Long Beach, California, August 2001.

1917. She was not sure about her age or whether 1917 is the year she was born. She verbally confirmed that all the people she knew who were about the same age as she were no longer alive. Also, some of the people who were younger than she had died. She came to the United States in the year the Ban Vinai Refugee Camp was closed by the Thai government. In Laos, she lived in Louangphrabang and Xainabouri Provinces. Below is Elder Mai's story.

I was born in a Mong village called Dlej Cawm Sav (stream to rescue life). There was a stream in my village that tasted very delicious. This was the only stream near the village. If people traveled between villages, then they had to go for two to three hours without water. They needed to carry water with them if they got thirsty fast. But, if people came to my village and they started to get very thirsty then they reached the Dlej Cawm Sav. They got a drink there before they came into the village. The people who lived in the village got water from this stream. This was why our village was named after the stream. My parents moved to Pham Num village when I was about four years old. I grew up in Pham Num and married there. Pham Num had lots of peach trees. During the peach season we got lots of peaches to eat. When I got married, I moved to live with my husband in Naj Neeb village. There, we did not have peaches to eat but we had lots of guava fruits. These fruit trees were planted by people who lived long ago and some grew by themselves.

When I was a young girl I was very shy. I did not learn any of the courtship songs or play any musical instrument. I did not even know how to whistle. My mother taught me some of the sewing techniques, and I learned all my sewing skills from the wife of my husband's older brother, *pwj laug txawj yeeb*. My father died when I was about two to three years old, so I did not remember what he looks like. My mother died when I was about eight or nine years old. I lived with my oldest brother *Ntxhoo Tsu Vaaj* (Chong Chou Vang), his wife, and children until I got married. While I was living with my brother, I learned to work hard in the plantation and to take care of chores around the house. Usually, I learned all my skills by watching my brother, his wife, and the elders work and participated with them. My brother and sister-in-law encouraged me to know all the necessary farming skills in order for me to carry on my life after I married. They wanted me to work hard so I would build a good reputation of being an obedient person. In this way, I would get a husband and parents-in-law that would love me.

In my childhood, I loved to *ua kawj nyaab* (play dolls), *kov aav* (play with dirt) and *dle txwv noj* (pick wild berries to eat). I remember the times my mother and I went to collect firewood in the forest. We picked wild berries and fruits. We went to get bamboo shoots and banana buds. When I did not go with my mother, then I gathered with my friends and we played dolls or played in the dirt. We used old rags, leaves, straws, sticks, and mud to make dolls. We pretended that these dolls were married and had children. As I grew older and my mother passed away, my life changed so quickly. I focused my work around the house such as bringing water into the house, collecting firewood, feeding animals, and farming. I no longer had time to play with my friends. I did not want my brother and sister-in-law to think that I was lazy and disobedient.

When I was about six or seven years old, I had a pain under my left ear. It was swelling and my mother had to carry me on her back to a man to break the swelling. He used a long sharp nail to pop it open. He put the sharp point into the fire until it turned red, then he quickly took it out to pop my swelling. After that, he showed my mother the herbal medicine to put on my wound. It took several months to recover from my pain. Later, after I married I had a similar pain on my left leg and it was swollen. I had to go through the same procedure to pop the swelling and used the same type of medicine plant. We did not have modern medicine and doctors like in the United States. When a person became ill we believed that either it was caused by the spirits, diseases or by internal injuries. We consulted with a Shaman and also found herbal medicine to cure our illness. In my mountains, we did not have as much disease as in the United States. There are all kinds of illness in America. I believe that the food we eat, water we drink, and air we breathe in this country are not as good as those in my mountains. In our mountains, we did not need *chiv* (fertilizer or manure) to help our crops grow. We did not need chemicals to protect our crops. We did not get medicine to help our animals grow. The things we ate or drank were natural, whereas in this country the things we eat, drink and breathe contain chemicals. This was the reason why we have lots of overweight people in this country. I did not look like this in my mountains. My body was thin and healthy. Now, my weight changes a lot and I am losing my eyesight and hearing.

My life in the mountains was very hard work. We used hemp to make our clothes. I remember how difficult it was to turn the hemp into fabric. We planted fields of *maaj* (hemp). We cut the hemp and dried it. After it was very dry, we peeled the skin. We spun the skin into thread. We boiled it with charcoal ashes for several hours. Then, we took it to the stream and washed the thread. At this time, the skin of the hemp or thread turned white. We used the handmade powerloom to weave the thread into fabric. If you wanted the fabric to be black then you dyed it with the plant called *nkaaj*. We planted *nkaaj* just to dye our handmade fabric. It took too many steps to turn the hemp into fabric. I made only two to three skirts and seven to eight blouses in one year. The men's clothes were easier to sew. We used to make our clothes, and it was very difficult to find the clothes that fit me in America. The clothes I bought from the stores were either too small or too big. I had to redo them in order to fit me. I did not see well, so sometimes my grandchildren helped me. If they were not around then I did it myself.

When I was in my mountains I did most of the men's work. My husband was not able to do heavy work so I cut trees, built houses, fences, etc. My oldest daughter, *Lag* (La) helped me to do all these heavy jobs. We did not have electricity and gas like in the United States. We did not have lighters or matches. We made fire from rubbing bamboo, wood, or rock. We used pork oil lanterns to see at night. If we ran out of pork oil, then we used bamboo torches. Usually, before we went to bed, we buried the hot charcoal under the charcoal ashes. In the morning, we dug out the charcoal and put bamboo hair or wood chips to start the fire. I had been working hard all my life until we moved out of Laos. I gave so much credit to my oldest brother and his wife who trained me in all the skills that I obtained. I learned so much from them. I remember when my family, my brothers' families with other few families were the first to establish a new village called Pham Phuv in the middle of a jungle. There were lots of tigers. At night the tigers came close to my house. The tigers killed our horses and mules in the barn. All my horses and mules were killed. Later in a couple of years more new families came to live with us in Pham Phuv. All of a sudden, we had many families living in Pham Phuv. Pham Phuv became a large village. Then the tigers were afraid to come near the village to make their kill. My brother *Ruj Tuam Vaag* (Chou Toua Vang) was a village chief in Pham Phuv.

From Pham Phuv to a nearby Laotian city took about two walking days. During this time, my people were afraid to go to the city because those who went to the city tended to get sick and some died. We believed that there were evil spirits in the lowland or city. We called these *dlaab lostsuas* (Laotian evil spirits). These spirits haunted the Mong if they went to the city. There were certain rules to follow when we went to the city, especially for the men. In the city, men must sleep on their sides only and be careful of what they eat or drink. When we went to the city we entered the house or place that we knew was safe. After we got home, we avoided certain food, and the men did not sleep with their wives for several days. If one did not follow these rules then one became ill and sometimes died. We needed to be sure the Laotian evil spirits could not enter our body by following these rules. Many years later, when the Mong began to get used to the climate of lowland or cities, they no longer feared the Laotian evil spirits. After that, Mong went to the city and there nothing happened to them.

In my mountains, it was beautiful. There were all kinds of edible wild plants, berries, fruits, etc. You would not starve if you got lost in the jungle or forest. Even if you ran out of food you could go get these edible things in the jungle. In this country, I do not know what would happen to me if I ran out of food. I saw poor people pick cans to sell but there were no cans to collect. I think if I ran out of food in this country, there is no chance that I could survive.

When I told my stories about how hard we had to work in my country and the skills I had to my grandchildren, they did not believe me. They said I lied. I told them that if they did not work hard in school then they would have a difficult time bringing resources into their family once they became adults. The hard work my grandchildren must do in school is like the hard work I had to do to learn how to farm and do house chores in my mountains. We need to have the proper skills in order to become successful people. My biggest concern for my grandchildren is that they no longer believe in me nor their parents. They think they have freedom and they can do what they want, but once they reach an adult age, then it becomes too late for them to go back to learn all the skills in order to fulfill their life.

My grandchildren no longer know how to cook, take care of house chores, and baby-sit their younger brothers or sisters. My life as a young girl to teenager was different. I listened to my parents, older brothers, uncles, and aunts. I respected what they told me. I kept a close relationship with them. All the skills I knew were through interaction and being with them. Now, my grandchildren are no longer interested in my culture and language, and they do not want to talk to me and listen to me. I feel like my life living in America is turning upside down because I am no longer worth anything to my grandchildren and the Americans. When I correct my children's language or show them something, they say I am dumb. I need to let them alone. It is really difficult for me to see my grandchildren make all the changes in my culture.

Elder Cha Shoua Hang

This is an interpretation of a story by Elder Cha Shoua Hang, who is about seventy years old. He said that he could not confirm his current age because in the Mong culture there is no record of his birthday. When he applied to come to the United States as an immigrant, he had to go through an interview with an Immigrant Naturalization Services (INS) Officer and this INS officer assigned him a birthday based on the interviews. Elder Cha Shoua's immigrant document shows that he was born on January 2, 1930. Now, he lives in Sacramento, California, with his oldest son. In Laos, he lived in Xaignabouri Province.

I will explain to you what I learned, know and remember. I want you to know that within the Mong society, we have twelve different original Mong clans. Each clan performs their rituals differently from the other clans so people do not get confused about why all the Mong do different things. Our rituals define our lineages of clanship. We cannot destroy this kinship system. All clans are related to one another through our marriage, *Moob neej Moob tsaav*. Marriage between the same clan members is a taboo for my people. We have to marry someone in the outside clans. Our customary kinship structure is our alliances and mutual support system. For example, my wife is a Thao clan member and I am related to you (the researcher) through my wife. It is no matter where the Mong people live. If they belong to the same clan then they are like family members, *ib tsev neeg*. I married when I was about eighteen or nineteen years old. I have six children. I have four boys and two girls. It is very important for you (the researcher) to know that a Mong person without culture is a person who no longer knows the Mong customary and religion rituals.

The sacred chants and rituals are always conserved within the knowledge of the Mong people, and that is an oral knowledge. Same clan members can lose part of their original clan rituals if they do not have a person who knows the foundation of all the chants within their clan. Therefore, they conduct whatever they know and this is why a similar clan sometimes performs its ritual a little different from the other clans. This is called *dlaab quas txawv* (all Mong rituals are not the same). But, our clan system always defines the membership of clan group in our culture.

I will start the story about my grandfather. He was called *Nyiaj Tuam Kaab Haam* (Nhia Toua Ka Hang). He was the only blacksmith in the region where we lived. He was a well-known person because of

Yawm Txhaj Suav Haam (Elder Cha Shoua Hang) in front of his shaman altar, holding his shaman licensure. Sacramento, California, March 2001.

the tools he made for the Mong people. He could make Mong rifles, knives, shovels, axes, etc. His nickname *Kaab* was given to him by the people who lived around the area; it referred to his blacksmith skills. His works were like machine-made but they were actually handmade. We did not have machines in our mountains to help us make things.

Everything we produced from our own two hands. Back in my mountains if a village had a blacksmith who could make tools for people, then they did not have to worry about traveling a long distance from village to village to get the necessary tools for farming or to do other types of works. One reason why there were lots of people who wanted to live near my village was because they brought their old tools for my grandfather to repair. Besides a blacksmith, each clan member that lived in our village had a person who was a religious leader. This person kept the clan together and helped the household of his own clan to perform any necessary rituals, because if you make a mistake while you performed a ritual, that could cause serious harm, possibly death to you or your family. These religious leaders protected us from illness and guided us about how to perform our rituals. A *kws neeb* (a Shaman), *kws tshuaj* (a medicine man or woman), *coj dlaab qhuas* (a person who is in charge of the religion rituals in a family or clan), and *kws hlau* (a blacksmith) received the highest respect by the Mong people similar to the way the Americans respect their doctors. We looked upon these elders who knew many things as our advisors and healers.

My yearly lifestyle in the mountains of Laos ran like this. January was the month to sharpen my tools and necessary equipment in order to clear my plantation, *phaj taus phaj txuas*. When February came I started to clear out my plantation, *luaj teb*. I had to clear three plantations. One plantation was to grow rice, *teb npleg*, one plantation was to grow corn, *teb pob kws*, and one plantation was to grow vegetables, *teb zaub*. In my vegetable plantation I grew a small garden of opium for medicine purposes. Opium was good for a pain-killer, stomach ache, etc. When the *suab tuam tshoj* (Mandarine Chinese) came to my village, they looked to buy opium from my people. They bought a lot of opium and we do not know what they did with it. I want to make it clear that opium cultivation was not only by the Mong. The *puj thawj* (khmu), *cu* (mien) and other minority groups also grew opium. Please do not think that my people grew opium. My grandfather told me a story that opium was introduced to us by the Chinese a hundred years ago in China. When my people escaped the Chinese persecution to Laos they brought opium seed with them. This was how we learned to cultivate opium. I will not discuss more about opium. I do not want people to think that my people cultivate opium for economy.

In my mountains, there was no one who could read or write like in the United States. We did not have written knowledge like the Americans. Our knowledge involved *tswv yim* (creative ideas), *tug dlaag tug zug* (the strength/energy one has), and *lub ncauj* (spoken words).

We passed our knowledge to our younger people by taking them with
us to places so they could observe our skills. Then as they performed
we provided them with guidance until they were ready to begin to
do the work themselves, *peb swv cov txuj ci nuav coj lug xyum ua neej
xwb*.

People *luaj teb taag* (finished clearing their plantation) by the end
of March. In the middle of April we *hlawv teb* (burned the cut bushes
and brushes). Then we started to plant in the month of May. June and
July were the months we *nthuav teb* (pulled weeds). The *nplej caug*
(fast-growing rice) was ready to be harvested in October. Also, the
corn was ready to be harvested. November to December were the two
busiest months for crop harvesting. Finally, we celebrated our New Year
toward the end of December. In the Mong calendar, we are one month
ahead of the American calendar. For example, the month of November
in America is the month of December in the Mong calendar. In my
culture, we have *noj peb caug* (New Year feast) before we have *dla peb
caug* (New Year celebration). For our New Year feast, we cook food and
call our family members, relatives, and friends to eat together. Each
family had a feast. During the New Year feast we go from house to
house to eat, because everyone tends to have this feast in the same
evening. If you have a New Year feast and you do not invite anyone
then people will say you are too selfish. After that, if you have any
problems your family members, relatives and friends will not come to
help you or you will not get invited to their feasts. You need to *pauv
dlaag zug* (exchange services) such as eating, ritual performing, works,
etc. If you are greedy and you do not *paub dlaag zug*, no one wants to
know you or be friends with you, because they know that when they
need your help you will not help them.

In my mountains, we did not have such things as watches or
calendars to help us tell time, months, and seasons. We looked at the
moon and sun to tell times and months. Also, insects, animals, plants,
and the changing weather were other ways to help us know how to
move between times, months and seasons. For example, when the night
insects are calling, then we know that it will get dark soon. When the
rooster crows then we know it is morning. When the leaves are falling,
then we know it is fall.

I learned my skills and gained my knowledge by observing my
parents, uncles, and elders. In my mountains the things we learned
are not associated with anything that is written. It was completely
oral. We learned everything by ear, participation, and observation. If
I wanted to learn my religion's rituals, I asked someone such as my

uncles or the elders who mastered all the rituals to be his apprentice. In my culture, we respect anyone who is older because we often depend on him or her to teach us something or expect to learn something from him or her. Each person knows different things and has different roles. For example, my father taught me all the rituals, chants, hunting, tool-making, and house building skills whereas my mother taught me all the farming, housemaking skills, and how to raise children. My grandfather and grandmother always substituted for my parents' roles if my parents were not around or if there were things that my parents did not know.

My father said to me that it is important to know how to perform my family's rituals and build my own house. These important skills need to reside in my knowledge. They are the foundation to start a family. When I was about ten or eleven years old my family moved to a different village. There we had to build a new house. My father took me with him to the forest and he showed me the kinds of trees, bamboo and thatch to make our house. He explained that in building a Mong house, there were only three main poles to hold the top roof. One pole went in the center. This pole was set in the middle of the house. The center pole was the *ncij tsu* (house spirits' pole). In the house, there were different places where different spirits live. For example, the door spirits lived on the main entrance door, the ancestors' spirits lived on the altar on the wall facing opposite the main entrance door, the bed's spirits lived in the door entering to the bedroom of the head household (which is usually the parents' bedroom), and the spirits of cooking lived on the *qhov txus* (main stove). There were two fireplaces in the Mong house. One was the *qhov txus* (main stove) and the other one was the *qhov cub* (stove). Mostly all the cooking was done on the main stove. The other stove was to heat up the house and boil small pots of hot water and food.

In Laos, I do not remember being afraid of other people who would hurt me or rob me like when living in America. The only thing that I worried about in Laos was not being able to grow enough crops to last a whole year for my family. My life in Laos gave me so much freedom. There were no such thing as laws and regulations to control or to protect the people, animals, trees, land, etc. The Mong people lived on the mountains and the Laotians lived on the lowland. The Laotian government did not pay attention to those people who lived in the mountains like they did to the people who lived in the cities. Therefore, we had a very independent life.

I went to the city to buy items that my family needed such as salt, black pepper, fabric, sandals, etc. In the city, the Laotians had cars, bicycles, and motorcycles. I saw cars for the first time when I was about 35 years old. This car was so huge. It was the *ntsheb thauj ntoo* (logging truck). When I saw this logging truck, I did not remember being scared but it was so noisy. I first saw *dlaab hlau* (eagle metal bird or airplane) when I was about eight or nine years old. My father and I went to get *zaub neeg* (horse's food) and I saw this airplane flying in the sky. I asked my father to look at it. I asked him what is this thing? He said it belonged to the *Fuablaab* (French). We called this flying machine *dlaab hlau* (eagle metal bird).

I became a Shaman many years ago. I became a Shaman in the United States. When I was ill for a long time the American doctors could not find my symptom, so I asked my family to call a Shaman to trace my spirit to see why I never got well. A Shaman performed a ritual and he found that the Shaman spirits had chosen me to be a Shaman. My family and this Shaman helped me to become a Shaman. After that, my illness was gone. My American doctor asked me what kind of medicine I took to get well. I told him that I took no medicine. I became a Shaman to get well. He still does not believe me.

As a Shaman, sometimes I can tell what kinds of symptoms a person has when they become ill. The shaman spirits guide me to understand the ways to diagnose a sick person. For example, when I feel the person's pulse on their wrist or feel his/her temperature by touching the ears, sometimes the spirits tell me what is wrong with this person. Usually, when a person is sick and you feel that the lower part of the ears are cold, then this person is *ceeb* (a major frightening moment caused a disturbance to the spirit to make the person sick). When I cannot determine the symptom, then I have to *ua neeg saib* (perform a Shaman ritual to find out the cause of illness). My culture has many elements, so in order for the Mong children to appreciate them, they must know how to speak Mong fluently and respect the customs and values.

In America, people have different values and beliefs. Our children no longer respect their elders, customary values, language and culture. When you ask them to learn the Mong traditional values, they say these traditions are no longer important to them. These traditional skills do not help them to get a good job. I am afraid that one day in the future our children will no longer be able to identify their culture. My people came to live in the United States only twenty-five years ago, and I begin to see Mong children losing the culture already.

Elder Chai Xiong

Elder Chai Xiong lives with her son in Fresno, California. She came to the United States with her son *Tsuj Kawv Vaaj* (Chou Ker Vang) in 1979. Elder Xiong and her family first resettled in the U.S. in St. Paul, Minnesota. In 1982, they moved to the California Central Valley. Her husband *Nkiag Looj Vaaj* (Kia Long Vang) passed away over forty years ago. She did not remarry. She remains a widow. She had two sons and two daughters. Her oldest son died when he was a small boy. One of her daughters lives in Thailand, and the other daughter lives in Laos. Mr. Chou Ker Vang was her baby. According to Elder Xiong's immigration document, she is only eighty-three years old. She said her real age is probably over ninety years old. In Laos, she lived in Xaignabouri Province.

I was born in a Mong village called Pam Kaam (Pacome). When I grew up my mother taught me everything from house chores, to working in the plantation, to taking care of animals and sewing. Besides my mother, I learned some more skills from a few of my aunts. My aunts taught me things when my mother was not around.

My village was very different from here in the United States. We did not have cars. We went to places only by walking. We lived in houses made of bamboo, wood and thatch. Our houses were not made of concrete walls, glass, and paper. In the houses we used pig oil lanterns to see at night. We cooked our food with firewood. We did not have gas and electricity. The first time I learned how gas and electricity work was in the United States. In Laos, when my family moved to live in a different village called Phuam Hoos (Pahorn), this village was closer to a big city called Npov Theeb (Bob Theng). I went to Bob Theng and saw electricity light up the streets and people's houses. When I saw it the first time, I wondered what makes electricity. Then my aunt told me that the *Lostsuas* (Laotians) had light. She said to me that she was not exactly sure how they made the light but she heard the Elders say that the Laotians had electricity. Also, I saw cars for the first time in Bob Theng. The cars looked very different. I saw lots of people ride on them like people ride horses in my village. I remember I was not afraid of cars because my aunt and my friends were with me. They already knew about cars so they explained them to me. They took me to ride in a car the first time. I was so nervous. I felt dizzy and the trees and houses on the side of the road looked so funny. It seemed like the trees and houses were falling down. From Pahorn village to the city, it took a full day's

Puj Ntxhais Xyooj (Elder Chai Xiong). Fresno, California, June 2001.

walk. When we went to the city, we had to spend a night with my aunt's friend who lived there. While I was growing up in Pacome Village, I did not see airplanes until I moved to Pahorn. I saw airplanes later after I already had all my children.

I only knew how to sing *lug txaj* (sung poetry). I did not know how to play the bamboo flute, jews harp and blew leaf song. I learned how to sing by watching and listening to other people sing. Then, I practiced myself and just knew it. I remember one time I practiced singing and my mother heard me. She came over and taught me how to project my voice. I was embarrassed in front of my mother so I learned to sing myself. When I was still single, I did not want to let my parents know anything about my courtship. This was typical for Mong people. Our parents only learned about our courtship during the Mong New Year celebration.

A memory that I never forget while growing up was playing dolls, *ua nkauj nyaab*, with my friends. We loved to get together and play dolls when our parents were gone to work in the plantation. We stayed home and we went to play in the bushes. We used sticks and wrapped them with *khaub hlaab* (rag) to make dolls. We made boy dolls and girl dolls. Sometimes we pretended that the dolls were married and they had children. If we did not play dolls, then my friends and I pretended to act like husband and wife and my other friends played as our children. We used tree branches and straw to build houses. We imitated our parents' roles by going to the farm to work and do house chores like cooking and cleaning. When my friends and I grew older we stopped playing dolls and acting because we learned to become embarrassed. We did not feel comfortable acting childish in front of our parents and elders.

I remember during the Mong New Year celebration, a lot of old and young people dressed up in their new outfits and we went to *zog taav toj*, meaning a village on the slope which is located in the middle of nearby Mong villages. We celebrated New Year on this *zog taav toj* every year. We tossed a soft fabric ball, *pov pob*. The boys tossed to the girls and the girls tossed back to the boys. This was the only time for us to have our youth courtship. Sometimes, we played tossing ball games, *swb pov*, meaning play to lose. Whoever dropped the ball had to give an item to the opponent. These items could be silver coins, bracelets, rings, necklaces, handkerchiefs, etc. At the end we got our personal items back by exchanging them. If you had nothing left to exchange, then each item is worth a song so you had to sing in order to get them back. All the boys and girls practiced their songs year round to prepare for these fun activities. During this courtship, young boys and young girls, *tug hluas hab ntxhais hluas*, got to know each other especially from the games. If you found a boy you liked and he liked you, then a relationship began. You continued dating after the New Year until you fell in love, then you got married.

I got to participate in the New Year for only two years, then I met my husband. We went out for a while and I married him. At the New Year festival, White Hmong, *Moob Dlawb*, and Mong Leng, *Moob Leeg*, came to celebrate together. People came from different tribes and clans. They brought their young people to have fun together.

Now, living in the United States, I always think about all the fun I had in my homeland, the daily activities of working in the farm and house, and gathering wild berries, bamboo shoots, etc. It is very hard for me to forget these things.

My life story while living with my biological parents taught me to work hard and listen to them. My parents taught great lessons to prepare me to start my own life. I remember the first time my husband brought me to live with his family: the wife of my brother-in-law and my mother-in-law set me up to see if I could perform their chores by pounding their heavy rice pounder. They wanted to check me out to see if I could do the job alone. It was an easy job for me, because when I lived with my biological parents I used to work by myself. My mother constantly reminded me that one day I was going to be on my own when living with my husband's family. Therefore, I needed to know all the necessary skills. This way my husband's family would like me because of my duty.

Anyway, the story began when there was no pounded rice for me to cook for dinner. So I went to get two baskets of rice from the rice storage and poured them into the rice pounder's hole, *qhov cug*. Then, I began pounding the rice. My mother and sister-in-law sat there in the living room staring at me. They pretended they did not know that there was no rice to cook for dinner. I assumed that they only wanted to see if I could perform the job by myself. I put my feet on the rice pounder and began to pound the rice. I did it in a few minutes and the rice was all ready. I took the rice out from the rice pounder's hole, *qhov cug*, and cooked dinner. My performance surprised my mother and sister-in-law. The next day, my sister-in-law told me that the rice pounder was heavy to her. She could not pound rice herself. She always had someone to help her. I asked, "Why? The rice pounder does not seem heavy to me." I used to do this kind of work with my mother. Mother would say to me that when you marry and you pound rice, be sure not to make the rice pounder sound *dlej dlawg ntawg*. This sound means you were working too slow. You need to pound fast to make the rice pounder sound *dlaaj dlawg dlaaj dlawg*. If you pound slowly, then your parents-in-law will not like you. I took my mother's words and kept them in my heart.

My mother taught me everything she knew except sex education. This was common in the Mong culture because all my friends said the same. Sex was one of the most embarrassing topics to discuss in my culture so we never shared it. I learned it myself as I was growing up. If I had questions I asked my aunts, but they also did not want to talk much about it. Sex was a privacy issue and we never talked about it in public.

I first learned about print text when I already lived in the United States. I saw my grandchildren go to school. This was how I realized that there are schools. In Laos, I did not know that people have print language. We did everything orally. I knew how to work in the plantation and took care of house chores, *ua noj ua haus hab ua dlej ua num huv lub vaaj lub tsev*. In my homeland, one year seemed to be very long, not like in America. I remember I had to wait for a long time for the New Year event. Here in the United States, suddenly the New Year comes and goes by so fast. I think because in Laos, we were busy working year round and a year seems longer. For example, one year going by feels like two years. In America, one year going by feels like a few months. The world is changing because the year goes by faster, the earth receives less rain, which is not like it used to be, and the earth's natural resources slowly disappear.

In Laos, the world was wonderful. In the forest, there were all kinds of wild berries and animals. I loved to go into the forest to pick berries and collect bamboo shoots. My favorite berries were: *txiv phuab, txiv lauj tauv, txiv ntsuag thood*. I did not see these berries in the United States. Besides berries, in my homeland there were all kinds of fruits. There were no apples. I ate apple the first time living in America. At first, I did not like it. It tasted milky and crunchy. In Laos, we had banana, mango, papaya, grapes, etc.

While I grew up with my parents, they taught me to work hard and to respect my elders. I always listened to my parents. For this reason, in my life history, I never got myself into trouble. The way Mong children grow up in this country they have no respect for their parents and their elders. Furthermore, they are no longer interested in the Mong cultural tradition. My grandchildren told me that they did not want to listen to my stories because in America the things I know are not important to them. They said the Mong culture does not prepare them to get a good job or become a successful educator. They said learning the American culture and language applies to their life. My ways of life do not help them like the American ways of life, *Miska kiv cai*.

The new life living in America is very difficult. These last two years, I have been thinking a lot about my life. I asked my son and grandsons to go to the Americans and to apply for legal papers to return me to my home country. I want to go back to my homeland. I do not want to live and end my life in this country. I have been thinking everyday that this country is not a home for me. I do not want to put my body to rest in the American soil. I feel very sad because I want my body to be put to rest in my mountain, the soil where I was born. Now, I am trapped in this country. I became a U.S. citizen five years ago. I knew that when I died they would not let my body be buried in foreign soil. I was so angry with myself that I had become an American citizen, *ua mivkas*. I should not have come to this country in the first place. I already know that when I die my spirit will not be able to find my ancestors. I will not be able to reincarnate to be a person again. My spirit will become animals, rocks, etc, because I cannot find my way back to live with my ancestors.

The soil in this country has so much value. My son and I do not have lots of money in order to afford a large land space for my grave. I have seen other people buried in very small space that barely fits a coffin. In my homeland people were buried in a free soil with a big space. Also, I do not like the American system and what they do to dead people. I do not want people to destroy my body when I die. When you die, your grave is dug very deep, and they put concrete to seal your coffin. There is no way your spirit can get out. I do not want to be buried in this country at all. I keep thinking to myself that if I could fly then I would already have flown back to my home country. I want to be buried in the soil of my parents and grandparents so I can be with them. My parents and grandparents told me that when a person died, the body needs to be treated with good care so the spirit can reincarnate to become a person again. In my homeland, we had our own freedom and there were no laws to restrict us like in America. The ways I see people's life in this country is like living in a cage. We all are being watched by American laws like prisoners. Our choices are limited. When I think about these things I do not want to live here in America. I want to return to Laos because one day when I die I can go live with the spirits of my parents and grandparents.

Elder Tong Yao Her

This is an interpretation of a story by Elder Tong Yao Her who lives with his wife and his youngest son in San Diego, California. He is eighty-four years old. He came to the United States in 1980. He came from Ban Vinai Refugee Camp. In Laos, he lived in a Mong village called Moos Pheeb. His oldest son also lives in San Diego. Most of his close relatives live in Rhode Island and Yuba City, California. Some of his relatives had lived in San Diego but they moved to Rhode Island to work. Those who moved to Yuba City did so to find land to farm and raise animals. He has lived in San Diego for over twenty years, and the house he now lives in is his third house. He only travels in California to Yuba City to visit his close family members. He went to Rhode Island once to visit his relatives. He has never traveled out of the country. When he applied to come to America he told the INS officer that he was seventy-two years old. Elder Tong Yao thinks his age was about right, but he is still not too sure because he does not have a record of it. He could be older or younger. No one really knows. His age was based on what his parents and the people who saw him born told him. In Laos, he lived in both Houaphan and Xiangkhoang Provinces. Below is Elder Tong Yao's story.

My parents had only three children. I was the middle child. My youngest brother was called *Pov* (Pao). He died when he was about two years old. My sister *Phuab* (Phoua) was the oldest child. She died when she was nine years old. Then my mother died when I was about fifteen years old. My dad passed away twenty-five years ago. According to my historical account, I was the fourth generation to live in Laos and third generation born in Laos. My great-great-grandfather and his brother came from China. He was called *Yawm Nplaj Xau* (Elder Bla Xao) and his brother was called *Yawm Ntxhab Dlua* (Elder Xe Dou). They both escaped from the Chinese to Vietnam then to Laos. My father's father was born in a Mong village called Zog Vaaj Pheej in Vietnam. My father was born in a Mong village called Pwj Num Xaab Cum in Laos. Then, I was born in a Mong village called Phaj Laim in Laos. I was born during the *Rog Npeb* (Crazy War). I did not know the year but it could be during Word War I. In this Crazy War, *Paaj Cai* (Pa Chay) led the Mong to fight against the French because the Mong did not like the French tax policy.

When I was about twenty years old, my relatives from a Mong village called Moos Pheeb (Xiangkhoang Province, Laos) came to help us move to live with them in Moos Pheeb. I lived in Moos Pheeb for

Yawm Tooj Yao Hawj (Elder Tong Yao Her). San Diego, California, July 2001.

over forty years. I got married when I moved there. My wife and I had one daughter and two sons. Then my wife died. I remarried a widow. My second wife did not have any children with her first husband. My second wife and I had one daughter. Altogether, I had four children. My oldest child was born during the *Rog Nyaj Pooj* (Japanese War or World War II).

As I was growing up my parents were *tub laj tub teb tub qoob tub loo* (farmers), and I was a farmer all my life until we moved to Thailand. I learned all the farming skills from my parents. I could not stand under the sun long so I learned to get up very early in the morning to work in the field to avoid the heat. When the sun got hot, then I rested. I went back to work in the afternoon when the sun cooled down. I got so much work done working early in the morning. In Moos Pheeb, I raised crops and animals to sell to people. Most of the people who lived in my village did similar things. I did not have good luck in raising cows. Tigers killed all my cows, and I did not get one to sell. The tigers could not kill my water buffalo because buffalo are strong animals. They know how to protect themselves from danger. Every year I made about ten or more silver bars (Mong money) after I sold my pigs, water buffalo, and crops. I had sixty silver bars one time. In my village, if you have a hundred silver bars then you are the richest person. Most families had thirty to forty silver bars.

My cousin had one hundred silver bars (Mong dowry). He made his money from selling his crops. I asked him to show me how he cultivated in order to produce good crops to sell. He refused to tell after he looked at my plantations. His recommendation to me was to work harder and to be very careful of selecting my plantation. I needed to get a plantation that had good soil. He did not say anything more.

I did not know much about the Mong rituals and chants. I could play musical instruments such as *tsaaj nplaim* (free-reed bamboo flute), *tsaaj ntsa* (bamboo flute) and *has lug txaj* (sing sung-poetry). I knew some *lug ntsuag* (folktales) but I did not know how to play the Mong sacred *qeej* instrument. My father was a *qeej* master. I did not like it so I never asked him to teach me. I had taken the *Mej Koob* (wedding negotiator) position before but did not know how to perform the wedding chants. When it was time to perform the chants I asked someone who knew how to do it for me. I was not interested in learning the rituals and chants. They were too difficult to learn.

I loved hunting. I was an expert hunter. I had two Mong rifles. I paid a Mong gunsmith by the name of *Txawj Suab Thoj* (Cher Shoua Thao) to make them for me. Each rifle cost *plaub choj* (four silver bars).

During this time, we did not have automatic rifles. We only had *Phom Moob* (Mong rifles). We got automatic rifles after the *Rog Nyaj Pooj* (World War II). After all the Mong joined General Vang Pao's army we began to have access to automatic rifles, grenades, and machine guns. I was in the army for two years. My two sons joined the army longer. After we got all these automatic rifles, all the wild animals disappeared. We did not know if they went away or became extinct. When we only had the Mong rifles there were lots of wild animals.

There were lots of forest and jungle in our mountains. I never went to school. There were no schools, electricity, and running water in our village. Everything we had was manmade, not machine made. Our mountains did not have *nqeeb* (thatch plant) so we used *nplooj kum yim* (palm tree leaves) to cover the roof of our houses. We used bamboo to make the walls and trees for the poles. I learned to build houses, play musical instruments, sing songs, tell stories, and farm mostly from my uncles. I watched them, then I just followed them. My father taught me some stories. My uncles taught me some musical lessons. I quickly picked up these skills, as I grew older.

After the Japanese War or World War II, the Mong who lived in the villages near the Lao city called Xiêng Khoung came to our village to teach our children to read and write in Laotion. We called the Mong who lived in the region near Xiêng Khoung *Moob Xeev*. The *Moob Xeev* went to school because they lived near the city. When they graduated, the government sent them to my village Moos Pheeb and other Mong villages to teach Mong children to read and write. School was only taught in Laotian. When there were very few teachers, we had to pay the teachers. If any families wanted their children to learn faster, then they hired private teachers. In a few years more and more teachers came to the Mong villages. We built the schools and the government paid teachers mainly from General Vang Pao. These teachers came to recruit the Mong parents to send all their children to school. They told us that being educated through school was the future of the Mong people. Education was the only way for the Mong people to become educated like the Laotians. All the parents in my village put their children in school. This was the reason why I had my two sons go to school. When my sons went to school my oldest was about sixteen and my youngest son was about ten or eleven years old.

The first time I saw *dlaav hlau* (metal bird or airplane) come to my mountains I was about fifteen to sixteen years old. I asked my parents and they told me that this airplane belongs to the *Faabkis* (French). *Faabkis yaaj tuaj suaj teb suaj chaw* (The French ride on this airplane to check out the country). I did not remember being scared of the airplane. I liked to watch it on the sky. I did not see cars until I was in my forties. I came to a Lao city called Vangvieng. There, I saw cars the first time. It took two days to walk from Vangvieng to my village Moos Pheeb. When I rode in cars the first time in Vangvieng I was very dizzy. It seems like all the bushes and trees on the side of the road were falling so fast, but when you got out of the car, there was nothing wrong with the bushes or trees. There were only dirt roads. Pavement roads were in the center of the city. I rode an airplane for the first time when we came to America.

When I first came to the United States everything looked very different. It was a very difficult life. I had to learn everything from the beginning. For example, I had to learn how to use the bathroom, to cook, to shop and to wash my clothes. I was lucky that my oldest daughter and her husband were my sponsors. When my family arrived in San Diego, they were there for us. In 1980, there were already a lot of Mong families living in San Diego but lives were difficult for everyone because our lives back in our mountains did not prepare us to live in an industrialized country such as America. My life in America is like living in a cage. I cannot go out because I do not know the ways things work in this country. I do not drive, speak English, read or write. I am afraid if I got lost, then who would help me?

Elder Ying Yang

This is an interpretation of a story by Elder Ying Yang, who came to the United States in 1980. Currently, she lives with her youngest son (the author) in Beaverton, Oregon. According to her immigration document, she was born in 1920. However, Elder Ying Yang said this birthday may not reflect her right age. An immigration officer who interviewed Elder Ying Yang during her application to the United States gave her this birthday. In Laos, she lived in Xaignabouri Province. Below is the story collected from Elder Ying Yang.

I have eight children. I have five daughters and three sons. My two older sons lived in Stockton, but my first oldest son passed away two years ago. I have one daughter who lives in France with her husband. I have three daughters who live here in the United States, and one daughter died in Laos. I have no family members left in Laos.

I was born in a village called Naj Neeb. I was the sixth child in the

Puj Yeeb Yaaj (Elder Ying Yang). Montclair, California, April 2001.

family. I have eight siblings. Six of my siblings have passed away. I have one brother still living. Now, he lives in France and one sister lives in Sacramento. I did not know exactly how old I was when I got married. Probably, I was about sixteen years old. In my mountains, the girls got married when they turned fifteen, sixteen and seventeen years old. If you stayed single until you passed eighteen years old, then people began to think that you were too old. It would be more difficult for you to get a young husband. Mostly the girls who were older married the men who already had a wife or were widowed. If you married a man who already had a wife, then you became his second wife. We have *nam hlub nam yau* (a polygamy system). The men can marry more than one wife. The young girls try to avoid getting a widow or married man. Therefore, if they find someone they love, then they tend to marry right away.

When I married, I moved in to live with my husband and his family. We lived in a village that took a day's walk to my parents' village. My husband's family was very poor. I had to work extra hard in order to bring crops and other goods to the family. For this reason, I missed all the times when I was still single and lived with my parents. My father was the village chief. We had lots of food. My family was wealthy. My life after marriage was very different. People no longer respected me the way I used to live with my parents. When they respected my father, they respected all his family members. I remember my father often had many guests. Every time we had guests, we cooked a meal for them. My father had many people to *ua zug* (work for him so they could get food from us). These people worked in the plantation to help us grow our crops. My family never ran out of food. When I went to live with my husband's family, we worked so hard but we were still *ntshaib plaab* (starving, ran out of food).

My husband died while I was still carrying my last child inside my stomach. My parents-in-law, brother-in-law and husband's side of the family asked me to marry my husband's younger brother. He already had a wife. I did not want to marry him, but they were afraid that as a widow I would remarry someone else. Then, my children would lose their father's clan membership and family name. So, I was forced to be my brother-in-law's second wife. I never loved him and I was too old for him. I did not have much choice so I married him. His family made him to *pe* (bow with his knees) to my husband during his funeral and promise him that he would look after my children and me. He had to go through this ritual in order to take me as his second wife. Once my brother-in-law went through this ritual, no man could date me and I could not date anybody because I already had a husband.

I lived with my brother-in-law and his wife for a few years. Then, my children grew up. My oldest son got married. My oldest son, his wife, my children and I moved to live in our own house. My family and my brother-in-law's family separated when my family moved out. I looked on my children as my family. They were all married. Now, I live with my youngest son. My brother-in-law and his family live in Stockton.

I miss the lifestyle in my homeland very much. There, it had all kinds of wild fruits, berries, beautiful rain forest, and many types of animals as well as birds. It was a *haav zoov nuj txeeg* (a jungle forest). Birds sang and monkeys called beautifully. I remember I loved to go with my sisters to pick fruits, nuts, and berries. They were delicious. During *lub caij luaj teb* (clearing plantation for farming season), there were many kinds of insects calling that are so beautiful. There were different insects that called during the different seasons of the year.

I know how to play several musical instruments, the *ncaag* (jews harp), *tsaaj* (bamboo flute), *tsaaj nplaim* (bamboo free-reed flute) and *hais lug txaj* (sing sung-poetry). Now, I am too old and I no longer can play these instruments or sing. I learned how to play musical instruments and sing sung-poetry by watching my older sisters, sisters-in-law and aunts. First, I got myself interested in knowing how to play musical instruments and sing sung-poetry. Then, I began learning myself. I sought advice from my sisters, sisters-in-law and my aunts. Suddenly, I realized, I already knew how to play. I think whatever you study if you *muab sab tsau ncua* (put your whole heart) into it, you learn it. I did not ask my parents to teach me all these courtship songs and activities. I was shy to them.

In my culture *kev ua nkauj ua ntsaug* (sexual information or activities and dating) we often ask other people for advice, not from our parents. We did not want our parents to learn about our sexual behaviors. My parents, especially my mother, taught me the skills to work in the plantation, to sew, and to do house chores. Again, I learned my working skills by watching my mother work. Then, I quickly picked them up as I grew up. While I was working, if I did something not right, then my mother showed me. There was no formal lesson taking place. We did not learn things like the way now the Mong children learn in school. We had no schools.

I did not know how to turn the hemp into fabric after I got married. After I was a married woman I needed to sew clothing for my children, husband, and me. There was no fabric so I needed to make my own fabric. The process to turn hemp into fabric was very difficult work. Also, it took so much time, but we had to do it. This was the only way we got fabric.

When the *Suav Tuam Tshoj* (Mandarin Chinese) and *Lostsuas* (Laotian) came to our village to trade, they brought fabric, threads, needles, salt, black pepper, cooking pots, and other goods to trade for opium. Then we stopped making our own fabric. We bought it from them. The traders came to set up tents in our village to do their business. They used horses and mules to transport their goods. Some traders used *nyiaj dlaim hab nyiaj maaj* (silver bar and silver coin money) to pay us if we did not want to trade. We also sold them animals such as water buffalo, cow, and pig. We did not know what they did with the opium and animals after they bought from us. The traders taught us the values of opium. First, we grew only a small garden of opium just for medicine. When these traders saw that we knew how to grow opium, they encouraged us to grow more opium so they could continue to trade with us. We did not know that growing opium was illegal. Besides that, there were other hill tribes who grew opium to sell to these traders. It was not only the Mong people.

In the early days before the traders came to trade in our villages, we used bamboo knot, trees, and coconut shell to make spoons, plates, and bowls. We made cooking pots from clay. We used bamboo to make torches and used pork oil lanterns to see at night. After the traders came to trade in our villages, we began to have silverware, metal pots, and flashlights. We had no television and radio. A few families had radio but not until many years later.

My people were very intelligent. They knew many things. We did not know how to read and write, because we did not have a written language. Reading and writing are the only things that we did not know, but now all children already know them. I learned that the Laotians have a written language after I was already an old lady. I went into the city to buy goods and there were Mong families who live in the city who told me. The Mong people who lived in the city sent their children to school. My brother *Vaam Ntxhais Yaaj* (Vang Xai Yang's) brother-in-law *Num Kais Lis* (Nou Ky Lee) was the first man I knew that went to live in the city. First, he learned to *ua luam* (trade). Then, he saved enough money. He moved to live in the city so he could continue his business. One of his sons became the first Mong dentist. Several years later, my brother went to live with his brother-in-law in the city. He sent his children to school. One of his sons became the first Mong teacher in Xaignabouri Province.

However, the Mong parents including myself who lived on the

mountains believed that if we sent our children to school, they would grow lazy and would not want to help their parents farming. Also, Laotian education was not as important to our children as the Mong tradition. In addition, you had to have money to pay for your child's education. In this way, we did not send our children to Lao school. There were very few wealthy families that sent their children to school. I learned about the importance of schooling only for a few years, then we moved to Thailand.

I did not even know how to use the Laotian money until I went to the city and my brother showed me. In the city, the Laotian money was made of paper. In our mountains, we used only silver money. When I went to the city I brought with me a basket of green mustard, chili pepper, green onion, and other vegetables to sell to get the Laotian money to buy the items I needed. I saw cars for the first time when I went to the city. I was in my late forties before I went to the city and learned that there were school and cars. When I was about six or seven years old my mother and I were in the plantation. We saw an airplane for the first time. This airplane flew very high in the sky, and it made a very strange sound. My mother told me that she heard people talk about the *Fuablaab* (French) flying machines. This could be the French flying machine. When we got home, I asked my father. He said this thing I saw on the sky is a *dlaavhlau* (metal eagle). It belonged to the French. Then, a few years later, more airplanes flew over our mountains. People said the French and Japanese went to war. The French used these machines to fight against the Japanese.

I miss the life I had on my mountains very much. I miss all the beautiful sounds that the birds, insects and monkeys made. In this country, I hear only cars running, airplanes flying, and people's noise. Life living in America is very difficult because I cannot go to places because I cannot drive and I don't read, write, and speak English. On my mountains, I did not have to worry about other people hurting me or getting myself lost. There were no burglars. We did not even lock our doors when we went somewhere. We lived in a very peaceful community. Of course, I had to work hard in order to produce enough crops for my family, but I worked for myself. When I got tired, I could rest anytime I wanted. There was no one there to monitor me to make sure I did my work right. Usually, a Mong family had three different plantations. One was to grow rice, one was to grow corn, and one was to grow vegetables. The rice plantation was the biggest farm. Sometimes, we had to work in the rain in order to keep up with the crop season and the weeds. If we worked hard, we got our work finished quickly, then we got to rest for a few days. If we had nothing else to do, then we did our sewing. Sewing was a year-round thing. If we had to do work in the field, then we did our sewing at night. We used a pork oil lantern to see. People tended to get their work in the field finished quickly so the women could have extra time to do their sewing and the men extra time to go hunting or to do other gathering. We did not have machines to help us to do our work like in America. Everything we had was made by our own two hands. I had a brother-in-law who was a good blacksmith. He made good farming tools and jewelry. He used the silver money to make beautiful necklaces, neck rings, and bracelets. His work was like machine made.

When I was a young girl, I loved to play *nkauj nyaab* (play dolls). My sisters and my friends often played around and went into the forest to pick wild fruits, berries, and nuts. I loved to go crab hunting. My sisters and I often went to dig mud crabs. Digging mud crabs was fun and mud crabs were very delicious. We cooked them with all kinds of spices. My parents did not let us climb trees or swing because we could get injured from it. I never climbed a tree. We asked the boys to climb the trees to get the fruits and berries. Also, we could pick them from the ground, because when they are ready then they fall onto the ground.

When I was a teenager I was not lazy like the Mong teenagers now living in America. I helped my parents do all kinds of work. I performed my work like an old woman. Now, I see the Mong teenagers no longer can perform the tasks that I did when I was a young girl. They cannot do simple tasks such as sweeping the floor, cooking food, and washing dishes. They are thirteen, fourteen, fifteen, sixteen years old but they act like a four, five, and six year old child. I always showed my respect to my parents, uncles, aunts, and anyone who is older than I. I was an obedient child. I never said anything that would hurt the old people's feelings. The young Mong people in this society change so much. They have strange behaviors. I heard people say that some Mong parents got beaten by their own children. This is very sad to learn that the Mong children no longer show respect to their parents, to their elders and to their own culture tradition like the way we used to back on our mountains.

Elder Xao Cheng Lee

This is an interpretation of a story by Elder Xao Cheng Lee who lives with his youngest son in Merced, California. He came to the United States

Yawm Xauv Tsheej Lis (Elder Xao Cheng Lee). Merced, California, June 2001.

in May 1978. According to his immigrant document, he was born in September 1928. However, he said his birthday may not be right. He believes his age is much older than what it says on paper. He lived in both Xaignabouri and Louangprabang Provinces. Below is his personal story.

I was an early mature boy. I remember everything since I was four years old. I remember what things looked like and what was happening. I was born in a Mong village called Haav Naaj Kais (City of Long River). The closet big city to my village was Laav 52 (City of 52). But the distance from my village to the city was still a day's walk. Later, my family moved to a new village called Fwm Xaib. I grew up in this village. All my life, I did not hunt much because I was not good at hunting. When I was about six or seven years old I already knew how to make *looj thawj kiv neeg* (horse lash). My father bought a male horse for me as my pet. I named him *txov lauj*. He was a young horse and very nice. I liked riding him.

My brother *Num Khais* (Nou Kia) and I were *nquag heev* (hard workers). I have four brothers. Each of my brothers has a special talent. I was the one that had the least talent. I only knew *txwv xaiv* (funeral chants), *zaaj tsoob* (wedding chants) and *miv ntswv dlaab qhuas* (some of the ancestors' chants). My father was a professional *qeej* player. He taught me but I did not get it. My father also knew all the Mong rituals and chants. I began to study the Mong rituals and chants after I married and already had two children.

I married my sister-in-law's younger sister. We lived in the same village. When my brother Nou Kia married his wife, his younger sister-in-law often came to visit us. My parents learned about her talents and working habits. They liked the types of work she did, her attitude, and personal characteristics. They asked me to marry her so I listened to my parents. I took her to be my wife. The Mong older generation, our parents, liked to get a daughter-in-law who was a hard worker and knew how to treat them nice. My parents said they liked my wife because she knew how to respect old people, *cov laug*.

I got married when I was about sixteen years old. A year later, my wife had a baby. We lost our baby when he was a couple of months old. Then, my wife stopped having babies. My parents gave her herbal medicines. I called the Shaman to perform ceremonies for her. Four years later, we had our oldest daughter. I have eight children.

I learned the funeral chants from my brother *Ntshoo Ntxawg* (Chong Yer). He lived in Naj Neeb village. He came to visit us for a few days. At night he gathered my other brothers and me together. He taught us the funeral chants. When I first listened to the chants I began to feel in love with it. After a few nights, I began to pick some parts of several chants. Then, my brother Chong Yer went back home. In a few months, I decided to go stay with him in his village to learn more about the chants. I went to stay with him for several months. My uncle *Tsaav Yeej* (Chang Ying) was the old master. He was Chong Yer's father. While I stayed with them I studied with both of them. The lessons took place during the evening after we ate dinner. We stayed up until midnight or sometimes until morning for the lesson. When I mastered the funeral chants, I came home, and an elder by the name of *Nyiaj Ntxawg* (Nhia Ger) died. I was asked to be a *Txwv Xaiv*. This was the first time I performed at a funeral. I remember I was kind of nervous to stand in front of a large crowd to say the chants. But, I did it successfully. My second time to take on the *Txwv Xaiv* position was in the funeral of brother *Suav Maiv's* (Shoua Mai) father. At that time I was about twenty-five or twenty-six years old.

When I was about thirty-five years old I went with my oldest brother Nou Kia to *ua luam* (trade business) in the Mong villages. We went to several Mong villages to sell spices. There was an elderly man who died in a village called Taj Kub Lub. In the village, there was nobody who knew the funeral chants. The family was looking for a *Txwv Xaiv* (a funeral chants expert) to stand before their father's funeral to sing the chants. There was a man by the name of *Xeeb* (Seng) who came to visit his relatives at the same time my brother and I were there. Seng saw me perform the funeral chants in my uncle's funeral. He told the family that I was a funeral chants expert. He had seen me perform once before. In Laos, usually a person who takes the role of *Tub Coj Xai* (a man who was chosen by the dead person's family members to be their keynote chanter and blessing) is about fifty to sixty years old. I was only thirty-five, and my age made some people think I was too young to be their *Tub Coj Xai* or *Txwv Xaiv*. The family could not find anyone so they asked me to be their *Txwv Xaiv*. Before the night that I was to perform the chants, I heard people say I was too young to be a *Tub Coj Xai*. They thought I might not know what I was asked to do. During that night there were lots of people who attended the ceremony. I performed the rituals all night until the morning. The people who expressed their concerns that I might not be able to take on the position came to congratulate me for the work I did. I overheard people saying that I may look young but I knew what I was doing. (This is what people called the expert).

My uncle Chang Ying who is my master told me that since I knew everything he had taught me I needed to maintain it and pass it on to the younger generation. When he died he wanted me to be the *Tub Coj Xai* (the *Txwv Xaiv* position) in his funeral. I promised him that I would do that, but unfortunately when he died I had moved to Thailand. My uncle was still in Laos. I could not attend his funeral.

I also learned the wedding chants from my uncle Chang Ying. When my father taught me the chants and rituals he knew I had a difficult time getting them but I did not have this problem of learning with my uncle. I also like to tell stories. I learned to stories by listening to the Elders. When I was a young boy I liked to listen to story telling. I often asked my grandfather, grandmother and other old people to tell stories to me. It was very easy to pick up a story. I said it was one of the easy things to learn in the Mong culture. I learned to tell the story from listening to the story a few times. I believe stories are important because they help us keep our tradition since we do not have a written tradition. There are different morals to the stories. They can be good or bad. Stories taught us how to live and take responsibilities.

When I was about fourteen years old, I went with my oldest brother to a *zog plog* (Lao city) to buy goods to sell in the Mong villages. There, I learned that the Lao people had a school. My brother and I walked by a school where I saw lots of children go, but at that time I knew nothing about school. When I was about twenty years old there was a Lao man named Sengma who came to my village. Sengma was a teacher. He was looking for students. He requested that if he could get at least five students and charged each student *kaum tswb maaj* (15 silver coins) a year, then he would stay in the village to teach Lao reading and writing to those students. During this time nobody could afford to hire him, so he left. I went to *ua luam* (trade business) a few trips and came back to be a farmer all my life.

I gave a lot of credit to my parents. They taught me all the good and bad things. I learned how to work in the plantation from my parents. My father constantly reminded me to learn how to take good care of my wife. My wife is the person who will take care of me, help me bring resources into the house and, most importantly, have babies. If she was not healthy, then she cannot provide these things for me. Also, when I make an offering to the house spirits and perform rituals, I need to know how to do it right or it can cause damage to the spirits, and then the spirits will make my family members become sick and possibly die. I need to learn how to be careful and respectful to the house spirits, the spirits of nature and spirits of my ancestors.

I miss my old life back in the mountain of Laos very much. There, everything I had I owned. Everything I produced or made belonged to me. In America, this society operates differently. I no longer can do things that I used to do in my homeland. For example, the things that my grandparents passed down, such as my culture, rituals, artifacts, language, and food have changed very much. The print society adds many new things to my culture which take away some of the values within my oral tradition. Now, in the print society, the pens do the talking for people. People like myself who cannot read or write have become worthless living in America.

In my oral tradition, we stored all the information in our heads, not on a piece of paper or in books. The Mong children who live in this new society no longer want to memorize information. They trust the print system more than anything and this makes our children want to stop learning what is in the oral tradition. I see that as our children are becoming educated in the print culture they begin to *ntsauj dlaab ntsauj qhua* (divorce their culture, language, religions and customs). I think in our future living in America, soon our children will become *ntsauj dlaab ntsauj qhua, ntsauj neej ntsauj tsaa, ntsauj kwv ntsauj tij* (disconnected to their culture, religion, language, relatives and family).

It is important to know that in the Mong culture, our father and mother were the two most important persons in our lives. They gave us life and we must respect them for the rest of our lives. Even though our parents had passed away, their spirits are still with us. Whenever we need their help or protection we call them and they will be present to support us. Furthermore, the Mong people must not forget to continue honoring the house spirits, the ancestors' spirits, and the nature spirits. The importance of *Neej* (living side) and *Dlaab* (dead side) is that everyone likes to receive gifts. If the evil spirits or spirits who are in the dead side are not happy, then these spirits will cause people who live in the living side to get sick and possibly die. The people who live in the living side must know how to make offerings to the evil spirits so these spirits stay within their own boundaries. For example, the purpose of Mong rituals and ceremonies is to keep our close relationship between the living side and dead side. If the Mong no longer can perform these types of rituals and ceremonies to keep the evil spirits happy and remain within their boundaries, then the Mong will be in serious trouble. The evil spirits or spirits who are on the dead side will invade the living side. Therefore, Mong must not lose their traditional customs and values. These values are the important guidance to our lives.

7

Keeping Oral Culture Alive
Through the Mong Elders

The voices of the Mong Elders and their profound oral tradition, custom, religion, language and culture within a non-literate society offer a great contribution to this literate society. The Mong Elders play a very important role in the Mong society. They pass down important heritage, knowledge, wisdom and information about Mong tradition from one generation to the next generation. They continue to pass on this tradition to the Mong children in the Mong-American community. The Elders' stories were very compelling. The Mong have a legacy of oral tradition preservation and it has been a continuing success to the Mong people for thousands of years. This legacy helps them to maintain their cultural identity, heritage and their strong family. Through oral tradition, the integrity of Mong culture, language, religion, custom, social harmony and sacred knowledge lives today. The Mong oral tradition survived through the Chinese persecution and the Lao Communists' genocide. There is no doubt that the Mong oral tradition will vanish quickly in the United States as long as the Mong Elders do not keep their strong oral traditional practices within the community. The Elders are the most important people in the family as community members who pass along their knowledge. An elderly man states, "Every old man who dies is like a library destroyed" (UN Department , 1982, p. 86).

The Mong Elders were wise and orally educated people. Their knowledge and skills (oral credential) ranked equivalent to the people who hold doctoral degrees (written credential) in this literate society. Ong (1980) uses the term "oral credential" to refer to the educators that have only a primary oral culture. In the United States, the Mong's medicine men, medicine women, Shamans, wedding and funeral rites experts, *qeej* master players, musicians, religion practitioners, storytellers and artists are highly respected in the Mong community, similar to how the American general community has respect for doctors and lawyers. Elder Xao Cheng Lee said:

> Even though we do not have the American credential (a piece of paper) to prove the types of skills or knowledge we know, our people respect us by our performances, honesty and the treatments we offer. We do not depend on other people from the outside community who have the American credential to perform our rituals, take care of our people and teach to us our tradition. The only time we need a person who has the American credential is if we deal with the Americans. Some Mong who have the American doctoral degrees do not know about Mong tradition like an elder man or elder woman who has never gone to school. When it comes to Mong tradition, these Mong doctors have to depend on the elders [personal communication, Merced, California].

Elder Tong Yao Her pointed out a similar issue:

> Some Mong people who become educated in America no longer know how to do the thank you ritual (*ua tsaug*). When it is time to perform the thank you ritual they look at you like they were in some kind of trouble. They do not know how to begin or how to end the ritual [personal communication, San Diego, California].

The stories told by the Elders show that the Mong are very peaceful. The Mong are very generous people. They always treat their people and the people outside the Mong culture with loyalty and great respect. They are compassionate, unselfish people. They have always offered and given to others of what they know and have. They share resources wisely with their family, extended families, relatives and friends. When I traveled to visit the participants I did not have to worry about finding a motel to stay in or place to eat. The Elders and their families treated me as their special guest. They offered me food, drink and their home to stay in. I learned that due to their peaceful, independent and self-sufficient lifestyles, the Mong people prefer to live with no outsider contact. This way they can maintain their indigenous tradition and culture values.

Unfortunately the Mong are unable to keep their beautiful indigenous tradition and culture because industrialized and literate culture has replaced their oral reality. The notion of literate culture changes the Mong's indigenous traditional modes of thinking to the colonial ideology. The written knowledge and information the Mong younger generation learns from school become a weapon to destroy the Mong oral tradition. Smith Tuhiwai (1999) writes that there are two basic forms of colonial education that impose indigenous values. She describes them as:

> Missionary or religious schooling (which was often residential) followed later by public and secular schooling. Numerous accounts across nations now attest to the critical role played by schools in assimilating colonized peoples, and in the systematic, frequently brutal, forms of denial of indigenous languages, knowledges and cultures [Smith Tuhiwai, 1999, p. 64].

Smith Tuhiwai's statements describe the issues that create difficulties for the Mong Elders' oral tradition I found in their stories. After the French colonized and introduced school to the Mong people on the mountains in Laos, the missionary came to live with the Mong and the U.S. Central Intelligence Agency (CIA) came to recruit the Mong people to fight in the secret war in Laos. The Mong began to be influenced by Western cultures, beliefs, policies and practices. Some families started to convert to Christianity, and some Mong began to incorporate the Western system to control the Mong people. Smith Tuhiwai states that when indigenous people went through the colonial education they tended to form an elite group to control their indigenous society in following the Western system. A similar model was used as a strategy to kill the Mong oral tradition.

This fundamental issue of a school-based knowledge system continues to be the driving force in the Mong community in California as well as throughout the United States to eliminate the Mong oral tradition, language and culture values. Increasingly, the Mong older and younger generations begin to self-segregate from each other based on cultural values and beliefs. The Elders believe that maintaining their tradition, language and culture are very important. The Mong younger generation needs them in order to hold onto their identity. The Elders told me that their grandchildren are losing their culture integrity. The loss of Mong tradition, culture and language causes the Elders to be harmed physically, mentally and spiritually. The power of institutions such as school teaches Mong children to deny their identities and stop supporting the Mong Elders' sovereignty rights to keep the Mong tradition. The Elders expressed a concern about what school has done to the Mong children. They said school does not educate Mong children to recognize and respect their parents and grandparents' culture. Instead, school educates Mong children about the values outside Mong culture. The Elders were shocked to see the way their grandchildren use school knowledge to rebel against the Mong oral tradition. School knowledge encourages Mong children to oppose their parents and grandparents' knowledge and their tradition. Elder Lee Xiong talked to me about her grandchildren:

> My grandchildren ask me why I do not want to become an American. I keep telling them to learn the Mong culture and tradition and want them to be Mong. I need to leave them alone because the knowledge of Mong culture is useless in America [personal communication, Stockton, California].

The way school educates Mong children fits well with the condition that Paulo Freire calls *cultural invasion*. Freire (1993) describes cultural invasion as an act in which

> The invaders penetrate the cultural context of another group, in disrespect of the latter's potentialities; they impose their own view of the world upon those they invade and inhibit the creativity of the invaded by curbing their expression.... The invaders act; those they invade have only the illusion of acting, through the action of the invaders.... All domination involves invasion ... [a] form of economic and cultural domination [pp. 133–134].

Antonia Darder (1991) argues the same pedagogical value saying, "Resistance is clearly linked to notions of structure and human agency and the concept of culture and self-formation, and situating these in a new problematic for understanding the process of schooling" (pp. 89–90).

The Elders' conversations and stories provide strong reflections of the way primary oral culture functions. The oral discourse discussions I had with the Elders helped me to gain tremendous concrete information about the Mong oral tradition. This information provided me with better understanding about the structure of Mong society. I found that the kinship system is the safeguard of the Mong tradition and constitutes the Mong as a powerful group of people. In the Mong society, everyone knows each other, has great respect and supports one another based on their strong kinship ties and cultural pride. The profound kinship relationships within the Mong society define the Mong people as one big family. The Mong people are living with their good reputation of being self-supported, self-sufficient, hardworking, committed to family and independent people. The Mong want to live having a good name. They would prevent anything that will ruin their family or people's good reputation. There is a strong mutual support system within the Mong society. The Mong believe that earning and maintaining a good reputation reflects the positive image of their people, tradition and culture. The Elders said that keeping their oral discourse of social and religious functions brings support and gives a good name to the Mong people. It is important to pass this oral discourse on to the younger generation so the Mong can maintain their strong culture pride and perform their rituals. Ong (1982) notes, "In most religions the spoken work functions integrally in ceremonial and devotional life" (p. 74).

The Mong Elders are feeling tremendous frustration and devastation about their grandchildren beginning to lose their oral tradition. They said that a primary oral person could take their knowledge with them everywhere they go whereas a literate person has to depend on books. A literate person does not function well without books. The Elders were doubtful that books could contain accurate information like oral discourse. They told me that some text translations of Mong sacred wedding and ritual songs which they came across do not have the same truth and meaning as the oral version. Also, once oral discourse is translated into text, then the person who did the translation becomes the owner of the text. When the translation is not done right, that information stays in the wrong form, and then it paralyzes the Mong culture for a lifetime. The ideology of text fixes meaning, manipulates sacred knowledge and develops new interpretations, so people can sell, duplicate and own them. Literacy is only a tool invented by humans to set up rules to control information and knowledge. This is not true of human intellectual knowledge. The Elders prefer to keep the Mong sacred knowledge and wisdom in the form of oral discourse. This way no one can sell, take ownership, have control or place copyright on them. Ong (1982) describes that the condition of oral discourse is quite different from text. He states that the oral codes of language are not like the writing codes. Ong (1982) adds that the primary oral culture had its unique ways to infiltrate things. He elaborates Plato's position against writing:

> Writing destroys memory. Those who use writing will become forgetful, relying on an external resource for what they lack in internal resources. Writing weakens the mind.... A written text is basically unresponsive. If you ask a person to explain his or her statement, you can get an explanation; if you ask a text, you get back nothing except the same, often stupid, words which called for question in the first place.... The written word cannot defend itself as the natural spoken work can: real speech and thought always exist essentially in a context of give-and-take between real persons. Writing is passive, out of it, in an unreal, unnatural world [Ong, 1982, p. 79].

Havelock (1986) states that translating an oral culture to mostly written texts affects the people who grow up in a primarily literate society. They were disconnected from the oral society. His comments describe most Mong children who were brought up in this literate culture, and who have little sense of an oral culture because their thinking processes function differently from those who grew up in an oral culture. The Mong children who were born and raised in the literate culture have had to the Elders bizarre behavior in which they often question their parents and resist their parents' oral values. The Elders stated that people who become literate often create ideas to make problems for society. They invent chemical and destructive weapons to harm humans, animals and nature. People abandon their family members in the literate society. The Elders said it is sad to see the Americans send their elders to live in the nursing home to be abused by the system. The family is being destroyed because people follow the system that has been set up based on literacy.

The Mong Elders' conversations and stories strongly witness that the Mong children who grow up in the literate culture have a difficult time relating to their parents' or grandparents' social skills as well as how informational knowledge works in the oral culture. It is difficult for the Mong younger generation to balance themselves between this tension of cultural conflict among the Mong Elders. The printed texts are what the Mong Elders think is a waste of time and it is a new way to record information. The Mong younger generation has to use writing in order to help them remember. But this makes the Mong younger generation look stupid when they are around the Elders, trying to write down what they say instead of just listening and recording it in their heads.

The Elders stated that the Mong sacred knowledge and wisdom must be kept in the oral form. This way it can continue to enrich the Mong understanding of the self and the cosmos. Also, it continues to be the spiritual guidance and education that helps the Mong people understand their reality. It helps the Mong to maintain commitment to family, harmony, happiness and peaceful life. In order to be healthy and have prosperity one must know the proper way to honor the spirits of ancestors and understand the true connection he/she has with the ancestors' spirits. This type of education must be done orally. The Mong cosmos is centered on the power of spirits. Therefore, it is important to know the necessary oral skills and philosophical knowledge to conduct rituals to protect people from illness that is caused by spirits. Chants, prayers and narratives are profound and provide the mystical way of life in the Mong culture. They are part of the Mong daily spiritual practices.

I learned from the Elders that Mong traditional religious beliefs are strongly anchored with ancestors' worship for spiritual protection. Their beliefs are similar to the nomads. Berman (2000) describes nomads' religious values as passed along from generation to generation since the Paleolithic period. Researchers point out that the practices of shamanism are common among the nomads' tradition (Khazanov, 1994; Basilow, 1989; Weissleder, 1978; Berman, 2000). Basilov and Zhukovskaya (1989) state:

> Shamanism is one of the most ancient types of religious cult. It is based on a belief that certain people (Shamans) can serve as intermediaries between humans and spirits (deities) [p. 161].

The Mong Shamans are the spiritual healers that cure illness. They are busy like the American physicians. Cooper, Tapp, Lee and Schworer-Kohl (1996) add to this notion:

> A shaman practices for the benefit of a sick person who has consulted him, or for whose benefit he has been consulted by somebody else (such as the father of a sick child), who is not a member of his family (a shaman will usually call in another shaman if he or a member of his family is sick) [p. 58].

Chindarsi (1976), Thao (1986), Lemoine (1986), Cohen (1987), Tapp (1989), Symonds (1991), Davidson (1993), Ensign (1994), and Cooper (1998) all support this idea that the Mong have their own unique belief system. Researchers Geddes (1976), Mottin (1980), Cooper (1984), Bliatout (1986) and Thao (1986), Symonds (1991), O'Connor (1995), Cooper, Tapp, Lee and Schwhorer-Kohl (1996), Cooper (1998) and Thao (1999) agree that Mong traditional lifestyles consist of such elements as agricultural practices, spiritual ceremonies, and social structures. O'Connor (1995) asserts, "In the Hmong cosmology, spirit in Nature may cause sickness in response to having been either purposefully or inadvertently angered or mistreated" (p. 91). Anthropologists Cooper, Tapp, Lee and musicologist Schworer-Kohl (1996) state: "The Hmong house is a reflection of the Hmong cosmos. The roof and rafters of the house represent the vault of heaven, the earthen floor represents the world of nature, and between heaven and earth is the world of men" (p. 56).

Mong traditional healing consists of Mong Shamanism, traditional herbal medicines, magic healing and the soul calling ceremony, which are common practices within the Mong society. Chindarsi (1976), Tapp (1989), Davidson (1993) and Ensign (1994) add that a Shaman is one who can trance a Mong sick person's soul to find out what is happening. For example, if the soul was lost and could not find its way back to the person's body, then a Shaman will perform rituals to bring the soul back to the sick person's body. Tapp (1989) elaborates about the Shaman:

> The shaman, like a modern psychotherapist, restores the balance of the psyche by first identifying, then retrieving, the absent or lost parts of the

self; Shamans divide the self into five parts: the chicken self (ntsuj qaib ntsuj noo), the self of the bamboo (ntsuj xyooj ntsuj ntoo), the self of the bull (ntsuj nyuj rag ntsuj nyuj rhi), of the reindeer (ntsuj nyuj cab ntsuj nyuj kauv), and of the shadow (ntsuj duab ntsuj hlauv) [p. 75].

The Mong cosmology includes birth, marriage, illness and death ceremonies. Everything the Mong believe is a reflection of the cosmos and it is a complex system. For example, souls are present in both the living or light world and death or darkness world. Mong refer to this as *yaaj ceeb* (living or light world) and *yeeb ceeb* (death or darkness world). Only a Shaman with his *qua neeb* (Shaman spirits and power) can communicate between the worlds. Tapp (1989) and Symonds (1991) state that only the spirits from both worlds can meet and all things are interconnected. These two divided worlds connect to complete the cycle of life and death. Chindarsi (1976) elaborates on the Mong view of cosmos:

> The Hmong believe in many supernatural beings — gods, spirits of places, household spirits, malicious spirits, and spirits of the dead. They also believe that men and all living things have souls which return to an afterworld when they die, and there await reincarnation [p. 17].

Geddes (1976), Chindarsi (1976), Mottin (1980), Lemoine (1986), Thao (1986), Bliatout (1986), Cohen (1987), Quincy (1988), Tapp (1989), Symonds (1991), Davidson (1993), Ensign (1994), and Cooper (1998) point out that Mong religion consists of many elements: a Mong person's body, symbol and house are the places where the souls are united. Mong believe that things in this world are protected by spirits. Therefore, the spirits should not be disturbed. Symonds (1991) says:

> The reality of spirits is a large focus in Hmong life and the intricacies of the universe are connected by natural, ancestral, supernatural, and wild spirits of the outside and tame spirits of the inside [p. 52].

Mong Oral Tradition and Culture Elements

There are many ceremonies in the Mong oral tradition. These ceremonies are to honor, make offering and respect the spirits that protect them. The Mong who still practice traditional rituals believe that souls are their only sources of life guidance and healing. For example, Mong have to perform a ceremony called *hu plig*, meaning calling the soul. During this ritual a soul is called to protect the person. This soul can be a new soul that needs to be welcomed to the souls of the house. This soul is called for a newborn. When a Mong family has a new baby, a ceremony is performed on the third morning counting from the day the child was born. After this new child is announced to the souls of the house, then they will protect the child. Cooper, Tapp, Lee and Schworer-Kohl (1996) state, "At birth, a child's body is not in full possession of, or possessed by, its souls. If the child survives for three days after birth, a *hu plig* ritual must be conducted to summon the soul into its body" (p. 60). Furthermore, Quincy (1988) supports this by stating, "Whatever its sex, the birth of a child was a great event. In one sense it meant a family had a new member, and for the Hmong the family was nearly everything. Children in particular were cherished and enjoyed" (p. 90).

When a person is sick as a result of a major frightening event, then it is a belief that this sick person's soul no longer embodies the person, so a soul calling is needed to call the soul to return to the body, or a Shaman is called to perform a healing ritual to guide the soul back. There are different chants in each ceremony. These rigorous chants are very difficult to learn. It takes many years for a person to master some of them. A master usually takes a few apprentices and teaches all the chants he knows to them. The master is usually the uncle or grandfather. The apprentices are the sons, grandsons or nephews. There are different chants like wedding chants, funeral chants, New Year chants, birth chants, Shaman's chants, healing chants, sickness chants, blessing chants, medicine chants, etc. Each chant has a different meaning, which serves a different purpose depending on the ceremony that takes place.

The Mong traditional wedding ceremony is considered the central occasion in life because the souls of families, relatives, friends and ancestors are present to bless and support the souls of the bride for a long lasting, happy and strong marriage with her new husband. This wedding serves many purposes, such as letting the people know that the bride and groom are married, informing the bride's ancestors' spirits that she is leaving the home and no longer needs their protection. After the wedding ceremony at the house of the bride's parents, the groom family needs to inform their ancestors' souls to let them know that they are adding a new person to their family for protection when they get into their home. A wedding ceremony is a time for elders, relatives, friends and family members to give *koob moov* (blessings, prayers and advice) for the married couple. The Mong Elders' view of marriage is as a very serious ceremony. This is the reason why the Mong people have a very intense and promising wedding ceremony.

When a person dies, the house's souls must be notified so the dead person's soul can join the dead ancestors' souls in the ancestors' world. This dead person's soul is carefully guided by chants and rituals back to the ancestors' world. Quincy (1988) says, "Shortly after the washing of the deceased's body, a rite was held to prepare it for the long journey in the spirit world to the place of its ancestors" (p. 96). A funeral rite is very important and it must be conducted with extreme care so it creates no harm to the soul of the dead. This way the soul can depart to the other world to be reincarnated. If the soul cannot depart to the other world, then this soul curses the living family. After the deceased's body has been buried for thirteen days, the family members who still live return to the grave site to call this dead family member's soul to make his/her last visit to the home of the living family. There is a ceremony performed called *Ro Plig* or releasing the soul. This "releasing the soul" ceremony is to allow the soul of the dead to be reborn after he or she has completed the journey back to the ancestral world (Chindarsi, 1976; Cooper, Tapp, Lee and Schworer-Kohl, 1996; Cooper, 1998).

Besides the chants, traditional songs and stories also play an important role in the Mong's oral tradition. Mong learn to sing sung-poetry, play musical instruments, tell stories and sing sacred songs by becoming an apprentice for their elders. Usually the Mong elder men and women know all this sacred knowledge. They pass it down to their children and grandchildren orally. For example, mothers pass down to daughters, granddaughters and nieces. Fathers pass down to sons, grandsons and nephews. In addition, the Mong's oral tradition involves a beautiful custom. They make their own outfits, instruments and tools. These oral skills are their reality. They have a long history of being independent people and have had their own tradition, culture, language and religion for hundreds of years. Living in the primary oral culture keeps the Mong close knit to their kinship and strong culture roots. Music is mainly used for courting, comforting sadness, releasing personal hardship and entertaining. Mong music can be very difficult to understand if one does not know the Mong language, culture and tradition. Amy Catlin (1997) has conducted extensive research on Mong music, saying:

> Listening to Hmong music requires specialized perceptual tools, many closely linked to linguistic skills. The Hmong has a number of unique musical systems for presenting verbal texts in non-verbal or para-verbal form. Listeners must puzzle out the underlying verbal content in order to understand and enjoy these coded semantic messages, sometimes responding in kind during spontaneous dialogues. Culture bearers listen emically to these materials, with varied results [p. 69].

The Elders stated that if Mong American educators do not do something to help preserve the Mong language, culture, religion and tradition they will disappear quickly due to the way school and American culture influence Mong children. Soon the Mong educators and their children will no longer have a culture heritage of their own. Once they realize this about the Mong tradition, it will be too late because the Elders who know the tradition will no longer be living. The Mong younger generation should not become too American and devote their time to study the American culture. They also need to know the concrete information and knowledge of the Mong tradition. This way they can pass on the culture tradition. The Elders were counting on the Mong pioneer educators like myself who need to help them reach out to the Mong children to conserve the Mong tradition. They suggested that the Mong American educators must look into the detail of Mong rituals in order to understand how important it is to keep the Mong language and culture values. Mong need to speak their language and know their culture to be able to conduct their rituals. If the Mong children no longer speak and understand Mong, they cannot practice and carry on the Mong rituals. Mong American educators need to create institutions in every Mong community across the United States similar to the churches for Mong Elders and parents to teach Mong cultural tradition to Mong American children. This way the Mong American can have a place to learn Mong traditional values. The Elders said that every Mong member needs to devote time to their institutions as the people who believe in Christianity do with their church organization. If these institutions are not formed, Mong Americans will lose their language, culture and tradition very soon because they are getting closer to the point where they no longer know their culture tradition. The Mong Americans are too busy with work and school. They need to have these institutions so they can make time and commitment to study the Mong tradition. This way the Mong will not become a lost generation living in a highly technological country such as the United States.

Understanding the Interconnectedness of Mong Oral Culture

It is important for the literate people not to have a mental picture of the non-literate people as unintelligent and unskillful. The Mong Elders who once lived in a primary oral culture have different knowledge than the people who have only the written culture. Therefore, the Mong younger generation needs to conserve their Elders' knowledge and infuse them into their own literate knowledge, so they do not become disconnected from the indigenous tradition and culture. They need to become bicultural and bilingual in order to maintain both the Mong and American cultures.

The Mong Elders were happy living in the oral society because there seemed to be more freedom for them to relate their mind and body to where they really were and they had a close-knit community, which made them feel secure enough to be themselves. Their life was wrapped with oral, not written tradition. In the literate culture, they became insecure because they felt the pressure to learn how to read and write in order to prove the necessary skills and establish a secure life. This issue created major obstacles for the people who were not literate. Literate people need to recognize and understand the values of oral tradition so they can realize the beauty of human culture. Knowledge of primary oral culture serves as an important contribution to society. Since our society is moving forward to a transdisciplinary globalized society, we need to look back to the past in order to bring forward ideas to help societies solve current issues. Increasingly, people are becoming detached from family, tradition, culture and homeland. People no longer have a sense of culture balance and have no respect for others living in a society that heavily relies on written policy as the control system. The Mong younger generation living in California as well as in the United States is constructing a new community which brings a different perspective to their culture, society, and tradition. They are losing the Mong Elders' community of neighbors that provides care to one another. In order to preserve their culture root and tradition values Mong Americans must be willing to sacrifice a generation change by learning the mainstream culture and their own at the same time to embrace their community with the Elders' community.

For thousands of years the Mong people lived in a nomadic society and they had their own culture that reflected their way of life. This lifestyle has given them the freedom to be Mong. They lived as a homogeneous group and they did not depend on other cultures to protect as well as to support them. Basilov (1989) writes about nomads:

> Nomadic societies were always characterized by a strong order based upon principles of kinship. The individual was a part of the "clan" (a group of blood relatives), and the clan was a part of more distantly related communities, which in turn constituted the tribe. This organization guaranteed a reliable defense against enemies ... Tradition traced the origins of the clan back to a single ancestor and frequently even several tribes were considered kinsmen, since they also shared an ancestor. This belief in a common origin promoted political alliances [pp. 5–6].

The Mong oral tradition began to change after the West came into contact with the Mong people and introduced them to the literacy system. The Mong's traditional customary law and social norms no longer have values to Mong children and the literate people. The notion of literacy caused both Mong older and younger generations to face violence and cultural resistance within their family and community. Mong American educators, the Mong younger generation, the American general community and institutions such as schools need to understand and develop full respect for the importance of Mong oral tradition and moral values. Information passed down from oral tradition provides a significant representation of Mong history and culture. Mong values are embedded in their oral tradition and religion. Parents and Elders are the people who hold onto these values. It is important for an individual to be committed to understanding the complexity of the Mong culture, religion, ways of life and beliefs in order to know the Mong world-reality. The Elders said:

> *Nkauj txawg hab tub txawg tsis noog nam noog txwv qhuab, nkauj txawg hab tub txawg txaj tsis paub lug taab nwg lub yig hab lub cuab.*

> Young women and young men who are educated but they do not listen to their parents' advice will not know how to begin their life.

They stated that these are the universal principles of important Mong customs:

- *Paub coj kwv coj teg coj neej coj tsaav* (Knowing how to lead family, clan, kinsman and kinswoman)
- *Paub coj dlaab coj qhua* (Knowing how to manage the principle of religion)
- *Puab tu tub tu kiv* (Knowing parenting)
- *Paub khwv noj khwv haus* (Knowing how to work and bring resources into the family)

These are the immoral acts that will cause a person to become self-destructive:

- *Kiv haus yeeb haus tsuaj* (Becoming a drug addict)
- *Kiv quav dlej qhuav cawv* (Becoming alcoholic)
- *Kiv twv txaj yuam pov* (Becoming a gambler)
- *Kiv ua pleeg ua yig* (Having an affair)
- *Kiv tsis hwm nam huv txwv hab hwm tej laug* (Having no respect to parents or the Elders)

The Elders said that their grandchildren who grow up in this literate society have no Mong tradition and culture meritocracy. Their grandchildren believe in the values that they learn from the school and the outside culture. This lack of knowledge about Mong tradition and culture will force them and Mong future generations to withdraw their culture, language and religion. Then, they will become a Mong lost generation. They will no longer have a culture identity. The Elders do not want to see the Mong culture and tradition demolished and cause future Mong generations living in America to have no cultural root. The young Mong Americans and their Elders need to have a traditional cultural training center to preserve their important heritage and oral knowledge.

Summary

The research in this chapter and the book was limited to thirteen Mong Elders who live in California. It cannot be generalized to other Mong Elders who live in different countries and it makes no claims of universal generalization. The author hopes to provide a microcosm of the dilemma faced by Mong Elders who have only a primary oral culture background but live in a literate society while trying to conserve their oral tradition.

It is important for the print culture people to understand the oral culture elements and listen to the tradition beliefs of the Mong people before they begin to make any judgments. Herda (1999) adds, "If a person learns to listen, and not only hear, what is already understood, opportunities come into play to open new worlds" (pp. 62–63).

The Mong culture is one of the very few oral indigenous traditions existing today in the world. I encourage educators and researchers to become sensitive to indigenous tradition and culture values. Information collected from fieldwork that contains sacred knowledge of oral indigenous tradition should not be documented to be sold or owned by researchers. Educators and researchers need to assist the Mong in conserving their oral tradition, rather than threatening and eliminating it. It is very important to write about Mong sensibility so as not to destroy the culture and tradition.

Afterword
by Marianne Pennekamp

I, too, come from immigrant roots and arrived in the United States as a teenager. The pressure was great to forget everything about the "old country" and take advantage of the opportunities here. I rebelled and tried, instead, to understand these roots and to build my adult life upon them. When I met Yer Thao in Humboldt County, I recognized a kindred spirit and supported his community building efforts. I still do.

In my work as a school social worker–school psychologist in the Oakland Public Schools, I had observed that the oral languages our students brought to school were key ingredients of their identities. Being respectfully listened to made it possible for these students, and their families, to bridge their lives from home to school, to own their own learning and to keep from feeling alienated and marginalized. Over the years, many outreach efforts — school or community based — succeeded through listening to their stories, their interpretations of their realities and their hopes. This process was an essential ingredient in their ability to partner with the informal and formal communications from the schools. Fadiman (1997) illustrates similar patterns in building bridges between Mong families and their medical providers.

Mong stories as told by the elders are an example of validating cultural groups' histories and identities. I heard similar stories from inner-city black grandparents, Latino grandparents, Vietnamese grandparents, Russian Jewish grandparents, and so on. I watched the struggles of the next generation to keep their children and youth safe from the street and its temptations. The overarching task was, and is, to find ways, in the mainstream society of neighborhood, school, playground, police, health and human services, public libraries and employment services to explore the skills and attitudinal assets of each generation of newcomers, so that these generations — the parents of the grandchildren, still foreign born, and the grandchildren, American born — can find their own voices, and can empower themselves in defining their trip from their family origins to their generational futures.

The key contribution of works like Professor Thao's is to prepare bridge staff during their academic pre-service curricula to take on the challenge of bringing honor to the elders, visibility to the culture they embody and a place at the table for ethnic group members who can speak on behalf of the group, negotiate accommodations, explore concerns and celebrate shared successes.

I am aware of a number of organized efforts that concretize this general task. A collection of examples, from all over the country, would be a most useful next step for the frontline practitioner/bridgers who are the essential resources in making sure that the current youth generation does not drift into a marginalized, alienated position in communities, one vulnerable to gang recruitment and negative reputations. With support, the young people will discover their own hopes and opportunities. Professor Thao challenges us all to take these next steps.

Marianne Pennekamp, MSW, Ph.D., is Adjunct Professor of Psychology, Retired, Humboldt State University, Arcata, California.

Bibliography

Adler, Julie. September/October 2000. "Hmong Students: A Quarter Century of Progress in the United States." *ESL Magazine*, pp. 26–28.

Bakker, Egbert, and Ahuvia Kahane (eds.). (1997). *Written Voices, Spoken Signs: Tradition, Performance, and the Epic Text*. Cambridge, MA: Harvard University Press.

Ballenger, P. Bruce. November 1997. "Methods of Memory: On Native American Storytelling." *College English*, 59, 789–800.

Banks, A. James, and C.A.M. Banks (eds.). (1993). *Multicultural Education: Issues and Perspectives*. Needham Heights, MA: Allyn & Bacon.

Basilow, Vladimir N. (ed.). 1989. *Nomads of Eurasia*. Seattle: University of Washington Press.

Basilow, Vladimir N., and N.L. Zhukovskaya. 1989. "Religious Beliefs." In V.N. Basilow (ed.), *Normads of Eurasia* (pp. 161–181). Seattle: University of Washington Press.

Berman, Morris. 2000. *Wandering God: A Study in Nomadic Spirituality*. Albany: State University of New York Press.

Bliatout Thowpaou, Bruce. 1986. "Guidelines for Mental Health Professionals to Help Hmong Clients Seek Traditional Healing Treatment." In G. Hendricks, B.T. Downing and A.S. Deinard (eds.), *The Hmong in Transition* (pp. 349–363). Staten Island: The Center for Migration Studies of New York, Inc.

Bliatout Thowpaou, Bruce, B.T. Downing, Judith Lewis, and Dao Yang. 1988. *Handbook for Teaching Hmong-Speaking Students*. Folsom Cordova, CA: Folsom Cordova Unified School District, Southeast Asia Community.

Boyes, Jon, and S. Piraban. 1990. *Hmong Voices*. Chian Mai, Thailand: Trasvin Publication Limited Partnership.

Brower, Reuban. 1959. *On Translation*. Cambridge, MA: Harvard University Press.

Cajete, Gregory. 1994. *Looking to the Mountain: An Ecology of Indigenous Education*. Durango, CO: Kivakí Press.

Catlin, Amy. 1997. "Puzzling the Text: Thought-Songs, Secrete Languages, and Archaic Tones in Hmong Music." *The world of music*, 39 (2), 69–81.

Catlin, Amy. 1986. "The Hmong and Their Music." In J. Cubbs (ed.), *Hmong Art: Tradition and Change* (pp. 11–20). Sheboygan, WI: John Michael Kohler Arts Center.

Catlin, Amy. 1985. "Harmonizing the Generations in Hmong Musical Performance." *UCLA Selected Reports in Ethnomusicology,* 6, 83–97.

Chindarsi, Nusit. 1976. *The Religion of the Hmong Njua.* Bangkok, Thailand: The Siam Society.

Cohen, Erik. 1987. "The Hmong Cross." *Peabody Museum of Archaeology and Ethnology,* 14, 27–45.

Cohen, William D. Winter 1989. "The Undefining of Oral Tradition." *Ethnohistory,* 36 (1), 9–18.

Conquergood, Dwight. 1992. "Fabricating Culture: The Textile Art of Hmong Refugee Women." In E.C. Fine and J.H. Speer (eds.), *Performance Culture and Identity* (pp. 207–248). Westport, CT: Praeger.

Cooper, Robert N. (ed.). 1998. *The Hmong: A Guide to Traditional Lifestyles.* Singapore: Times Editions Pte Ltd.

Cooper, Robert, Nichohlic Tapp, Gary Yia Lee, and G. Schworer-Kohl. 1996. *The Hmong.* Bangkok, Thailand: Artasia Press Co., Ltd.

Crawford, W. Lisa. 1993. *Language and Literacy Learning in Multicultural Classrooms.* Needham Heights, MA: Allyn & Bacon.

Darder, Antonia. 1991. *Cultural Culture and Power in the Classroom: A Critical Foundation for Bicultural Education.* Westport, CT: Bergin & Garvey.

Davidson, Jack. 1993. "Hmong Ethnohistory: An Historical Study of Hmong Culture and Its Implication for Ministry." Unpublished doctoral dissertation, Fuller Theological Seminary, California.

Delgado-Gaitan, Concha. 1990. *Literacy for Empowerment.* New York: The Falmer Press.

Delpit, Lisa. 1995. *Other People's Children: Cultural Conflict in the Classroom.* New York: W.W. Norton & Company, Inc.

Dickinson, Paul. 1994. "'Orality in Literacy': Listening to Indigenous Writing." *Canadian Journal of Native Studies,* 14 (2), 319–340.

Dundes, Alan. 1965. *The Study of Folklore.* Englewood Cliffs, NJ: Prentice-Hall.

Einhorn, J. Lois. 2000. *The Native American Oral Tradition: Voices of the Spirit and Soul.* Westport, CT: Praeger.

Ensign, John S. 1994. "Traditional Healing in the Hmong Refugee Community of the California Central Valley." Unpublished dissertation, California School of Professional Psychology, California.

Faderman, Lillian. 1998. *I Begin My Life All Over.* Boston, MA: Beacon Press.

Fadiman, Anne. 1997. *The Spirit Catches You and You Fall Down: A Hmong Child, Her American Doctors, and the Collision of Two Cultures.* New York: Farrar, Straus and Giroux.

Fine, Elizabeth. 1984. *Folklore Text: From Performance to Print.* Bloomington: Indiana University Press.

Finnegan, Ruth. 1992. *Oral Traditions and the Verbal Arts: A Guide to Research Practices.* New York: Routledge.

Finnegan, Ruth. (ed.). 1978. *A World Treasury of Oral Poetry.* Bloomington: Indiana University Press.

Finnegan, Ruth. 1970. *Oral Literature in Africa.* Nairobi: Oxford University Press.

Finnegan, Ruth. 1967. *Limba Stories and Story-Telling.* Nairobi: Oxford University Press.

Foley, Miles John. 1990. *Traditional Oral Epic: The Odyssey, Beowulf, and the Serbo-Croatian Song.* Berkeley: University of California Press.

Foley, Miles John. 1988. *The Theory of Oral Composition: History and Methodology.* Bloomington and Indianapolis: Indiana University Press.

Freire, Paulo. 1993. *Pedagogy of the Oppressed.* New York: The Continuum Publishing Company.

Geddes, William Robert. 1976. *Migrants of the Mountains: The Cultural Ecology of the Blue Miao (Hmong Njua) of Thailand.* Oxford: Clarendon Press.

Gold, Peter. 1994. *Navajo & Tibetan Sacred Wisdom: The Cycle of the Spirits.* Rochester, NM: Inner Traditions International.

Goldstein, Beth L. Summer 1988. "In Search of Survival: The Education and Integration of Hmong Refugee Girls." *The Journal of Ethnic Studies,* 12 (2), 1–27.

Gollnick, Donna M., and Philip C. Chinn. 2002. *Multicultural Education in a Pluralistic Society.* Upper Saddle River, NJ: Merrill Prentice Hall.

Goody, Jack. 1987. *The Interface Between the Written and the Oral.* New York: Cambridge University Press.

Graham, D. 1954. *Stories and Songs of the Ch'uan Miao.* Washington, D.C.: Smithsonian Institution.

Guss, David M. August 1986. "Keeping It Oral: A Yekuana Ethnology." *American Ethnologist,* 13, 413–429.

Hall, Edward T. 1976. *Beyond Culture.* New York: Doubleday Dell Publishing Group, Inc.

Havelock, A. Eric. 1986. *The Muse Learns to Write: Reflections on Orality and Literacy from Antiquity to the Present.* New Haven and London: Yale University Press.

Hayes, Christopher. 1984. "A Study of the Older Hmong Refugees in the United States." Unpublished doctoral dissertation, The Fielding Institute, California.

Hendricks, Glenn L., Bruce T. Downing, and Amos S. Deinard (eds.). 1986. *The Hmong in Transition.* Staten Island: The Center for Migration Studies of New York, Inc.

Herda, Ellen A. 1999. *Research Conversations and Narrative: A Critical Hermeneutic Orientation in Participatory Inquiry.* Westport, CT: Praeger Publishers.

Hones, Donald. 1999. *Educating New Americans: Immigrant Lives and Learning.* Mahwah, NJ: Lawrence Erlbaum Associates, Publishers.

Johnson, Charles. 1992. *Dab neeg Hmoob: Myths, Legends and Folk Tales from the Hmong of Laos.* St. Paul, MN: Macalester College Department of Linguistics.

Khazanov, Antoli Michailovich. 1994. *Nomads and the Outside World.* Madison: The University of Wisconsin Press.

Kohler, John Michael. 1986. *Hmong Art: Tradition and Change.* Wisconsin: Sheboygan Arts Foundation.

Kroskrity, Paul V. Summer 1985. "Growing with Stories: Line, Verse, and Genre in an Arizona Tewa Text." *Journal of Anthropologist Research,* 41, 183–199.

Lee, Pao. 1999. "Language Maintenance and Language Shift among Second-Generation Hmong Teenagers." Unpublished doctoral dissertation, University of San Francisco, California.

Lee, Yia. 1986. "Culture and Adaptation: Hmong Refugees in Australia." In G. Hendricks, B.T. Downing and A.S. Deinard (eds.), *The Hmong in Transition* (pp. 55–71). Staten Island: The Center for Migration Studies of New York, Inc.

Lemoine, Jacques. 1986. "Shamanism in the Context of Hmong Resettlement." In G. Hendricks, B.T. Downing and A.S. Deinard (eds.), *The Hmong in Transition* (pp. 337–348). Staten Island: The Center for Migration Studies of New York, Inc.

Levinson, David, and Melvin Ember (eds.). 1996. "Encyclopedia of Culture Anthropology." *Oral Tradition* (pp. 887–891). New York: Henry Holt and Company, Inc.

Lewis, A. Judith. 1993. "Hmong Visual, Oral and Social Design: Innovation within a Frame of the Familiar." Master's thesis, California State University, Sacramento, California.

Lewis, Paul, and Elaine Lewis. 1984. *Peoples of the Golden Triangle: Six Tribes in Thailand*. London: Thames and Hudson, Ltd.

Liu, Theresa. 1995. "Relationships of Acculturation to the Academic Achievements and School Adjustment of Hmong-American Youths." Unpublished doctoral dissertation, Marquette University, Wisconsin.

Livo, J. Norma, and Dia Cha. 1991. *Folk Stories of the Hmong*. Englewood, CO: Libraries Unlimited.

Lyman, A. Thomas. 1974. *Dictionary of Mong Njua: A Miao (Meo) Language of Southeast Asia*. The Hague: Mouton & Co. N.V., Publishers.

McLuhan, Marshall. 1962. *The Gutenberg Galaxy*. Toronto, Canada: University of Toronto Press.

Meredith, William H., and George A. Rowe. 1986. "Changes in Hmong Refugee Marital Attitudes in America." In G. Hendricks, B.T. Downing and A.S. Deinard (eds.), *The Hmong in Transition* (pp. 121–134). Staten Island: The Center for Migration Studies of New York, Inc.

Michaud, Jean, and Christine Culas. 2000. "The Hmong of the Southeast Asia Massif: Their Recent History of Migration." In G. Evans, C. Hutton, and K.K. Eng (eds.), *Where China Meets Southeast Asia* (pp. 98–121). New York: St. Martin's Press.

Morrow, Robert D. 1989. "Southeast-Asian Parental Involvement: Can It Be a Reality?" *Elementary School Guidance & Counseling*, 23, 289–297.

Mottin, Jean. 1980. *History of the Hmong*. Bangkok, Thailand: Odeon Store Ltd. Part.

Nasr, Seyyed Hossein. 1989. *Knowledge and the Sacred*. Albany: State University of New York Press.

Ni, Ching. August 4, 2000. "China's Other Wall." *Los Angeles Times*, pp. A1, A10.

Nielsen, Eduard. 1954. *Oral Tradition: A Modern Problem in Old Testament Introduction*. London: SCM Press.

O'Connor, Bonnie Blair. 1995. *Healing Traditions: Alternative Medicine and the Health Professions*. Philadelphia: University of Pennsylvania Press.

Okpewho, Isidore. 1992. *African Oral Literature: Backgrounds, Character, and Continuity*. Bloomington: Indiana University Press.

Olson, R. David, and Nancy Torrance (eds.). 1991. *Literacy and Orality*. New York: Cambridge University Press.

Ong, Walter. 1977. *Interfaces of the Word: Studies in the Evolution of Consciousness and Culture*. New York: Cornell University Press.

Ong, Walter. Winter 1980. "Literacy and Orality in Our Times." *Journal of Communication*, 30 (1), 197–201.

Ong, Walter. 1982. *Orality and Literacy: The Technologizing of the Word*. New York: Routledge.

Pollard, Samuel. 1919. *The Story of the Miao*. London: Henry Hooks.

Porter, L.M. Fall 1995. "Lost in Translation: From Orature to Literature in the West African Folktale." *Symposium (Washington, D.C.)*, 49, 229–239.

Quincy, Keith. 1988. *Hmong: History of a People*. Cheney: Eastern Washington University Press.

Randall, Joan. (ed.). 1985. *Textiles, Silver, Wood of the Hmong-Americans: Art of the Highland Lao*. Davis: C.N. Gorman Museum, University of California–Davis.

Relyea, Kie. August 3, 1994. "Sacrifice Part of Faith, Hmongs Say." *The Times-Standard*, p. A1.

Riessman, Catherine Kohler. 1993. *Narrative Analysis*. Newbury Park, CA: Sage Publications.

Savina, F.M. 1924. *Histoire des Miao*. Paris: Société des Missions Étrangères.

Scott, George M. 1986. "Migrants without Mountains: The Politics of Sociocultural

Adjustment among the Lao Hmong Refugees in San Diego." Unpublished doctoral dissertation, University of California, San Diego.

Smalley, William A. 1994. *Linguistic Diversity and National Unity: Language Ecology in Thailand.* Chicago: University of Chicago Press.

Smalley, William, Chia Koua Vang, and Gnia Yee Yang. 1990. *Mother of Writing: The Origin and Development of Hmong Messianic Scrip.* Chicago: The University of Chicago Press.

Smith Tuhiwai, Linda. 1999. *Decolonizing Methodologies Research and Indigenous People.* New York: St. Martin's Press.

Soto, Lourdes Diaz. 1997. *Language, Culture and Power: Bilingual Families and the Struggle for Quality Education.* Albany: State University of New York Press.

Strouse, Joan. 1985. "Continuing Themes in U.S. Educational Policy for Immigrants and Refugees: The Hmong Experience." Unpublished doctoral dissertation, University of Wisconsin–Madison.

Sweeney, Amin. 1987. *A Full Hearing: Orality and Literacy in the Malay World.* Berkeley and Los Angeles: University of California Press.

Symonds, Patricia V. 1991. "Cosmology and the Cycle of Life: Hmong Views of Birth, Death and Gender in a Mountain Village in North Thailand." Unpublished doctoral dissertation, Brown University, Rhode Island.

Tapp, Nicholas. 1989. "Hmong Religion." *Asian Folklore Studies,* 48, 59–94.

Thao, Paoze. 1999a. *Mong Education at the Crossroads.* Lanham, MD: University Press of America, Inc.

Thao, Xoua. 1986. "Hmong Perception of Illness and Traditional Ways of Healing." In G. Hendricks, B.T. Downing and A.S. Deinard (eds.), *The Hmong in Transition* (pp. 337–348). Staten Island: The Center for Migration Studies of New York, Inc.

Thao, Yer Jeff. 2003. "Empowering Mong Students: Home and School Factors." *The Urban Review,* 35 (1), 25–42.

Thao, Yer Jeff. 1999b. "Multicultural Learning Environment for Mong Children in the California North Coast: Home and School Collaboration." Master's thesis, California State University, Monterey Bay.

Thao, Yer Jeff. 2002. "The Voices of Mong Elders: Ways of Knowing, Teaching, and Learning with an Oral Tradition." Ph.D. Dissertation, Claremont Graduate University, California.

Timm, Joan T. 1994. "Hmong Values and American Education." *Equity & Excellence in Education,* 27 (2), 36–44.

Timm, Joan T., Berttram Chiang, and Brenda Doherty Finn. April 1998. "Acculturation in the Cognitive Style of Laotian Hmong Students in the United States." *Equity & Excellence in Education,* 31 (1), 29–35.

Tollefson, James W. 1991. *Planning Language, Planning Inequality.* New York: Longman.

Trueba, Henry T., Lily Jacobs, and Elizabeth Kirton. 1990. *Cultural Conflict and Adaptation: The Case of Hmong Children in American Society.* New York: The Falmer Press.

UN Department of Public Information. 1982. "Oral Tradition: Deep Well of African History." *UN Chronicle,* 19, 85–86.

Vang, Anthony. 1999. "Hmong-American Students: Challenges and Opportunities." In C. Park and M. Chi (eds.), *Asian-American Education: Prospects and Challenges* (pp. 119–136). Westport, CT: Bergin & Garvey.

Vang, Lue, and A. Judith Lewis. 1984. *Grandmother's Path, Grandfather's Way.* Rancho Cordova, CA: Southeast Asia Community Resource.

Vansina, Jan. 1965. *Oral Tradition: A Study in Historical Methodology*. Chicago, IL: Aldine Publishing Company.

Vansina, Jan. 1985. *Oral Tradition as History*. Madison: The University of Wisconsin Press.

Weissleder, Wolfgang. (ed.). 1978. *The Nomadic Alternative: Modes and Models of Interaction in the African-Asian Deserts and Steppes*. The Hague: Mouton Publishers.

Wilson, Karen Harper. 1995. "'In Hmong Mountain': See Lee's Oral Narrative as History and Poetry." Master's thesis, California State University, Long Beach.

Wong-Fillmore, Lily. 1991. "When Learning a Second Language Means Losing the First." *Early Childhood Research Quarterly*, 6, 323–346.

Young, Russell, and MyLuong Tran. 1999. "Language Maintenance and Shift Among Vietnamese in America." *International Journal of the Sociology of Language*, 140, 77–82.

Zipes, Jack. 1984. *Breaking the Magic Spell: Radical Theories of Folk and Fairy Tales*. New York: Methuen, Inc.

Index

1937